PRINCETON
MANAGEMENT
CONSULTANTS
Guide to Your
New Job

PRINCETON MANAGEMENT CONSULTANTS
Guide to Your New Job

NIELS H. NIELSEN

John Wiley & Sons, Inc.

Published by John Wiley & Sons, Inc., Hoboken, New Jersey.
Published simultaneously in Canada.

No part of this publication may be reproduced, stored in a retrieval system or transmitted in any form or by any means, electronic, mechanical, photocopying, recording, scanning or otherwise, except as permitted under Sections 107 or 108 of the 1976 United States Copyright Act, without either the prior written permission of the Publisher, or authorization through payment of the appropriate per-copy fee to the Copyright Clearance Center, 222 Rosewood Drive, Danvers, MA 01923, (978) 750-8400, fax (978) 750-4744. Requests to the Publisher for permission should be addressed to the Permissions Department, John Wiley & Sons, Inc., 111 River Street, Hoboken, NJ 07030, (201) 748-6011, fax (201) 748-6008, e-mail: permcoordinator@wiley.com.

Limit of Liability/Disclaimer of Warranty: While the publisher and author have used their best efforts in preparing this book, they make no representations or warranties with respect to the accuracy or completeness of the contents of this book and specifically disclaim any implied warranties of merchantability or fitness for a particular purpose. No warranty may be created or extended by sales representatives or written sales materials. The advice and strategies contained herein may not be suitable for your situation. The publisher is not engaged in rendering professional services, and you should consult a professional where appropriate. Neither the publisher nor author shall be liable for any loss of profit or any other commercial damages, including but not limited to special, incidental, consequential, or other damages.

For general information on our other products and services please contact our Customer Care Department within the United States at (800) 762-2974, outside the United States at (317) 572-3993, or fax (317) 572-4002.

Wiley also publishes its books in a variety of electronic formats. Some content that appears in print may not be available in electronic books.

Library of Congress Cataloging-in-Publication Data:

Nielsen, Niels H.
    Princeton Management Consultants, Inc. guide to your new job / Niels H. Nielsen.
       p.   cm.
    Includes index.
    ISBN 0-471-23174-6 (pbk. : alk. paper)
    1. Job hunting. I. Title.
    HF5382.7.N54 2002
    650.14—dc21

                                                          2002026728

Printed in the United States of America.

10 9 8 7 6 5 4 3 2 1

To Ruth, my beloved wife

Acknowledgments

I am grateful for the help and encouragement I have received from many people in the conception, writing, and preparation of this book.

I am especially indebted to my son, Niels, a Managing Consultant with EDS, for his advice and for editing chapters related to business strategy, marketing, advertising, and sales. Thanks also to my colleague Harvey Steinberg for editing the chapter on compensation and to Dr. Robert Karlin of Rutgers University for writing *How to Avoid Getting Down While You're Out*. My wife Ruth was invaluable in her dedication and long hours she spent preparing the book for the publisher. I want to thank Tony Lee, Editor-in-Chief of Dow Jones's careerjournal.com, for recommending me to Michael Hamilton, Senior Editor, John Wiley & Sons.

Finally, I am grateful to the thousands of executives, managers, and professionals who have attended JobSeekers, which I founded in 1982 and continue to lead at Trinity Church in Princeton, New Jersey. It is the longest continuously running job club in the country. The experiences of the participants, as well as those of my many outplacement clients, have proved a rich source of materials for this book.

N.H.N.

Contents

PRINCETON
MANAGEMENT
CONSULTANTS, INC.

Dear Job Seeker:

I'm sorry you are out of work, whether you were downsized, terminated, or quit. It's tough. You are probably hurting emotionally as well as financially. If you have been totally involved in your job, you may even feel that you have lost some of your purpose in life.

However, this is a wonderful opportunity to start fresh. Now you have to take on a whole new career, that of

Interim Entrepreneur

For the time being, you are going into business for yourself with the single goal of getting one customer—your next employer. The process of finding the job is the same as if you were starting a new business. You are going to write a business plan *just as if you were going to seek venture capital*. This book shows you how to:

Set up Shop. You need dedicated home office space, equipment, computer hardware and appropriate software, an Internet Service Provider, supplies, stationery, a separate telephone line and voice mail, and access to fax and copy machines. Chapter 2 tells you how to do all this.

Prepare a Financial Plan. It costs you money to find a job. It may be difficult for you to contemplate spending money when you do not have an income. But you have to budget for job hunting expenses, and you have to keep records for income tax purposes. Chapter 2 provides you with a budget and control worksheet.

Get Started and Stay Motivated. You cannot waste a moment. Every day that goes by without a job is a day of lost income. It is also another day of potential discouragement and even depression because you are out of work and you are being rejected by employers. Chapter 2 tells you how how to discipline yourself to maintain a routine, and how to stay motivated.

Define Your Business Strategy. Write up your job-getting strategy. Determine your vision and mission. Know what your near- and long-term goals are and how you are going to get to them. Chapter 3 guides you in how to approach the job hunt strategically.

Consider Changing Your Business Model. You may want to (or have to) change your career. Reinvent yourself anywhere on the spectrum from upgrading or repackaging your skills through creating a new version of yourself to embarking on a whole new career. Chapter 3 outlines the range of options open to you in choosing a new career.

Catalog Your Stock in Trade. The best predictor of future success is past success. Describe all your accomplishments in a way that demonstrates the benefits you can bring to prospective employers. Chapter 4 shows you how to prepare a catalog from which you can create your advertising (cover letter and resume) and sell your services (interview) as a top performer.

Determine Your Marketing Strategy. Start from the premise that you are doing Business-to-Business (B2B) marketing. This book shows how to do the market research, define your market concept, package your services and yourself, and get the word out through the distribution channels. Chapter 5 leads you through the processes of building your marketing strategy.

Prepare Your Advertising. Now—and only now—that you know what you are going to sell, to whom, and at what price, you are ready to prepare your advertising materials: cover letter, resume. E-mail newsletter, and Web site. Chapter 6 gives you step-by-step instructions on how to create an effective ad campaign.

Price Your Services. What to charge for your services is an elaborate and complicated issue. There is an enormous array of salary plans, incentives, stock ownership programs, employee benefit plans, human resources policies, and perquisites to consider and negotiate. Chapter 7 shows you how to make your way through the minefield of all the different compensation plans and prepares you to negotiate the best deal.

Launch Your Sales Campaign. All this preparation is for only one purpose: to get a job with one employer. You need to build leads through networking, develop an elevator speech to get attention and be remembered, get appointments for interviews, make effective use of middlemen such as recruiters, and know how to sell your services in the interview. Chapter 8 shows you how do these things so well that when you ask for the job, you are likely to be given an offer.

Manage Your Customer Relations. Once you start on the job, you have to hit the ground running and produce measurable accomplishments for your new employer. Chapter 9 tells you how to find out what is expected of you from day 1, how you will be measured and evaluated, and how to keep adding to your catalog of achievements.

This book comes out of both my personal and my professional experience. I have been unemployed several times in my corporate life, sometimes voluntarily, other times involuntarily. I have set up my own business as a *permanent entrepreneur* in management and human resources consulting to Fortune 500 and Inc. 500 clients as well as start-up companies. I have counseled thousands of people who were changing jobs or careers. I have survived the ups and downs of several business cycles over more than two decades.

You *are* going to get a new job—even if it takes some time. To get it, you are going to draw on the realities of your career and job accomplishments instead of on psychological tests. You are going to succeed in your new job and learn how to manage your career based on your experience as a job getter.

Now, get going in your new venture.

Best of luck,

Niels H. Nielsen
President

1

Introduction

Job Seeking as a Start-Up Business

Question: What difference is there between a start-up small business entrepreneur and a job seeker?

Answer: A job seeker is looking for only one customer.

Otherwise, the processes are almost identical.

I realized this when I was simultaneously providing consulting services to both an entrepreneur and a job seeker. I was going through the same steps with each of them in their different contexts. The only difference seemed to be the vocabulary:

Outplacement Counseling	Business Planning
Job hunting plan	Business strategy
Self-assessment	Catalog of products or services
Changing career	Reinventing business model
Resumes and cover letters	Advertising
Networking and referrals	Lead generation
Executive recruiters	Middlemen
Researching companies	Market research
Targeting employers	Marketing strategy
Interviewing	Sales calls
Compensation	Pricing
Negotiating the terms	Making the deal
Starting on and keeping the new job	Customer relations

There Is No One Right Way

Most job hunting articles and books tell you that the only way is the way the author advocates. They are filled with words like "always . . . never . . . only . . . secret. . . ." This may be good for marketing books, but it is poor job hunting advice.

There are simply too many variables for any one formula to work. Each country, geographic region, industry, company, business unit, division, office, interviewer, manager, and coworker is different. In fact, the culture, the incumbent, or the mood of the interviewer can change, whether imperceptibly or dramatically, from time to time. Similarly, each job seeker's work experience is different and cannot be made to fit a mold.

The Legend of the Bed of Procrustes

There is a Greek legend about a giant named Procrustes who lived in a remote area beside a road between two cities. According to custom, he welcomed any traveler who came to his house at nightfall to stay overnight. When the traveler had fallen asleep, Procrustes went into his room to see how well the traveler fit the bed. If he was too short, Procrustes stretched him until he was long enough and, of course, killed him. If he was too long, Procrustes cut off part of his body until he was short enough and, of course, killed him.

The message for you in this legend is that if you try to make your methods fit arbitrary rules, you may kill your chances of getting the job that is right for you.

The alternative is to find out what is needed and what the job, place, and person you hope to work for are like, and to be sure there is a fit. If you do your homework, you have a better chance of succeeding. However, because things will change, be prepared to be flexible enough to change with them, or astute enough to recognize that you may need to move on.

Job Getting Is an Art, Not a Science

Job getting is an art, just like playing the piano. When you start taking piano lessons, you learn techniques such as scales, arpeggios, fingering, reading music, and so on. You gradually become proficient by practicing the techniques . . . and practicing . . . and practicing.

However, to become a musician, you go beyond the techniques. You interpret the music and make the performance your own. You become a master.

This book gives you the tools to become proficient as a job hunter. It is up to you to become a master. Practice the methods in it and practice some more. Then use your good judgment based on facts and hunches to be as good as or better than the employer in the employment process. Both of you will win.

The Style Used in This Book

Even though I have written this book in a way that implies imperatives, I use action verbs as a style that is short and punchy. Interpret the advice based on your own situation and adapt or discard what is written according to your own research.

To repeat what paradoxically does amount to a rule:

THERE IS NO ONE RIGHT WAY

Ten Ideas to Get Jump Started

1. Visualize the accomplishment.
2. Move into action—do it now.
3. Identify obstacles and worst-case scenarios; figure out how to deal with them.
4. Surround yourself with supportive people.
5. Identify your skills and the skills needed.
6. Set a goal consistent with motivating vision.
7. Prepare a thorough action plan.
8. Write a goals and action plan timetable.
9. Stay flexible; adjust action plan as needed.
10. Define benefits to employer.

2
Business Operations

Set Up for Business

As a job seeker, you are now running a start-up business to sell your services. Granted, you are only looking for one customer—an employer—but in every other respect, you are in business for yourself.

This means you have to set up operations exactly the same way you would if you were going to be in business permanently, even though it is only a matter of time until you return to the world of employment.

You may already be in this situation if you were telecommuting, employed by a virtual corporation, working out of your home because you were in sales or otherwise traveling extensively, or taking a lot of work home from the office.

Dedicated Home Office

Job getting is a full-time occupation. You need the facilities to pursue it effectively. Unless your former employer is paying for outplacement counseling services that include use of a time-shared office or you have the resources to rent space commercially, you have to set up an office in your home.

The most important thing if you have a home office is to be professional. Children, pets, or household noises distract you from devoting yourself to your search. They reveal to anyone you contact by phone that you are not fully engaged in your job hunt. So, do whatever it takes to set aside space that lets you function efficiently.

Furniture, Fixtures, and Equipment

Much of the equipment you need relates to computer and connectivity capabilities. Technology is complicated and rapidly changing and beyond the scope of this book to describe. Do your research thoroughly before you buy anything or sign up for any services. The wrong choices can be a serious impediment to your work and a drain on your finances.

Computer, Printer, and Modem

Most likely you already have a computer at home but you need unimpeded access to it during your working hours. If you have to, buy a computer for yourself. They are so inexpensive that you ought to make that investment. Purchase the very bottom of the line because you need only minimum power and capacity to run the software and store the data that relate to your search.

Desk, Chair, and Table

You will be spending most of your time working at your computer or telephoning prospects. Make sure you have an ergonomically correct computer desk and chair. Have enough space to organize and do your work.

Filing Cabinet

You will need a filing cabinet to store and access all the files you will create in the course of your search. You may have copies of files from your former jobs that you had a legitimate right to take with you that also need to be stored.

Lighting

You will need excellent task lighting that allows you to work efficiently without eyestrain.

Supplies

Consider all the supplies you had in your former office as a guide and buy enough supplies to last you for the duration of your search.

Stationery

You may be able to create your stationery yourself on your word processor, but make sure its appearance helps you create the professional image that you need to convey to the recipient. Use high-quality 25 percent rag content bond paper, preferably in a businesslike color. Include your address, telephone and fax numbers, and e-mail address on the letterhead. Otherwise, get letterhead and envelopes designed and printed at a print shop so that they look professional.

Get a business card designed and printed that is consistent with your stationery in style, font, and color. Computer designed and printed cards and stationery rarely look professional.

Software

If you do buy a new computer, try to avoid having to learn a new operating system and new software at this critical time in your life. Load what you are adept at into your new computer so that you can hit the ground running.

The job hunting process is built around creating a list of contacts, making contact with them, keeping track of what you have done, and scheduling what you have to do. It also involves sending letters, resumes, and e-mails and keeping track of contacts and appointments.

You can do this manually using an appointment calendar, a Rolodex, an index card box, a business card folder, an accordion file, a looseleaf book, and a file drawer with hanging files. These no-tech methods work very well and there is a very low cost and a fast installation and learning curve.

However, there are many powerful software packages that can automate these processes. Be aware, though, that installation can be complicated and there is a fairly steep learning curve for them.

Mass Mailings

You can mass mail letters and e-mails to your list using various kinds of software, depending on the size of your list.

Word Processor

Since you are going to send out mass mailings, learn how to use the mail merge function of your word processor program to write personalized letters and envelopes. You can create a data file of up to 100 records within your word processing program.

Spreadsheet

If you have between 100 and 500 records, you can use a spreadsheet to create your list and keep track of your interactions with people on it. You can mail merge using your word processing software.

Database Manager

If you have over 500 records, you may want to use database manager software instead. Again, you can mail merge using your word processing software.

Contact Manager Software

As an alternative to building your own system, you can use a contact manager software package that does all of the previously mentioned, as well as some additional functions. (The most popular ones are MS Outlook, Act!, and Maximizer.) They perform most or all of the following functions: database management, automatic scheduling, diary, menu-driven log of contacts made with room for notes, automatic telephone dialing and logging of call date and time, envelope preparation, mail merge, logging of mail recipients and dates, search and filter on database, and report writing. However, there is the learning curve to consider.

Internet Service

You will be using the World Wide Web extensively for your job hunt. Therefore, you need to get a high-quality, reliable Internet service provider. Use a screen name that identifies you in a professional way.

You may decide to create a Web site. AOL and MSN provide do-it-yourself capability. If you want something more sophisticated, shop for available Web design and hosting services in your area.

Telecommunications Systems

Separate Telephone Line

You need uninterrupted access to your telephone for voice, fax, and Internet. If this is not possible on your family line, consider adding one or more phone lines for the duration of your job search.

Voice Mail

Get a separate voice mailbox or answering machine for your home office. Carefully write a script for your outgoing message that is friendly and businesslike. Personal or cute messages do not fit the business image you need to convey.

Facsimile and Copier Machines

Many job advertisements ask you to fax or send copies of your resume. However, buying your own fax and copying machines may not be a good investment. Use copy shops or other resources in your neighborhood that provide such services.

Job Hunting Financial Plan

It will cost you money to hunt for a job. You may have to dip into your savings or borrow money if your severance pay and unemployment benefits run out. So budget for these costs rather than have them surprise you.

Budgeting and Control

Set up a budget to finance your job search. Don't do things yourself that others can do better for you at lower pay rates than you can eventually earn. You need to save your time to do those things you alone can do to conduct the job search.

Revise your personal budget to reflect the loss of income and the costs of your job hunt. Do zero-based budgeting and take immediate steps to cut unnecessary spending.

Chart of Accounts

Here is a list of the most common outlays you may have to make on your job search:

Furniture, Fixtures, and Equipment
    Computer
    Desk, chair, and table
    Filing cabinet
    Supplies and stationery

Computer Software
    Word processor
    Spreadsheet
    Contact manager

Internet Service Provider (ISP) and Web Site
Monthly ISP fees
Web domain registration and fees
Web site hosting services charges

Telecommunications Systems
Telephone equipment purchase
and installation
Telephone line monthly charges
Voice mail
Caller ID
Answering machine

Postage and Delivery
U.S. Postal Service
Postage
Post Office box
Express mail services (UPS, FedEx)
Mail Boxes Etc.
Mailing services for mass mailings

Secretarial Services
Typing
Copying
Fax

Marketing and Advertising
Cover letters and resumes
Advertising
Sales promotion
Web site design

Job and Career Counseling

Professional Training

Travel, Entertainment, and Meals

Bank Loan Repayments and Interest

Tax Deductions

Some of these expenses are tax-deductible. Refer to IRS Publication 529 for information on "Job Search" (see Index).

Return on Investment

The return on your investment in your job hunt (ROI) is potentially huge.

Every day that goes by before you get a new job costs you a full day's salary, bonus or commission, and the total cost of your benefits, whether insured under COBRA or self-funded.

Assume that adequately financing your job hunt will reduce the time you remain unemployed. Prepare best, average, and worst-case scenarios to estimate how many weeks it will be until you are employed again versus how long it would take without spending money on your job hunt efforts. Convert that time into dollars, which represent your return. Divide that number into your expenses. That will be your ROI.

For example, if you will earn $5,000 a month and you spend $5,000 on your job search, *each month* you cut from your time being unemployed represents a 100 percent return on your investment. Multiply that by your guess about the total number of months earlier you get back to work by investing in your search, and that is your ROI.

Alternatively, based on your research into compensation (see Chapter 7), determine what net *per diem* salary you can reasonably expect in your new job. Then calculate how soon you will recoup your after-tax job hunting expenses.

Staying Motivated and Disciplined

Self-Discipline

One of the biggest challenges you will face working in your home office will be self-discipline. There are innumerable distractions: refrigerator, family members, pets, errands, and chores. Conversely, lonesomeness can be a burden that can compound the depression you may be experiencing from losing your job.

Work Scheduling

When you went to work at your former employer's location, your work habits and routines were mostly set by other people. Now you have to be totally self-directed. Experiment to find out what your best rhythm is and establish the pattern that suits you. Then stick with it.

For example, I am a lark. I get up early and do my best thinking and writing in the morning—even before breakfast—and my best interacting with people in the afternoon. Therefore, I have adopted this pattern as a routine. However, I remain flexible to take advantage of opportunities that come up.

You may be tempted to abandon routine entirely, sleep in, stay in your pajamas, eat when your stomach moves you, and intermingle work and leisure. Don't let that happen. No matter what "shift" you work, follow a routine of getting up, dressing for work, doing your exercises, and "opening your business" at the same time every day. A set routine is one of the best ways you can avoid or mitigate nonclinical depression.

Planning

Prepare a daily, weekly, and monthly to-do list. At the end of every work day, plan what you are going to do the next day, preferably in the sequence and time that you will do each item. Use your pocket or desk calendar, your computer calendar, or PDA to do this. That way, you can start working on your job search immediately instead of spending a good part of the morning deciding what to do.

Many things will be repetitive: researching, phoning, and sending out cover letters and resumes. Do them according to a set schedule. Others will be mandatory, such as going to networking or interviewing appointments. Allow for flexibility in your routine for those events.

Leisure

Looking for work is a full-time job. It is every bit as demanding as a paid job. Therefore, it also requires leisure and recreation, otherwise you may burn out. To the extent your budget allows it, keep doing the things that give you pleasure. Besides, your family deserves your attention too, especially because they are under the stress of you being out of work.

On the other hand, avoid overdoing it. Many people who are out of work rejoice that they now have time to spend with their partner and children. However, the downside is that you may disrupt their obligations and routines. And you will presumably be reverting to much the same work pattern when you resume working for an employer, which means that they again have to adjust.

Managing Emotionally

Interviewers can smell if you are down and they don't want to deal with that in an employee. So it is essential that you stay "up." You can do many things to maintain a positive attitude and stay energetic. Read the advice on pages 13 and 14 from Dr. Robert A. Karlin, a practicing clinical psychologist and Associate Professor of Psychology at Rutgers University.

Join a Support Group

It gets lonesome when you are out of work. You used to have a boss, probably peers and colleagues, likely specialists from other departments to help

How to Avoid Getting Down While You're Out

It is natural, at least occasionally, to be discouraged and upset by unemployment. But when being upset interferes with your ability to solve your problems, make contacts, create and pursue leads, and hunt for the job, you may be depressed as well as upset and/or discouraged. The important question is whether your emotional reaction to the situation is getting in your way. One common biochemical/emotional reaction to the stress of unemployment or the need to search for a job is mild or moderate depression.

Here are some facts about depression:

1. *Depression lies to you.* It tells you that you just need to relax for a little while and just be left to yourself in order to feel better. Such feelings and thoughts may well be symptoms of depression. Following their dictates makes depression worse.

2. *Depression requires structured activity, preferably some of it with other people, and some of it physical in nature.* Make sure to spend some time interacting with others; don't let yourself become isolated. Exercise daily, keeping your heartbeat at an aerobic level for 20 to 30 minutes.

3. *One difficult thing about unemployment is that it removes the usual structure of one's life and one's daily contacts.* Set up structure so that you always have something to do. Build momentum by doing easy tasks for a few minutes to get going and then do the harder tasks you might otherwise avoid at first.

4. *Avoid mind-altering substances such as alcohol and drugs.* They aggravate the depression. Even television can be depressing if you use it to avoid activity and being with others!

5. *Volunteer.* Give to others who are less fortunate than you. Volunteering is a great self-esteem booster. It keeps you active and involved and helps you feel you can do whatever your new job will require.

6. *Keep a life.* Social and recreational interactions with people are "antidepressants."

7. *Learn to relax.* There are many good self-help books such as *The Relaxation Response* by Herbert Benson, M.D. (New York: William Morrow

(continued)

How to Avoid Getting Down While You're Out (continued)

and Company, 1975) that are based on valid research. An excellent book that helps with feelings of simple anxiety as well as panic is *Mastery of Your Anxiety and Panic, 2nd ed.* by Barlow and Craske (Westport, CN: Greenwood Press, 1994).

8. *Make sure your thinking is not unduly pessimistic.* Again, there are wonderful self-help books. My favorite is *Mind Over Mood* by Greenberger and Padesky (New York: Guilford Press, 1995).

9. *Get help.* If the depression is so bad that it prevents you from being effective, see a therapist. The treatments with the best evidence of effectiveness are antidepressant medications combined with cognitive-behavior therapy. One nasty symptom of depression is that you don't believe that anyone or anything (except the right job) can help you. Depression can be fatal, but it usually can be easily alleviated if it is treated. It is dumb to kill your career or yourself when treatment is effective and readily available.

---

you, and possibly subordinates. Even if you were in sales on the road or a telecommuter, you had interaction with other businesspeople.

Now, it is just you.

Fortunately, there are many job clubs. They generally provide instruction in job finding and career-changing techniques, networking and lead generation opportunities, and support. Many of them are sponsored by churches and nonprofit community groups. Some are under the aegis of government agencies. A few require paid membership or work in return for services.

There is a list of such groups and events in the *Wall Street Journal's* Web site careerjournal.com at the bottom of the home page.

Set Up a Board of Advisors

It can be difficult to adjust to being a solo operator, especially if you have been working in an organization where you had a boss, colleagues, perhaps subordinates, and experts from other departments and from outside the company to draw on for direction and help. Therefore, create substitutes. Set up a "Board of Advisors." Make alliances with people who can advise and encourage you while you are out of work. Ask them to meet on a regular basis to review your plans and progress. Offer to reciprocate by telling them what you have discovered during your networking and research that will benefit them in their jobs and careers. They can also learn from your experiences as a job getter.

Bottom Line: Stay Focused

I have a sign on my desk that reads:

HOW WILL THIS MAKE MONEY?

I recommend it to you as a great way to focus your job hunt and avoid wasting time.

3

Business Plan

Your Job-Seeking Business Strategy

Every start-up business should have a business strategy. There are two major purposes:

1. To crystalize the thinking of the entrepreneur and communicate a consistent strategy that everyone involved in the venture can understand and follow.
2. To get financing from banks, private investors, or venture capitalists (or for both purposes).

Business Strategy Statement

As an "interim entrepreneur," you too need a job-seeking business strategy. It should answer such questions as:

What "business" are you in?

What products or services are you selling?

What markets are you selling your services to?

What price are you charging for your services?

What is your destination and how will you get there?

What are the reasons you will succeed in your new job?

Niels Nielsen article reprinted by permission from careerjournal.com, © Dow Jones & Co. All rights reserved.

The answers to these questions are documented in a strategy statement. Although it appears at the beginning of your business plan, it is written only after you have done your research. The strategy statement combines the results of cataloging your products and services (Chapter 4), your market research (Chapter 5), your analysis of the total compensation package (Chapter 7), and your personal vision and mission statement (Chapter 3). In its final form, the strategy statement comprises a summary statement, a summary of the characteristics of your target market, and your Unique Selling Proposition.

Summary Statement

Open your strategy statement with a brief summary regarding what business you are in. This summary should sell you. It should also clearly tell recruiters and employers how you will succeed for them. It can be adapted for use as the career summary on your resume and for your elevator speech.

A dozen examples follow from a wide variety of occupations and levels. They are excerpted from resumes at the end of this book:

Sample Summary Statements

Chief executive officer with a record of growing revenues and profits through creative marketing, effective team leadership, and the use of Baldrige quality criteria.

International marketing and sales executive with record of discovering and exploiting worldwide market opportunities and creating rapid and profitable growth for consumer products.

Financial and market analyst with record of providing decision-making, profit-producing information to management. Especially effective in use of spreadsheet, database, graphics, word processing, local area network (LAN), and project control software.

Sample Summary Statements (continued)

Profit-creating, commission-building marketing and sales executive with record of accomplishment at corporate, regional, and agency level in insurance and securities industries.

Pharmacologist with unique combination of marketing, clinical, research, managerial, and teaching experience in industry, hospital, and academic settings.

Creative and energetic engineering and systems professional, with demonstrated leadership and organizational skills. Accomplished negotiator with diverse experience in manufacturing, design, and subcontract management. Successful record of meeting all technical and performance objectives.

Pension administrator with track record of reducing employer pension costs, cutting turnaround times, improving service to and increasing rapport with clients, and thereby raising billable revenues.

Hands-on troubleshooter in accounting and systems with record of improving efficiency, cutting costs, and moving operations to a higher plane.

Local and Wide Area Network professional with a record of increasing productivity, speeding up communication, reducing costs, meeting deadlines, and enabling companies to achieve their business goals.

Versatile, energetic, and problem-solving administration manager with record of achieving results—on time, on budget, and above expectations—in a wide variety of industries including high technology, finance, professional service, and not-for-profit.

Banker and financial executive with a record of starting up and building profitable businesses by identifying and exploiting attractive niche opportunities.

Turnaround marketing and underwriting executive with record of creating long-term revenue and profit growth and extensive market contacts in property and casualty insurance industry.

Market Characteristics Statement

There are several similar questions about the employment markets you are targeting. Look at them from a bird's-eye point of view rather than in specific terms at this stage of your planning:

What is the growth potential of your market?

What kinds of prospective employers do you plan to target?

What are the chief characteristics of your prospective employers?

Here is a sample statement by an international executive in a high-technology industry. Create your own version based on your market research (Chapter 5):

Sample Statement of Market Characteristics

The market for my abilities has significant future growth prospects because of the aging of the baby boomer population. I plan to target firms that are at the cutting edge technologically but not in the start-up phase in order to reduce the business risk elements that could jeopardize my job. The employers in these companies are experienced mature executives with a strong social consciousness coupled with a focus on their customers' needs, their communities' welfare, and their employees' well-being and work/life balance. These employers are rated highly as good places to work and therefore have many applicants for jobs.

Your Unique Selling Proposition

The right job has a great fit between a prospective employer's specific needs and what you do best. That's your "unique selling proposition."

Here are the questions to answer to describe what your Unique Selling Proposition (USP) is:

To what extent and in what ways is the market competitive in your field?

How do the services you offer differ from those of your competitors for jobs?

Why would your prospects hire you instead of your competitors?

What gaps are there to be filled in your market? Can you offer new services that employers need but cannot find candidates to provide?

What are the reasons you will succeed in this business?

What are the biggest benefits to prospective employers of your services?

How will you make prospective employers more profitable or effective?

What is there about you that would appeal to the prospective employers on an emotional level?

What are your strengths and weaknesses for the job you are looking for? What should you do, if anything, to overcome the weaknesses? Alternatively, what kinds of jobs or employers should you avoid so that the weaknesses do not matter or may even be strengths?

Here is an example of a Unique Selling Proposition statement:

Unique Selling Proposition

The market in my field is very competitive. I differ from the majority of candidates, however, because I have an unusual combination of successes in research, production, and marketing. Most of my competitors have had experience in only one of these functions. My versatility as well as my international expertise make me stand out from them.

I have a record of acting as a catalyst to bring the different players together to produce results. There are very few people in my field who can demonstrate achievements that cross organizational and national boundaries.

I will succeed in the job because of my record of accomplishments in the global high-technology business. My previous employers benefited from my multidisciplinary, multinational abilities because I built alliances with people in other countries who had patents and products that we

(continued)

Unique Selling Proposition (continued)

could adapt for sale throughout the world. I gained their trust so that we quickly negotiated mutually favorable contracts. After the initial costs of rolling out the products, we achieved profitability within two years.

In my previous company, I worked with many people at all levels in the industry and know what makes them tick. My perception is that I would quickly fit in to their culture and function effectively in the company.

My strengths include my ability to communicate fluently in several languages, my managerial, organizational, and people skills. I lack some technical knowledge, but I am a quick study and can soon get up to speed. I should avoid companies that are highly political.

Combine the Three Elements to Create Your Business Plan

Refine your three elements by adjusting them to conform to your findings in the others. For example, you will probably have to change your catalog of achievements as you do your market research and marketing and sales, and vice versa. You will probably adjust your personal priorities as you clarify your markets and targets.

After you have finished your analyses, write your strategy statement using your elevator speech, your market analysis, your Unique Selling Proposition, and your personal mission statement (see Chapter 3).

Your Personal Vision and Mission

Now that you are unemployed, this may be the time to ask yourself some hard questions:

What kind of career do you want?

Where are you going in it?

How are you going to get there?

Be opportunistic. You now have an opportunity to reconsider your career. For many people, this issue is easily answered. They are exactly on the track they want to follow and should stay the course. However, you may have had questions or doubts in your mind but were too busy to contemplate them while you were working. This is the time to step back and review the questions previously posed.

There are three interrelated elements to a decision to make a change:

1. Your personal values, needs, and aspirations.
2. The options that are open to you to reinvent your career. "Change Your Business Model," later in this chapter, guides you through this process.
3. The economics of the job market in terms of which industries, job functions, and companies are growing and which are stagnant or declining. Chapter 5, "Market Research," guides you through this process.

To maximize the efficiency of your decision making in considering which jobs to look for, start with your personal and family circumstances. Figure out where you will flourish and be content. Conversely, avoid looking at the kinds of jobs or businesses you would not be happy or effective in.

Your Values, Needs, and Aspirations

Take stock of yourself and, if relevant, your spouse or partner and your family. Ask yourself what is really important to you in your life and career. If there were no holds barred, if money were no object, what would you do? Write down your answers to the following questions. Show the degree to which each matters to you.

Do you want to work for a giant, medium, or small organization? Where do you function best, or think you would?

Do you want to work in a for-profit or not-for-profit organization? Do you believe in the capitalist way? Do you have a strong social conscience? Can you combine them?

Do you flourish in a political work environment?

Do you need or want a boss, a structure, a clear definition of goals, duties, responsibilities, rewards, recognition, and a stable environment?

Are you a risk avoider or are you a risk taker?

Do you want independence, autonomy, self-sufficiency?

To what extent do you need to affiliate with an organization, be part of a team?

How important is loyalty—both ways—to you?

How much does satisfaction in a-job-well-done matter to you? Do you seek recognition from other people?

How much or little interaction do you want or need with other people? What kind of people do you especially like to associate with?

What are your career goals and what is your time line to achieve them?

How important are money, power, or prestige to you? How ambitious are you?

Are you naturally a leader, manager, supervisor, or employee?

Do you want to manage, to achieve through others, to get satisfaction out of getting the best out of subordinates, to deal with the administrative responsibilities, to go to meetings?

What are your passions? What subject matter fascinates you? Do you have hobbies or interests that you could make your career?

What kind of work/family/community balance is important to you? Are you willing and eager to work long hours, travel on the job, bring work home, entertain business colleagues, think about work even when you are not at work?

Where do you want to live? What lifestyle do you want? Are you willing to commute and how far? Would you want to telecommute or work out of your home?

If you have additional criteria, write them down too.

Write Your Vision and Mission Statement

Based on your answers, write your personal profile. Here are two examples to help you get started:

I would work best for a global profit-making corporation that has a clear structure and definition of goals and responsibilities. I work well with the political aspects of getting ahead and am prepared to take some risks to get there. I want to be part of a team of corporate people like myself and take pride in being part of the company I work for. I expect that my loyalty will be reciprocated by my employer. I get satisfaction out of my work and am proud of my accomplishments. I seek recognition from my peers as well as from my boss for what I contribute.

Money, power, and prestige are very important to me and I want to be in a senior executive position by the time I am 45. I have strong leadership qualities and know how to get the best out of people. I am somewhat impatient with the administrative aspects of this level but know how to delegate.

My work is my passion and I am willing to give up time with my family, interests, and community so that I can devote myself to my job. However, I want my family to be comfortable and live in an upscale suburb near a large city. I am prepared to commute up to three or four hours a day if that is what it takes.

Here is a profile that is nearly at the opposite end of the spectrum:

I want to start a business and be a jack-of-all-trades to do whatever needs to be done whenever that happens. I am a risk taker and enjoy the thrill of making deals. I am a solo operator and do not want to work for anyone else. I am not at all political; what I take pride in is the solution of the challenge, not the process. I do enjoy being looked up to as successful in my occupation and my community.

If I succeed in my venture, the money will come and I expect to be well off. I hope to build a profitable business that I can sell in five years, when I will start another business. I will gather entrepreneurial colleagues to help me do this and will outsource staff functions so that we can concentrate on creating, making, and marketing the product.

My family is very important to me and I will make time to be with them. We prefer to live in a small town near my office and recreational facilities so that we can get away as often as possible. I know that my work will be on my mind, so I will allow time for staying in touch with the business while away. Until the profits become significant and steady, I will invest in the business rather than in an expensive lifestyle. That can come when I retire.

Now, build your own vision and mission. With the agreement of your family, use your statement to filter the possibilities open to you and narrow down your job search.

Your mission statement should be liberating and a basis for making choices. It should give you the strength to pursue the right job and the courage to reject all the wrong jobs. A test of your mission statement is: Would you reject a job offer if it didn't meet every one of the criteria you include? Which ones are deal-breakers? Which can be compromised? What are the trade-offs? Which don't matter at all?

Armed with your mission statement, you are liberated from the compulsion to accept the first job offer that comes along to "put the bread on the table." You can manage your career in a way that maximizes your work/life balance.

Words of Wisdom to a New MBA Graduate by Niels H. Nielsen

Dear Son,

As your father, I'd like to make a suggestion about your coming job search now that you're leaving graduate school. Before you start interviewing, clearly define your career goals. For example:

What industries would you like to work in? Are they growing, dynamic, international, profitable, and competitive, and likely to stay that way for some time?

Is your target company financially solid with good future prospects? Would you invest a large amount of your own money in it?

What kind of work do you want to do immediately, five years from now, and in the future? Would you be able to do it?

Is the position you're considering on the fast track to the top of the company? Can you become president by the time you're 35?

What kind of culture will you flourish in? Conversely, what kind of environment would frustrate or destroy you?

Will the job represent a step up from the position you held before returning to graduate school? In other words, will you get an immediate payoff for the two years and the money invested in your MBA?

Will you work for a mentor who can increase your knowledge and further your goals?

Will you be able to control your work environment and the direction of the company?

Will you be a businessperson, business leader, business bureaucrat, or business advisor?

Will you be able to make a large and measurable contribution that will be recognized and rewarded?

Will the job provide you with an equity position that will allow you to create wealth for yourself? Will you eventually earn enough to start your own business? It's often worth trading a higher salary, benefits, profit-sharing, or other retirement benefits for equity positions.

In case a job doesn't work out, is the employer located in an area where other opportunities are available, or would you have to relocate?

Does the area offer cultural, social, and recreational amenities that fit your lifestyle and values? Would you enjoy living there, and what would it cost you relative to your income?

You probably have other questions that should be added to this list. In fact, you'll have more concerns each time you interview. You can also explore your career goals retroactively by evaluating past jobs and internships. You might want to rank or weight your standards to determine what you'd be willing to give up to get what's really important to you.

The point is, you should accept a job offer based on objective criteria that you've identified in advance, not out of impulse or desperation.

Much love,

Dad

Change Your Business Model

Companies often change their original business models to:

> Sell the same products or services to new markets.
>
> Offer new product lines to their existing customers.
>
> Enter new markets with new products.

The reasons for such changes in direction are many: opportunities, competition, innovations, economics, and changing company strategy. For example:

> Microsoft's strategy is driven by technological and product changes from inside and competitive pressures from outside to expand and extend its offerings. It has gone from its original DOS operating system to Windows, from operating systems to applications software, from concentration on stand-alone personal computers to Internet server-client networks, from software to Internet service provider and content, from game software to game boxes, and from software to some hardware products. And all of them are repeatedly upgraded to new versions to create new demand.

The same dynamics and motivations apply to you as you and/or your job markets change. Your industry may be growing or shrinking due to mergers, shifts in buyer habits, changes in technology, stock market booms or busts, or many other reasons.

Alternatively, your career may be changing around and under you, either dramatically or almost imperceptibly. Your capabilities may have changed, or you may psychologically be ready for a new direction.

Reinvent Yourself to Change Careers

You therefore have to reinvent yourself. Do as companies do—change your business model. Your choices of career changes can range all the way from upgrading your skills to going into a completely different line of work in a whole new industry.

Upgrade Your Skills

Often as your skills become obsolescent, you have to change just to survive in your present job. In that case, there are various steps you should take. Keep up to date on your professional literature. Attend seminars and conferences. If you are unemployed, take advantage of the time you now have to get training in current techniques or methods. Some state governments pay for retraining if you meet their requirements, so ask your state unemployment office. Otherwise, consider your personal expenses on courses to be a necessary investment in making you more marketable. Do information interviewing to see what is going on elsewhere in your field. Attend professional conferences and trade shows.

Repackage Your Skills

If opportunities in your industry are declining or if they are growing faster elsewhere, it's time to cross industry boundaries to find work in your current field. This may be difficult because many employers feel that you have to have worked in their specific industry even though your occupation is totally transferable. But this is merely an objection to be overcome.

To do this, learn all you can about their business, the kinds of jobs they have, their culture, and their language. Delete industry-specific language and references from your resume and cover letter. When you meet such employers, acknowledge their concern and then show how your accomplishments apply in their industry. Become like one of them so that you can become one of them.

Create a New Version of Yourself

Upgrade your offering and issue a new version of yourself. The computer and automobile industries are great at doing this. Their marketing strategy is to sell the latest version, which makes the previous one obsolete.

Reposition Yourself

You may want (or have to) reposition yourself as you or your target markets change. Instead of looking for full-time employment, consider becoming an interim manager or working full or part time for a consulting or job shop firm.

Embark on a Totally New Career

You may want to make a complete career change and do something you have never done. Be aware, though, that this is the hardest and riskiest transition to make. Fortunately, there are many people who have done this successfully. (I am in my nineteenth career due to a combination of circumstances, luck, opportunity, desire for variety, choice, and necessity.)

Would You Rather Be an Entrepreneur?

Some of us actually decide to give up employment altogether and become entrepreneurs. "Entrepreneur" has many meanings, but the one I am using applies to someone who starts a new business of any kind and is self-employed. It includes solo-operator consultants or free-lancers working in their areas of expertise.

Be forewarned, this is not an easy way to make a living. It takes courage and persistence. It requires business smarts that very few corporate types have learned, no matter how high they have risen in the hierarchy. It is high risk and the failure rate is horrendous.

However, if you do have the entrepreneurial fire in your belly, the energy, the drive, and the financial resources to start on your own, this book will give you the basis for a preliminary business plan. However, it does not cover all the aspects of setting up a real business as compared to the interim entrepreneurship it advocates for job getters.

How Do You Change Your Business Model?

Here are several different methods to help you decide what new business model to adopt. All of them are based on economic and personal realities (rather than pop-psychological theories). They are interrelated—each influences all the others.

Your Values, Needs, and Aspirations

Refer to "Vision and Mission" in this chapter for a checklist of criteria to take into consideration as you think of changing your career.

Mine Your Catalog of Accomplishments

Go through your entire catalog of accomplishments and make a second set that is generic. (I am going to assume that you have them on the index cards I refer to in Chapter 4.) Remove industry-specific and company-specific labels and language. As you do this, think about other achievements and write them down on new cards. If you already have an idea of alternative careers, think about how each accomplishment could be transferred, and jot that down.

Now, sort the cards to see if there are any patterns. Shuffle them and lay them all out on a table. Pick them up and rank them 1 through 5 (where 5 is highest) according to criteria such as the following:

What made the biggest contributions to your employer?

What did your boss give you as a top rating in your performance reviews?

What got you raises, bonuses, or awards?

What skills did you use that gave you the greatest satisfaction?

What subject matter really grabbed you?

What are you proudest of having accomplished?

What did you really enjoy?

After you sort on each of these in turn, write the criterion and rank on the back of each card so you will remember it.

When you have finished, shuffle the cards and turn all of them over so that only the ratings appear. Now pick them up according to the weight you gave them. For example, you will find some cards that are predominantly 5 and others that are mostly 1. The remainder will have more scattered ratings, but try to put them in some average sequence.

Look for Patterns
Now look at the accomplishments that ranked highest and look for patterns. You will find that certain achievements really were great for both you and your employer. Do the same for those at the bottom and recognize that you should stay away from that kind of work, or alternatively go for the opposite. Check the in-betweens to see if they provide more evidence one way or another.

With this information, write up your second profile, this one about your career alternatives. It will tell you with real data from your catalog of your achievements what you ought to pursue in your new business model, that is, career. Remember, the best predictor of future success is past successes. (The profile will also give you answers for the inevitable interview question, "What are your strengths and weaknesses?")

This approach is far more effective than so-called psychology tests that claim to measure your aptitudes or personality and attempt to correlate them with occupations. Most of the authors of these tests have no idea what work or skills are involved in any occupation. There is, in fact, low correlation between personality and success. Look at all the people you know in your occupation who are successful and you will find very little similarity in their personalities or styles.

Market Research

Having determined what your career change strategy is, your next step is to find out what jobs there are in the field(s) you have identified. Refer to Chapter 5 on Market Research for guidance.

Integrating the Many Elements of the Process

Finally, go back and adjust the new catalog of your services to fit the reality of the marketplace. Select the fields where there is growing demand rather than those that are in decline.

Examples of Career Changes

Read the articles and case studies that follow this chapter for examples of career changes. They show the results of these processes in tangible form.

There are four cover letters and four resumes regarding career change in the Appendix to this book. They are all originals that I have created with and for clients. Client identities and the names of their employers have been changed for confidentiality reasons.

Use these examples to stimulate your own thinking. But do not imitate them. Hiring managers and recruiters, in particular, can spot boilerplate and phony statements. So, be original as a way of differentiating yourself.

Career Success Begins with Self-Evaluation
by Niels H. Nielsen

As a career counselor, I've advised many people on choosing a new occupation. On the premise that the best predictor of future success is past success, I help clients take inventory of their successes and then transform and transfer their accomplishments to other fields.

This sounds simple, but it's really complex. I need to know the kind of work my clients have been doing and even more about occupations they might consider. I have to uncover their interests and skills, some of which are hidden. Among these are the hobbies or outside activities that absorb them. I always ask about their career fantasies—their "Walter Mitty" dreams—so they'll stop straight-line thinking or worrying about feasibility.

I used this technique when I worked with an architect and urban planner. When he lost his job during a downturn in the economy, he was forced to change occupations. As I examined his successes, I noticed that he had a second occupation that sustained his primary one. He had secured the financing on all his projects. After we altered his perspective, he landed a job at a leading bank doing project financing at triple his former salary.

Another case involved a pastor who was burned out. In analyzing his duties, I was astonished by how many roles he had: inspirational speaker, teacher, chief executive officer, social worker, fund raiser, planner, organizer, politician, salesperson, public relations spokesman, community leader, facilities manager, small businessperson, financial planner and controller, entertainment coordinator, show business impresario, and others.

It's a great job, if you can do these things in the order they come at you. But he was overwhelmed by the complexity of his work. So using the techniques I described, I helped him zero in on what he enjoyed doing most and he became a social worker, a career he was well-qualified to do.

Not long after, my wife died prematurely and I had to consider my own career options. She left me with enough money to do whatever I wanted, no holds barred, cost no object. My choices ranged from doing nothing to making a radical life change.

Making this decision was a daunting proposition. My career has been rich and varied. In fact, I've had 19 different careers. The first seven were in large corporations where I was rotated through a range of functions. The other 11 were in occupations I had to learn after founding my human resources and general management consulting practice in 1979. At that time, I had to become a professional salesperson to avoid starvation. I also became a small businessman. Other occupations arose out of different assignments with clients.

While I had plenty of experience with career change, this was a unique challenge. I used the gamut of tactics career counselors apply when working with others, including paper-and-pencil tests, computer analysis, flash card tests, and my own techniques. Nothing worked. Some produced bizarre results; would you believe rocket scientist?

I explored alternatives I hadn't been able to try earlier in life for various reasons. I had once thought about arts management, but gave that up and remained a volunteer for economic reasons. I considered earning a degree in a new field to round out my intellectual life. I briefly contemplated retirement, but ruled that out as too boring.

This process, which took me to various advisors, lasted about two months. During this time, I felt both exhilarated and directionless. It was weird not having to take jobs that came up or follow a compelling timetable. It was a frustrating and freeing feeling.

Ultimately, I looked inside myself. I thought about what had given me the greatest satisfaction and joy over the years. Remarkably, I realized I was in my ideal job—solo operator management consultant. That discovery, after all the soul-searching, came in a flash.

Being asked to look at a situation that needs to be fixed, figuring out what's really wrong (often not what the client thinks initially), conceptualizing the best solution, and putting it into effect—that's what I love. And I'm paid to do it. What could be better?

The lesson here is to include your heart as well as your head when you're deciding on your next career. Follow your passion. You'll be much more effective in a job you love than in a position you choose for the money or because it seems like the right or only thing you can do.

4

Product Plan

Create Your Catalog of Service Offerings

Like any start-up company, the first thing you have to do is decide what services you are going to offer. You are probably selling your specialized brainpower. But how do you demonstrate that you have skills and knowledge and what you have done with them? They are not like cars, computers, toys, jackets, food, houses, books, life insurance policies, investment portfolios, or educational programs that the prospect can examine and choose.

As I said earlier, when it comes to brainpower, the best predictor of future success is past success. The way to demonstrate the value added of your experience and education is to illustrate it with what you have accomplished in your previous jobs.

Employers, for their part, are screening for top performers. They want to know what you can contribute to their success that will make them decide to hire you. Your accomplishments *by being factual* are very persuasive.

Sample Accomplishments

Your most powerful sales tool is a catalog of achievements that are tangible and quantified. An example that a marketing professional offered is:

> Mounted intensive marketing campaign to land a Fortune 100 company; used cold calls, direct marketing, telemarketing, and formal presentation to obtain request for proposal; prepared response—Result: Obtained a contract that was four times the average size for firm.

That is much more exciting than the typical job description task that most resumes contain:

Responsible for marketing to major corporations to obtain Requests for Proposals.

Likewise, a manufacturing executive wrote:

Took over loose operation, analyzed every stage of production, established uniform written procedures and tighter quality control standards, cross-trained all employees to be versatile—Result: In five years, increased production speed by 300 percent, cut chemical costs by 50 percent, reduced material consumption by 20 percent, and cut failure rate from 15 percent to less than 0.1 percent, even with the more demanding standards.

The job description simply said:

Manages factory production, quality control, and costs; supervises staff.

An information technology expert working at a newspaper stated:

Assembled a complex multiplatform, multiprotocol network, comprising Unix servers, Microsoft Windows NT software, and Novell Netware—Results: Enabled reporters to collaborate and to send rapidly breaking developments to news wires more quickly, thus enhancing company's reputation for timeliness in a time-critical business.

rather than just listing the hardware, operating systems, middle ware, and software with which she was familiar. What counts is what she accomplished for her employer by using the tools of the trade. (Note that the buzz or key words used by the computerized scanners are there, too.)

Even so-called "soft" occupations like Human Resources can come up with numerical measurements of their results:

Increased the annual rate of hiring by 65 percent while reducing cost per hire by 50 percent in the space of 18 months.

Set up in-house recruiting agency—Result: Saved $3,500 per permanent employee hired.

Negotiated with temporary help agency to set up on-site representative—
Result: Gave incentive to agency to keep temp usage to a minimum.

That's much more graphic than "Handles recruiting of employees."

Clearly, your job description tells nothing about how well you did your
duty nor what your results were. However, your job description is implicit
in your accomplishments, so you don't have to include it.

Take Inventory of Your Past Achievements

What achievements are you proud of? More importantly, which ones were
your employers satisfied with because you added value? They are your "catalog of services." You can probably come up with 10, 20, 30, or more, depending on how long you have been working and what your jobs were.
Even routine job descriptions can be turned into achievements.

The way to remember what they were is to go through your present
resume, your job description, your monthly reports, your performance reviews (especially those that got you raises, bonuses, awards, and promotions), your memories, the war stories that you told your partner or your
buddies that they can remind you about, and any other sources that come
to mind. Often, you will be reminded of your achievements during a job
interview in response to a question. Write them down right away or as
soon as they occur to you.

Go to outside sources, too. Read the classified and Internet ads in
your field and see what employers are asking for. They may remind you of
your past accomplishments that will fit the real needs the employers stipu-
late. Another source is the Occupational Information Network (O*NET),
a comprehensive database system for collecting, organizing, describing,
and disseminating data on job characteristics and worker attributes. Its
Web site address is http://www.doleta.gov/almis/onetnew1.htm.

Don't limit yourself to jobs you have been paid for. Include relevant
volunteer activities (they may show leadership abilities), hobbies and interests (sports can demonstrate teamwork), even household management
(ability to multitask), or personal financial management. Your accomplishments in those contexts can be rich sources of information about additional value you bring to the new employer.

Skills, Competencies, and Traits

Many people think—or are advised—that skills, competencies, and traits are what employers look for. It's possible, but those characteristics are implied by the achievements and scenarios illustrated earlier. For example, initiative, action-orientation, attention to detail, people skills, conceptual abilities, innovativeness, training and education, even hard work, can all be inferred from what you achieved in previous jobs and activities. On the other hand, what you achieved cannot be discerned from a list of competencies.

Style of Catalog Entries

Study the previous examples and the resumes at the end of this book for examples of catalog entries.

Start with an action verb in the past tense to indicate power. Words like "assisted," "liaised," "coordinated," and "contributed" leave the employer or recruiter wondering if you actually did anything. On the other hand, "devised," "initiated," "directed," and "implemented" connote active contribution.

Note that the "I" pronoun is implied. It does not matter whether you had help with your accomplishment. Claim credit if you can legitimately say that you were a key player. Forget what your parents taught you about not bragging. This is not the time to be modest. In any case, everyone knows that no one works completely alone, so it is not worth the space to write that others were involved.

There is an important exception to this suggestion. If the employer asks for teamwork, or if teamwork was what you were measured on in your old job, tell what the team achieved and what role you played in making the team succeed.

Then describe briefly what you did. This gives substance and credibility to your claim of meeting and overcoming the challenge you faced. It also indicates what your job and role were and what skills or tools you used. Make this really striking, it is the "feature" of your product.

Finally, state the measurable results—the "benefits"—of your services. These are most compelling if they are written in relative terms. For example, you may have saved $10 million. Who knows if that is impressive or insignificant? If the saving was out of a budget of $25 million, that's 40 percent. If it is out of $10 billion, it is only 0.1 percent. So, give a benchmark against which to judge the impact or state it in relative terms (or both).

Inventory Cards for Your Catalog

The best way to do this physically depends on your own preferences. You may be most comfortable writing the achievements on your computer. However, one technique that many people have found helpful is to use 3″ × 5″ index cards—one accomplishment per card. The cards force you to be brief. They give you flexibility. They are easy to sort, and you will sort them often. If you suddenly think of something, you can just write it on a card and find out where it goes later. This is especially valuable when you wake up in the middle of the night with a thought. It also works right after an interview to record what was said so that you can use it for the thank-you letter and to increase your catalog items. (I have written this entire book using index cards.)

The Many Uses of the Catalog

You will use your catalog of accomplishments to write your targeted resumes and cover letters, answer advertisements, develop your elevator speech, make a great impression in your interviews, and possibly select a new career.

Once you get used to preparing your accomplishments, you will find them indispensable in succeeding at your next job. You will develop a keen focus on what you are really doing your job for and how you are adding value for your employer. Their style is terrific for preparing your monthly reports and self-evaluations in performance reviews. They will help you in setting your goals.

5
Marketing Plan

Marketing Strategy

Business Vision and Mission

Your business vision and mission are very simple:

> Your vision is a great job, one that is as close as possible to your ideal.
> Your mission is to go get it.

Your success in achieving your vision and mission depends on your total commitment to marketing and sales. There are many marketing and sales tactics that make sense in the job market. Use all of them rather than limit yourself to any one or a few.

Business-to-Business (B2B) Marketing

As a job seeker, you are an "interim entrepreneur" in the business of finding employment with another business. Your job-hunt marketing strategy is very much like that used by a corporation launching a new service or getting a contract to perform a lengthy project. It involves:

- Dealing with relatively few prospects that need your qualifications at the time you are looking for a job.
- Using layers of intermediaries or middlemen to help you find each other.
- Investing in a long lead time to make the sale.

- Seeking ultimately only one buyer.
- Negotiating an elaborate contract that is subject to numerous company policies and practices as well as government laws and regulations.
- Pursuing a deal with a multiyear duration.

Therefore, you can adapt the same strategy and tactics that corporations use in their Business-to-Business (B2B) marketing to achieve success.

Relationship Marketing

There is one big difference between you as an "interim entrepreneur" and a start-up company, however. In this case, *you* are personally the product that you are selling. Ultimately, the hiring "company" is a collection of human beings and they are making a decision about another human being, not a commercial transaction:

> Are we making the right choice? Are you going to work out? Are you going to fit? Are you going to deliver what we need? Are you going to make us succeed? Or are you going to be a problem on top of the ones we already have and make them worse?

Those are tough questions to answer. They are what keep hiring managers awake at night. Survey after survey concludes that the CEO's biggest worry is whether they are getting the best people for the job. Human nature is so complicated and dynamic that the answer is quite unpredictable. The final decision—after all the processes have been thoroughly gone through—is based on gut feel.

The uncertainty is even greater on your side. You have less to go on than the employer does in making your decision. Despite all the information you have gathered about the company and the due diligence you have done, when you go to work on your new job, it will be with people. Lots of people—people with their own personalities, agendas, ambitions, degrees of desire to cooperate or compete with you, axes to grind, and maybe even with knives out. The cast of characters changes continually, all the way from getting a new manager to having the company acquired by a new owner.

There is no one right answer to the question of how to deal with such mutual uncertainty. However, the most likely way to succeed is to build relationships. Use relationship marketing to get the interview in the first place, interpersonal skills to land the job in the second, and alliances to keep it when you finally have it.

The tactics of B2B marketing have been described in the preceding chapters and will be further developed in the chapters that follow. As you use the suggestions about marketing and sales techniques in the rest of the book, remember to keep relationship marketing at the center of your strategy.

Market Research

As the opening number in "Music Man" says: "You got to know the territory." What you offer from your catalog of services is determined by what is being bought in the market. Demand can be volatile. A case in point was the boom market for dot.com experts. In the second half of the 1990s, there was an extreme shortage of people with skills in Web design and online sales and fulfillment. Then there was a sudden reversal at the beginning of the 2000s, which was called the "dot.com bust." Similar swings occurred in the telecommunications industry.

Stay alert to where the jobs are now and whether that area is growing or declining. To do this, you need to learn some elementary market research techniques. (You can start to learn about them from the Market Research cover letters and resumes at the end of the book.)

Primary Research (Information Interviewing)

There are two kinds of market research, primary and secondary. Primary research from your perspective is information you acquire while you are networking. Actually, *information interviewing* is similar to lead generation networking (see Chapter 8) in method but different in purpose.

Ask your contacts for an information interview to find out first hand about occupations, products or services, companies, industries, and regions from the people who work in them. You can also get information about the company culture, what role Human Resources plays, and who makes the hiring decisions. Say that you are considering going into that line of work (or whatever reason applies to you) and ask appropriate questions. If the meeting goes well, you can ask for networking referrals.

However, do not bait and switch by getting an appointment to obtain information and then asking for a job. If the contacts do have a job for you, they will let you know and they will switch the meeting into an interview. In case that happens, be prepared to seize the opportunity.

Secondary Research

The other main way to do market research is to consult the library or the Internet for information from published sources. Reference librarians are especially helpful and willing to show you how to do this effectively and efficiently with both the library resources and the Internet. Here is a sample of sources you can use for secondary market research:

Newspapers and Magazines
All business papers
Professional and association
    journals
Help wanted ads

Directories
Professional associations
Alumni directories

Financial Services
Bloomberg
Dun & Bradstreet
Standard & Poor's
Moody's
Value Line
Stockbrokers analyses

Business Directories
Chambers of Commerce
Municipal and county
    governments
State and federal governments

Mailing and Address Lists
Direct mail list services
E-mail list services

Trade Shows, Conferences, Conventions

Job Fairs

There are also academic, nonprofit, and government sources.

Doing this research will take time, but it will give you the kind of information that you need to target your markets. However, budget your time on the Internet, or your can find yourself sucked into a quagmire.

World Wide Web Sources

There are many sources of information about how to job hunt on the World Wide Web. Some of the better ones include:

ABC News   abcnews.go.com/sections/flash/Employment/WNT_employment _010627.html

AOL   aol://4344:690.cwmain.6168949.679116420

Business Week   www.businessweek.com/careers; www.businessweek.com/careers/resultlist/payarcho1.htm

Careerbuilder.com   www.careerbuilder.com/JobSeeker/Index.htm?siteid =ibcwwwcareerscom&zbid=X1333630D121743291DD25FE9641BBAE989 F06708CC57B09614DA560A4A9E1F460

CareerInfonet   www.acinet.org/acinet/default.htm?tab=wagesandtrends

Careerjournal.com   www.careerjournal.com

Direct Employers   www.directemployers.com

Fortune   www.fortune.com/careers

Free Edgar   www.freeedgar.com

Hoover's Online   www.hoovers.com

HotSheet.com Web Directory   www.hotsheet.com

Monster.com   www.monster.com

NETSHARE   www.netshare.com/executive_jobs/executive_overview.asp

New York Times/Job Market   www.nytimes.com/pages/jobs/?rd=hcmcp?p =0422YY0422YS48UzN012000mVHgEVHf5

Switchboard.com Yellow Pages   www.switchboard.com

Thomas Register   www.thomasregister.com

Vault.com   www.vault.com

There is also a metacrawler that lists all the job sites with hot links to them:

www.allsearchengines.com/careerjobs.html

www.worktree.com/?AID=4183518&PID=154779

However, you have to use your judgment about the content of what they publish. Some of it is excellent. Some of it is terrible. One clue to picking out the poor sites is if they say that they have the secret to the one right way. Remember: *There is no one right way.*

NOTE: Sites come and go. These sites were available at the date of publication. However, there is no guarantee that their URLs are the ones listed, nor even that they still exist.

Market Research Report

Write a report to yourself on the results of your market research. Make it explicit in terms of what markets you are selling your services to, the growth potential of your markets, what kinds of prospective employers you plan to target, their chief characteristics, and the extent to which and the ways the market is competitive in your field. Examine how the services you offer differ from those of your competitors for jobs, and why prospective employers would hire you instead of them. In addition, figure out what gaps there are to be filled in your market and what new services you offer that employers need but cannot find candidates for.

Package Yourself

The choice of the winning candidate is usually based on "chemistry," that is, decided on an *emotional* level. Most employers are most comfortable with employees who fit in. Do your research so that you know what personal traits and qualities fit into the employers' organizations and cultures. Knowing this, you can "package yourself" appropriately.

When I worked for JC Penney many years ago, there were 210,000 employees in the company, the vast majority of whom were women. Nevertheless, the hiring checklist for college recruiters ended with the question—the one that carried the most weight—"Is this a Penney man?"

Package Yourself to Fit In

The effectiveness of the packaging starts at the moment of first contact, whether that is by mail, e-mail, phone, or in person. Look, sound, exude the part that makes you the kind of employee who is successful in that environment.

However, if the culture is not comfortable for you, don't take the job. It is a sad fact that most terminations are based on interpersonal issues ("chemistry"), rather than on matters of competence. So, run, do not walk, to the nearest exit. You will not be able to transform yourself and therefore will not be effective.

Be Sure Your Written Communication Portrays Your Brand Image

Often the first thing a prospective interviewer sees about you is your cover letter and resume. You can control the stationery and the layout and readability of your materials. If you use a fax or e-mail, you are largely at the mercy of the receiving medium.

Check Your Personal Brand Image

Your appearance is your brand image. It includes everything about you; your clothes, your manners, your way of walking and talking, your hair; the list goes on and on. There used to be advice books on this subject to make everyone fit the same mold.

There is no longer a single standard. You do not dress the same way in an accounting or law firm as you do in an advertising agency or software development start-up. The standards change from time to time even within a company. Dress for work at one time means dress up and at another means dress down. So, before you go for an interview, ask what the appropriate attire for the interview is. You may even need a definition of "business" and "business casual" because they differ from place to place.

Bottom line: Look "professional," whatever that means, for the prospect.

Distribution

Top 11 Ways of Getting the Word Out

Here are the top 11 ways to get the word to employers that you are in the job market. They are subjectively ranked from high to low in their effectiveness:

1. Networking, lead generation (especially employees of target firms).
2. Targeted telephone campaigns to employers (list obtained from market research).
3. Targeted mailings to employers (list obtained from market research).

4. Mass mailings of unsolicited resumes to employers (postal and e-mail).
5. Mass mailings of unsolicited resumes to search firms.
6. Job fairs and trade shows.
7. Help wanted advertisements in:
   Employers' Web sites, career, or employment opportunities pages.
   Job sites on the Web.
   Trade and professional journals.
   Newspapers.
8. Visits to employers' offices without appointment.
9. Visits to search firms' offices without appointment.
10. Venture capital companies.
11. Job Wanted advertisements in:
   Job sites on the web.
   Trade and professional journals.
   Newspapers.

6

Advertising Plan

Prepare Your Advertising Copy

Now that you have created your catalog of services and have identified your target markets and their needs, it is time to prepare your advertising copy. There are many different ways for you to advertise your services to the job market. These include direct postal mail, direct e-mail, Internet job site posting, job wanted advertisements, e-mail newsletters, telemarketing, and Web sites. Whatever the medium, the same principles apply.

Make Your Advertising Sing

As the old saying goes, "You don't get a second chance to make a good first impression." Regardless of medium, your advertising represents you. It conveys your image or brand. Therefore, its appearance must be superb, inviting, readable, open, quickly assimilated, exciting. It must be free of grammar and spelling errors. Write as many drafts as it takes until the copy reads so easily that it seems spontaneous.

Perception Is Reality

Visualize your readers as you prepare your ad copy. Executive or in-house recruiters are confronted daily by a stack of mail—whether paper or electronic—that they have to dispose of before the next day's batch arrives. They give each piece about 20 seconds before they decide what to do: put it in pile A (call for interview), B (possible if nothing better shows up),

or C (dump). Most are discarded based on the appearance of the cover letter and resume, regardless of the quality of the applicant.

These same criteria apply to the people you network with. They have
no personal interest in your job hunt and are busy with their own jobs
and lives. So they are unlikely to give your material attention unless it
grabs them quickly and is memorable.

Finally, the hiring managers are really busy getting their work done,
probably short-handed because they have to fill a vacancy. Making a decision about who to hire has a high risk-reward ratio. If they make the
wrong choice, their own performance suffers. If they make the right one,
they look good and are rewarded.

Style Is Significant

Write powerful, succinct language that portrays what you have done for
your previous employers and therefore proves what you will do for your
prospect. Be as bold as the culture that you want to work in allows. For example, the way you write to a sales department differs from what is appropriate to accounting. Forget what your mother told you about being
boastful. Now is the time to blow your horn, to show why they should hire
you. Make the reader salivate.

Image Is Important

Everything you send or give to the decision makers ought to convey high
quality. For example, have your letterhead designed by a printer rather
than doing it yourself on your word processor. Use 25 percent rag content
bond paper, preferably in a businesslike color such as off-white. Do what
you can to make your e-mail look professional. You can select fonts and
sizes that are more attractive than the defaults. Serif fonts such as Times
Roman are easier to read than are sans serif like Arial.

Emphasize How You Can Contribute to
the Success of the Employer

As in all advertising, start with the prospects. The only thing that matters to them is what you can do for them that will help them succeed, not

what you want to satisfy your personal goals or career ambitions. Therefore, review your market research about your prospects. Find out who they are and what you can do to meet their needs, alleviate their fears and difficulties, and satisfy their desires.

With that information firmly in mind, prepare your ad copy so that it demonstrates what value you can add for the prospective employers. Show how you can be the solution to their problems and how you can make them look good. Make it obvious that you can hit the ground running. You may even make them aware of business opportunities they did not realize were available and that they need your help to exploit.

Speak the language of the trade so that you connect with the readers. Find out and use the buzzwords that are common to the industry and even the specific employer. In a technical field, you may want to have two versions of your advertising: one with and one without jargon and acronyms.

So put time and money into getting your advertisements right. If you are not an advertising copywriter or creative expert, get a professional to help you. The return on your investment is phenomenal in terms of getting a job faster (and therefore earning an income again sooner) and maybe even getting a higher income.

Bottom line, make it easy for the screener to select you from among the hundreds of applicants who are competing with you.

Direct Marketing

The most common form of Business-to-Business advertising for a job is a cover letter and a resume. They are similar to the direct mail pieces you receive that open with a cover letter enticing you to read an enclosed brochure and to make the decision to buy what is being sold.

Direct mail marketing is a powerful way of getting your word to potential employers. It allows you to reach your targeted audiences with the messages that apply specifically to them. In contrast to general advertising, such as, placing a classified "Job Wanted" advertisement in a newspaper or posting your resume on an Internet job site, direct mailing is extremely efficient. It goes only to the people you want to contact in the businesses you want to reach.

Like any kind of direct advertising, your cover letter and resume have to be outstanding to stand out from the crowd. You only get 20 seconds to get your message across and get selected for pile A. Make your direct marketing work for you. Make it excellent. It represents you to your prospective employer.

Cover Letters and Resumes Each Have Their Own Purposes

Although there are no rules, it is a good practice to give the cover letter and the resume each its own function.

A Cover Letter Is a Sales Letter

Your cover letter should arouse the interest of the recipient in what you are offering. The opening sentence should appeal to the needs and desires of the prospective employer. It is a teaser that makes the reader decide to go ahead and read your resume—the counterpart to a brochure.

A variation on the cover letter is your answer to an advertisement about a job opening. It should respond directly to the specifications contained in the ad. It is like an answer to a Request for a Proposal (RFP).

A Resume Is a Factual Statement of Your Accomplishments

A resume is advertising copy that differentiates you from the herd. It is *not* a job description nor a career autobiography.

Like a brochure, it tell the features and benefits of the services you can bring to the prospect as demonstrated by the contributions you have made to previous employers. It is factual, quantitative, results-oriented. It too should create excitement.

Both the cover letter and the resume should lead the recipient to make a decision in your favor. Generally, this means that it opens the door to a face-to-face sales call, that is, an interview. It does not usually produce an immediate job offer.

Test Market Your Advertising

Before you distribute your cover letter and resume, market test them. Ask an informal focus group of recruiters and hiring managers to read them.

See how they would react if they received them as prospective employers. A word of caution: Because there is no one right way, you will probably be given contradictory advice. Use your own good judgment about what to adopt in the end.

Production and Distribution

Word processing allows you to customize each cover letter and even each resume. Create boilerplate paragraphs for your cover letters (see the next section) and select the ones that apply and modify them for each person. If you are doing mass mailings, try to personalize them by category of recipient. Similarly, individualize the resumes as much as possible by selecting the accomplishments from your catalog of service offerings (see Chapter 4).

Mail merge your letters with your database to address and salute each individual by name (see Chapters 2 and 5).

Samples of Cover Letters and Resumes

There are 43 paired cover letters and resumes, plus eight resumes only in the Appendix to this book. They are all originals that I have created with and for clients. Their identities and the names of their employers have been changed for confidentiality reasons.

Use these examples to stimulate your own thinking. But do not imitate them. Recruiters in particular and hiring managers can spot boilerplate and phony statements. So, be original as a way of differentiating yourself.

Concept and Contents of Cover Letters

A cover letter is a sales letter. It is a powerful way to get the attention of your prospective employers because it is personal, targeted, and persuasive. Sent with a resume, "a letter becomes a focus of attention. It is perceived as more personal or individual than the copy around it, so the letter can set a tone, introduce a product or idea, and direct readers' attention to (your resume). . . . Next to the human voice, a letter is the most personal way to communicate" (*Do-It-Yourself Direct Marketing*, Mark S. Bacon. New York: John Wiley & Sons, 1997).

Show How You Can Solve the Readers' Problems and Satisfy Their Needs

In your cover letter, specifically address the subject that is most important to your readers. It may be growing sales, increasing or preserving share of market, cutting costs, adopting new technology, developing or introducing new products, finding financing, upgrading computer and connectivity security, or improving employee relations. Find out what these issues are in the recipients function, business, or industry from careful market research you do before writing your cover letter.

The letter shows that what you have to offer can benefit the recipients personally. It demonstrates why you are the one to hire because your accomplishments at former employers are what you can do for them. It indicates that you understand their needs by using their language, that is, their jargon, buzzwords, and acronyms. (You may need a second version that does not use insider language to send to executive and human resources recruiters.)

Go beyond the Conventional

First, a cover letter is *not* a transmittal letter, which is just thrown out, leaving the resume hanging out there by itself. Second, you need to take and keep the initiative. Otherwise, you will get the "Don't call us, we'll call you" treatment. Third, and most important, make your cover letter so good that you stand out in the crowd. Get the readers' attention so they realize that you go beyond the conventional.

Address the Letter to a Specific Person

Letters addressed "To Whom It May Concern" or other anonymous salutation run the risk of being blocked in the mailroom or thrown away unopened. Do your market research to find out who to address your cover letter to—name *and* title.

Contrary to widespread advice, you do not have to bypass Human Resources and send your material only to the hiring manager. Send your letter to both. Keep Human Resources in the loop, they often have veto power.

Start with Your "Unique Selling Proposition"

Grab the attention of the readers right away. Make a big claim in your opening sentence. Use an accomplishment from your catalog that they can immediately use to help them succeed. Or ask a question that gets them to think about you as the way to solve their problems such as "Do you need someone who. . . ."

Here are some examples of various kinds of openers that grab attention:

- *Accomplishments from Resume*

  As head of mergers and acquisitions and business development for the enterprise subsidiary of a multibillion dollar, multinational firm, I targeted the 50 largest telemarketers in the country for acquisition. I brought 10 of them—ranging in price from $4 million to $75 million—to the table in only 15 months.

  As Vice President of Marketing, Business Development and Sales, I turned around the company's long-term sales and profit decline. I analyzed the existing customer base to determine the profile of best buyers and focused on highest potential prospects—sales grew by $1 million in first year.

  I created three new CD ROM and six new print products—produced $1.5 million in annual sales growth.

  How did I accomplish these things? Leadership.

- *Management Style*

  An insatiable drive to beat yesterday, break the rules, press the limits, target perfection, create new solutions, analyze and master all aspects of the system, identify and solve problems, turn around operations, and thereby produce profits—does this sound like what you need in your Operations Manager?

- *Impressive Employers*

  Assistant to the president of one of the hottest start-up production companies at Disney Studios; assistant to Norman Jewison; casting assistant at Turner Network Television; assistant production office coordinator at von Zerneck/Sertner Films; staff assistant at the Virginia Governor's Film Office; and production intern at Marian Rees Associates! That is the track record I bring to you.

- *Interesting Career History*

  I began my career as a gourmet cook at the age of five when my mother taught me to bake the family's daily bread. By the time I was 10, I was preparing meals for feasts up to 20 people. You can say that cooking has been my life.

  If you need a gourmet chef whose experience ranges from cooking for wealthy individuals to cooking for a five-star hotel dining room and gourmet French restaurants, you may wish to read my attached resume.

- *Turnaround Challenges*

  "Boy, I'm going to sue your ass."

  That was what I heard on the phone within days of starting my new job as vice president of a deeply troubled insurance company from the president of one of our best clients. He was calling to complain about an unpaid refund of several million dollars for the past three years. It turned out that my predecessor had frozen the payment for negotiating leverage. Now he was gone, and so were our files on the account. After doing strenuous detective work, I found out that the balance was legitimate and paid it. This salvaged the relationship and we went on to grow the business volume.

  When the bottom dropped out of the global oil market, sales of the captive high-technology division I headed went from $14.4 million to $2.4 million in two years. Within five years, I had brought revenues back to their previous peak by aggressively entering new commercial and government markets. And I did it with 25 percent fewer people while improving quality.

- *Overcoming Obstacles*

  When constant turnover is the nature of your supervisory job, you really are much more of a trainer than you are a supervisor. In my position, raw recruits are assigned to me unpredictably and without my involvement, and employees leave this undesirable area as soon as they are qualified for something they consider better. Therefore, to succeed in my job, I train, and train, and train. I succeed in what I have been assigned to do—even with a crew that is constantly changing.

- *Unique Combination of Abilities*

   Imagine a systems test engineering supervisor with excellent people skills and excellent technical skills and excellent business skills and a dedication to Total Quality Management. This is the unbeatable combination I can bring to your firm.

- *Using Questions to Prove Ability*

   What does it take to satisfy insurance claimants so well that they write letters of appreciation? Getting their claims paid promptly and accurately. But it also takes good customer relations.

   What does it take to get a property or casualty claim paid promptly and accurately? Persistence, persistence, persistence. But it also takes building excellent relationships with the insurance carriers.

Enumerate Your Qualities

In the next paragraph, tell about your qualities. These augment the factual material in your resume and make you come alive as a valuable employee. Pick those qualities that fit the organizational culture of the employer you are targeting (based on your research). For example:

In addition to my ability to find, negotiate, and execute large-scale business opportunities that leverage my knowledge of new technologies, I can offer you the following capabilities:

- Versatility and adaptability in working and/or living with people of many nationalities and cultures including Bahrain, Japan, Korea, Philippines, Singapore, South Africa, Sweden, and Taiwan, as well as Texas and New York.
- Success at persuading governments, economic development agencies, investors, lawyers, key customers, partners, alliance members, and licensees to work together in order to initiate and bring major projects to completion.

- Participative management, leadership, and interpersonal skills with a history of identifying, diagnosing, and solving organizational, people, and team-building problems.
- Ability to hit the ground running, make the tough decisions, and produce results early and on a sustained basis.
- Record of leading large and small projects that come in on time and on budget.
- Strong written and oral communication skills, effective public speaker with the ability to think on my feet and handle difficult questions.
- Solid integrity, honesty, and trustworthiness.

Two things contributed to my success over the past four years:

1. The energy, persistence, dedication, hard work, communication skills, and enthusiasm that are essential to producing sales growth and profitability,

combined with

2. The application of the full range of marketing skills needed to back up the sales achievements including marketing strategy, market research, sales promotion, advertising, and marketing administration.

In addition to my commercial sense and managerial skills, my strengths include:

In-depth technical knowledge of IBM AS/400 and other mid-range computers, as well as personal computers;

Ability to organize people and tasks and deal with crises to get things done—right, on time, and within budget;

Interpersonal skills that produce results with employees, colleagues, vendors, and clients and customers;

A trans-Atlantic career that even involved directing a United States based project team from the United Kingdom;

Oral and written communication facility that enhances the capabilities of both technical staff and users; and

Ability to satisfy customers in ways that bring them back for repeat business.

Direct the Reader to Your Resume

Having piqued the readers' interest, the next thing you should do is direct them to your resume for more information about how you can help them succeed. For example:

> If you would like to learn more about my accomplishments in marketing management for some of the country's biggest and most successful retailers and direct mail marketers, please read my attached resume.

Ask for an Appointment

Close by asking for an appointment to elaborate on how you can contribute to the success of the prospective employers. Tell them you will call them instead of asking them to call you. AND THEN DO IT. You have in effect set up a telephone appointment for a face-to-face appointment. This ploy also gives you a way of getting through to the person you want to speak to because you can say, "So-and-so is expecting my call." Close with:

> I would appreciate the opportunity to meet you personally to discuss how my capabilities can contribute to the success of [name of company]. I will call you on [day] to set up an appointment for us to meet at a mutually convenient time.

Postscript

Postscripts are proven attention-getters. They stand out as separate information that recipients read. Use them to emphasize a benefit you bring to the employer. For example:

> PS: I am sure that my record and capabilities in marketing and public relations can contribute to the growth and profitability of your organization.

> PS: If you need someone in your department who can be really successful in hitting the ground running in ensuring effective interaction between IS and users, we should get together.

PS: If you can't wait until I call you, e-mail me at robertsj@aol.com or call me at 888-555-9999.

Other Types of Cover Letters

The cover letter just described is designed for an unsolicited direct mail campaign. It can be adapted for various other purposes.

Networking Referrals

The purpose of networking is to get referrals to other people who may know people who may have an opening. Ask permission to use the name of each person who gives you referrals. Then start your cover letter with the sentence:

> Our mutual friend, _____, suggested that I contact you because you may know of someone who might be aware of a company that needs a _____ .

Be sure to follow with the appropriate grabber in the next paragraph. Then conclude with words like:

> I would be very pleased if you and I could get together briefly to discuss how my record of achievement can contribute to the needs of your contacts or people they might know. I will call you on [day] to set up an appointment to get together at a convenient time. Many thanks.

Search Firms

In mass mailings to search firms, at the point where you direct the reader to your resume, use a phrase such as:

> If you have clients who need a _____ who has a demonstrated track record in _____, you may wish to look over my resume, which lists some of my other accomplishments.

Conclude with a sentence like:

> I [feel it would be beneficial to both of us or I would be pleased] to meet with you to discuss how my accomplishments and abilities can contribute to the success of your clients' organizations.

Customize Answers to Advertisements

First, and this is as close to a rule as I will come, answer only those advertisements in print or electronic media that "have your name at the top." In other words, do not waste time applying for jobs that you do not fit. Either your response will be discarded or worse yet, you will fool the employer into hiring you when you cannot deliver what you promised. On the other hand, if you can repackage your accomplishments to meet the specifications (see Chapter 3, "Change Your Business Model"), do reply to the advertisement.

Second, the most effective way to respond is to demonstrate how your accomplishments fit the criteria. Take each word or phrase and match one or more achievements from your catalog to it. (If appropriate, create new accomplishment statements that the advertisement reminds you about and add them to your catalog.) This is the acid test for how well you meet their needs and whether or not to respond.

Finally, write a cover letter using this raw material. The first sentence should be a grabber that identifies in it what job you are applying for. This is better than the conventional "In response to your advertisement . . ." It can say something like "As [job title in ad], I [accomplishment]." Then use an adaptation of the rest of your standard letter. If you do not know who the employer or recruiter is, omit the part about calling them and instead conclude that you look forward to meeting them personally.

Adapt your attached resume to the advertisement. Choose those accomplishments that precisely meet the requirements. Augment them with others that you know would enhance your chances. Use the right buzzwords from the ad as well as others that are typical for the job.

If you are sending your reply to a Web job posting by e-mail, you have no control over what it looks like to the recipient. Many e-mails look like modern poetry because of different margin widths, line breaks, and the browsers' settings. Your best bet, therefore, is to keep the style simple so that scanning software can read it. Attachments are most likely not going to be opened because of fear of viruses, so copy and paste your resume into the e-mail. If there is a postal mailing address, follow up with a hard copy (and say that you have already replied by e-mail).

Fax transmittal is also hazardous. The quality at the receiving end is unpredictable. So follow up with hard copy.

If you follow these suggestions, you increase the probability of getting an interview. But, answering advertisements is a high-risk/low-yield approach to finding a job. The employer or search firm probably places or posts the advertisement after having exhausted internal sources and databases of resumes they already have on file. The number of responses may be in the hundreds, the first screening is probably done by a computer or a clerk with precise instructions, and if you make the cut, you still have lots of competitors for the job.

But, that said, apply to the right advertisements anyway. People do get jobs that way. You never know.

Samples of Cover Letters

The 43 cover letters in the Appendix to this book are all originals that I have created with and for clients whose identities and employers' names have been changed to preserve confidentiality.

I have provided these examples as a stimulus to your own thinking, not to be imitated. Remember what I said earlier: Recruiters and hiring managers can spot boilerplate and phony statements. So, be original as a way of differentiating yourself.

Concept and Contents of Resumes

There Is No One Right Way

Contrary to popular opinion, there are no rules for writing resumes any more than there are rules for writing any other kind of direct mail advertising copy. There are opinions and there are conventions, some of which are reasonably good. But when you read one authority asserting that your resume must be only one page and another asserting that it should be two, you know that both of them cannot be right. In any case, there was never a "Resume Congress" that proclaimed rules and regulations that have the force of law.

I have done a fair amount of research into the preferences of recruiters and hiring managers. There is very little unanimity among them. About the only thing they agree on is that they want to be able to scan

Resume Conventions

Here are some of the *conventions* that I recommend to my clients:

- Increase readability by having enough white space. Tightly packed contents and small fonts are hard to read.
- Use 12 or 10 point type. Smaller type *seems* hard to read even though it is commonly used in periodicals and telephone directories.
- Use a "serif" font such as Times Roman or its variations. "Sans serif" fonts such as Arial are harder to read, according to research done by publishers.
- Use headings that clearly identify the subject matter.
- Start with a Professional or Career Summary that is one or two lines long so that the reader can quickly pigeonhole you. This statement also serves as your "Unique Selling Proposition." Alternatively, you can write your objective here, although I prefer to put it in the cover letter.
- In a chronological resume, put the most recent job first and work back from there. People expect that, so let them have it.
- Show all the jobs you held, but only show accomplishments relating to those that are pertinent to the position you are looking for. However, if you have held a series of jobs over a short period of time, group them as consulting or interim if they add to your credentials. Otherwise, leave them out.
- Give prominence to either your employers or to your job titles depending on which will impress the recipient more.
- Put the years of employment at the *right* margin so that they are not the focus of attention and so they take the least amount of space.
- Incorporate key words or buzzwords in the text so that scanners, whether computer or human, can easily spot them. In some occupations, such as Information Technology, it is conventional to have a separate section that lists hardware and software that you have expertise in.
- Avoid bullets, bold face, italics, underlines, and other highlighting devices because they may make electronic transmission and computer scanning more difficult.
- Put your education at the end of the resume. By this time, your experience is far more important than what you learned in school. (The exception

(continued)

Resume Conventions (continued)

to this convention is in the academic world where education is a primary basis for choice of candidates and should be at the beginning.)

- Include personal information and hobbies and interests as a way of humanizing yourself. They also give you a chance to show your off-the-job achievements, which may be useful in the job you are seeking. The personal data can also be an ice-breaker at the beginning of the interview. There are many conflicting opinions about this. But bear in mind that the hiring manager is judging how well you will fit in and what you will be like to work with day in and day out. Credentials being equal, "chemistry" is often the basis on which the final decision is made.

- A particularly sensitive question is age. My opinion, based on my research with recruiters and employers, is that if they want extensive experience they won't hire youth, and *vice versa.* So, tell them your birth date and save everyone trouble, embarrassment, and potential EEO complaints.

- On the other hand, leave out vital statistics such as height, weight, and health. They only apply in physical jobs.

---

the resume and make the first cut in about 20 seconds. From there on, it is subjective. And that's a problem. It means that you cannot be sure that your resume won't be rejected because of the individual screening techniques of the recipient.

The solution is to do the best you can according to reasonably acceptable criteria. The advice and the sample resumes in this book only provide a starting point. Exercise your judgment and creativity to fit your target markets as you produce a distinctive resume.

Types of Resumes

Reverse Chronological

According to convention, there are two types of resumes—reverse chronological and functional. Each has its pros and cons, but reverse chronological is preferred by most recruiters and hiring managers. They are used to reading them and finding what they want in a hurry. That has probably been your own experience as a hiring manager.

Functional Resumes

Functional resumes have their place for someone who has had a diversified career and wants to demonstrate the ability to handle a multifaceted position such as chief executive officer, chief operating officer, general manager, or chief administrative officer. They may also be useful if you want to change careers. Include your career history as well as other factual information at the end of the accomplishments.

The hazard with functional resumes is that they are often used by people with spotty work histories and may raise a red flag. If this is your reason for using a functional resume, forestall the question by addressing it in the cover letter. You can write something like, "I have gained experience in a wide variety of jobs and companies. I am now ready to establish my career in . . ."

Unconventional Resumes

Unconventional resumes are, by definition, creative. They work best in the creative industries and take the form that speaks most directly to their cultures, such as portfolios, video- or audiotapes, writing samples, design samples, and so on. No rules or conventions apply here because it is the creative work that sells the person.

Length of Resume

When you go to a mall and look in the display window of a clothing store, you generally see two suits or outfits, a jacket and slacks, a blouse or shirt, and some accessories. That represents the whole store to the browser. If you like what you see in the window, you go inside and check if there is anything you would like to buy.

Similarly, a resume is a microcosm of what you are offering to employers. The word *resume* literally means summary. It should only contain enough to whet the readers' appetites and give them sufficient information to make a decision about you as a candidate. For most people in professional, managerial, and executive jobs, a two-page resume is about right.

That gives room for about 12 accomplishments plus the other factual data enumerated in the box on pages 63 and 64.

Contents of Resume

Go to your catalog of service offerings (Chapter 4) and select the ones that fit where you want to work and what you want to do in the future. Put your highest achievements right up front under each of your positions and employers. If you had similar achievements at more than one job, show them only once, preferably where they first happened, so that you can show how your career has progressed.

Just as there are no promulgated rules about the structure of a resume, there is no law that says you have to have one generic resume. Word processing enables you to create as many as you want. Because you have a catalog, you can custom-build each. This is obviously not practical if you are doing a mass mailing, but come as close as possible to the needs of your target markets.

Testimonials

Many resumes contain the line, "References will be provided upon request." Because you no doubt will do that, it is an unnecessary statement, and can be left out. Letters of reference are rarely included with resumes in the United States. They are common in Europe and other countries. Find out what the customs are in your marketplace.

Salary Information

Leave out salary information unless you are answering an advertisement that stipulates that your resume will not be considered if it is not included. Salary is used as a screening device to determine if your pay is either too high or too low. You want to avoid being eliminated at the beginning of the application process.

Truth in Advertising

There is one inviolate rule: Tell the truth. There are good practical reasons for this rule. One is that you have to be able to deliver what you promise. If you don't, you run the risk of failing and even losing your job. The other is that if you are found out, lying could cost you your job or even make you subject to a lawsuit. There are companies that specialize in doing reference checks on behalf of employers and they are good at what they do.

Sample Resumes

There are 51 resumes in the Appendix to this book. They are all originals that I have created with and for clients, whose identities and the names of their employers have been changed for confidentiality reasons.

Use these examples to stimulate your own thinking. But do not imitate them. As I've said before, and it bears repeating: Recruiters and hiring managers can spot boilerplate and phony statements. Differentiate yourself by being original.

Electronic Marketing

E-mail and the World Wide Web are used extensively for marketing and sales of all kinds of products and services to businesses and to consumers. Electronic marketing is a viable way for you to market your services to employers. For good or for ill, it has extended everyone's work day. As a job seeker, you can legitimately conduct business into the night or early in the morning. There is a good chance that your recipient will be online before or after the work day to catch up on e-mail and will get your correspondence.

There is, of course, one caveat: Spamming and viruses have made many people and companies very wary about opening e-mail and downloading attachments from strangers. As a result, you have to use e-mail with finesse.

Purposes of Electronic Marketing

The primary purpose of electronic marketing is to open the door for an interview. You can also use it to stay in touch with your network on a regular basis to build your relationships. It is a vehicle for easy two-way communication. It can enhance your brand image as a computer-savvy individual, demonstrate your credibility, and convey your personality. Most important, it is a way to get people to write or call you back for more information or to invite you for an interview.

Electronic marketing is unique in terms of its immediacy. It is visual like television and interactive like the telephone. It is seen as a source of information. It is dynamic and easy to keep up-to-date. It alerts recipients to breaking news. It is a way to keep in front of the people on your database between the times you make personal contacts by telephone or in person. It can be linked to top job sites on the Web.

E-Mail Newsletter

Create a monthly newsletter to maintain contact with your network. It can contain news items from the business and professional press as well as nonconfidential information you acquire on your travels. It should also keep your contacts up to date on your progress and let them know you are still in the market. You can also ask for more networking referrals.

Because of the concern many people have about unsolicited e-mail, be sure to ask permission from each person to send your newsletter. Have an "opt out" line at the bottom that allows recipients to e-mail you asking to be unsubscribed.

Subject Line for E-Mail

To overcome the reluctance people have to opening unsolicited e-mail, craft a subject line that will identify you and your reason for writing. State the purpose of the e-mail and include your name (or the name of the person who has referred you). Gimmicky or deceptive subject lines do not work. People just delete those e-mails before even opening them.

E-Mail Signature

Remember, this is business correspondence! It's important to have a professional signature (no cute pictures or favorite quotes). Write e-mail messages with the same level of formality as your other written communications. Many people become very sloppy with their e-mail messages. They ignore grammar and punctuation and use slangy language. Above all, check the spelling on all e-mails before they go out. You must appear professional.

Web Site Design

You can create a Web site for your job search. If you plan to go this route, it is essential that you make your e-marketing and advertising look professional. You are a professional, and your Web site must reflect that fact. It is better not to venture into this territory at all than to send out amateur material. Unless you are qualified to design your own Web site, you are probably better off spending money to have a professional Web designer do it for you under your direction and with your participation.

Incorporate your newsletter into a "What's New?" button on your Web site. That way, it does double duty by going to your target list and by being accessible to your visitors. Use your Web site to show a portfolio of your work. If you have created software, developed Web sites, made presentations, published articles, or produced anything visual, the Web site is a great place to showcase your work.

While electronic marketing and advertising are still relatively new and untested, there are some fairly well-accepted conventions that are worth noting:

Electronic Marketing Conventions

Make the Site Easy to Locate. Register it on search engines and link it to similar sites.

Grab Attention on Your Home Page. Put helpful information on your home page to attract visitors to go inside. Make it interesting and exciting.

Use Key Words or Buzzwords That Will Be Found by Search Engines. Search engines look for key words the way resume scanners do.

Make It Easy to Navigate. Create links from every part of the site to every other part and back to the home page from everywhere.

(continued)

Electronic Marketing Conventions (continued)

Make Graphics Work for the Site. Tie graphics in with your message. But be certain that they are simple so that the site will load quickly. Browsers have the "patience of a New York cab driver."

Have Two-Way Communication. Make it possible to ask you questions about any part of your site. Make it easy to send you an e-mail.

Have Something New Regularly. Give an incentive to the visitor for returning to the site frequently, such as news that will interest them.

Ask for the Sale. Make it easy for visitors to buy your services, that is, to let you know that they want to follow up with an interview.

Test and Refine the Site. Pretend you are a customer. Ask a panel of the kinds of people you are targeting how easy it is to buy. Seek their input. Go back to the drawing board until it is very good. However, don't keep redoing it to get perfection. That can be a swamp.

To see these suggestions in action, please visit my Web site: princetonmanagementconsultants.com.

Do-It-Yourself Web Site Design Programs

However, if you are confident that you can do the design yourself, the following programs are relatively easy to use:

- Front Page version 2000 is very user-friendly and behaves like other Microsoft applications.
- Adobe Page Mill requires slightly more technical ability.
- AOL: click on People, Create a Home Page, Your Business.
- Microsoft bCentral:
    Marketing Strategy http://www.bcentral.com/default.asp?cobrand =msn&LID=78
    E-mail Marketing http://www.bcentral.com/products/lb/default .asp?lid=379

Domain Name

Choose a domain name that fits your advertising strategy. To find domain name registration services, use www.Google.com and search for "Domain Names."

Combine Electronic with Conventional Marketing, Advertising, and Sales Tools

Electronic marketing reinforces your other marketing, advertising, and sales tools. Use them together so that each refers to the others. For example, your written and e-mail correspondence should invite readers to visit your Web site. Your e-mail signature should look like your Web site design. Your stationery and business card should show your e-mail and Web site addresses as well as your postal address and phone number.

All of these tools should bear a consistent family resemblance to convey the same strong brand image: same typeface, same colors, same overall appearance.

All this advice is subject to my favorite caution: "There is no one right way."

7
Pricing

Pricing Your Services

What price should you charge an employer for your services? In other words, what compensation should you receive for the job you are seeking?

The first thought that comes to most peoples' minds is only what salary to ask for. That is too narrow. Salary determination is based on a very sophisticated process in larger companies. The total compensation package is much more elaborate and complicated because it also comprises a bewildering variety of incentive, benefit, perquisite, and stock owner-ship plans.

Employers provide a total compensation package for a variety of rea-sons, including:

- To attract and retain employees in a competitive labor market.
- To motivate and reward employees.
- To focus employees' attention on general corporate and specific per-sonal or product goals.
- To pass on to employees the advantages that employers have in bar-gaining for group benefit programs that would otherwise be more ex-pensive for individuals to obtain on their own.
- To take advantage of tax breaks available to employers and employees.

Here is a way to make sense of the total pay package. It comprises four subgroups:

1. Income creation plans.
2. Asset or wealth creation plans.

3. Income protection plans.
4. Asset protection plans.

This matrix defines each subgroup in terms of its purpose:

	Income	**Asset**
Creation	Plans that enable and encourage employees to increase earnings and purchasing power and earnings potential.	Plans that increase the financial or tangible assets of employees.
Protection	Plans that replace all or part of income when employees are unable to earn income for reasons beyond their control.	Plans that prevent a major drain on the financial or tangible assets or on the creditworthiness of employees.

Many of these plans involve contractual relationships between you and the employer. Except for income creation plans, the others supplement statutory plans such as Social Security, Workers Compensation, and Unemployment Insurance. Almost all of them are subject to employment, labor, and tax laws and regulations, Employee Retirement Income Security Act (ERISA), Generally Accepted Accounting Principles (GAAP), Securities and Exchange Commission (SEC) requirements, and New York and Nasdaq Stock Exchange rules imposed on you or the employer.

Be Prepared!

Pricing the services you sell to employers is comparable in complexity to pricing contracts for large projects or heavy equipment built to order. Employers have the advantage because they have access to creative consultants, in-house human resources specialists, lawyers, accountants, and tax experts.

Be really smart about the pricing conventions in the job market. Get your own experts to help you, such as your accountant, broker, financial and estate planners, lawyer, and human resources advisor. You can find general financial advice on the Web at http://money.cnn.com/pf/101. To get you started, the following sections synopsize and explain the purposes of the plans that fall into each category in the matrix. Study them carefully and use the descriptions to evaluate the offers you receive.

Income Creation Plans

When they think of how much a job will pay, most people concentrate on the part that goes into the bank such as salary, bonuses, and commissions. This is natural because it is the largest piece of the compensation pie. It is what you pay your bills with and, for many people, it is a measure of status and success. However, there are also hidden forms of income such as subsidized services, programs, and perquisites. All of them create income for you.

There are also costs of going to work that reduce the amount of salary you get to keep—your "take home" pay. There are differences in income taxes and in living costs and real estate taxes in various locations that affect your standard of living. This section describes briefly how income creation plans work.

Salary Determination Plans

When it comes to the design of formal pay plans, even a little knowledge is a valuable thing. It gives you the power to negotiate the best deal. Here is an overview of how many pay plans are designed.

As you read this description, the point to bear in mind is how subjective and arbitrary the whole salary determination system is and therefore may be open for negotiation.

In *larger companies*, salary determination plans consist of several elements that together produce salary ranges for the job and the amount you are personally paid.

Compensation Policy

Each employer makes decisions about its compensation policy based on its own business philosophy, costs, or relationship among various parts of the total compensation package. Most want to pay the average rate for their industry or geographic area. Alternatively, some choose to pay above average, others below. More broadly, some industries pay higher than average salaries, while others pay below average.

Before you meet a prospective employer, try to find out about its compensation policy. When you are being interviewed and the subject turns to pay, ask for an explanation of it.

Competitive Pay Surveys

To find out what their competitors pay for given jobs, employers obtain surveys of salaries in their labor (as compared to their product or service) markets. They use published data, often augmented by custom surveys. If there are many jobs in the company, they sample just the key ones called *benchmark jobs*. Then they price their own jobs accordingly, bearing in mind their pay policies.

Sources of Survey Information on the Web

You can do the same thing in preparation for your interviews. You can get salary survey information from Web sites such as those listed next. Some of these are free, others charge a fee. Be sure to check the job descriptions behind the titles to get the best match and figure out how the job you seek stacks up against them. Also, look for the dates the surveys were made; some data are too old to be helpful.

www.acinet.org/acinet/default.htm?tab=wagesandtrends

www.careerjournal.com/salaries/index.html

jobstar.org/tools/salary/sal-prof.htm

www.salary.com

www.salarysource.com

www.wageweb.com

www.workindex.com/salary

If your previous employer has a formal salary plan, your salary range for your old job is a good guide to what other employers pay for the same job (adjusted for their salary policies). Your previous employer's Human Resources department may be willing to help you.

Other good sources of compensation data are professional and trade associations you belong to or have access to. Check their Web sites and periodicals and call their offices for information.

Check your local library for other sources. Reference librarians are great resoures.

Pricing (Job/Position Evaluation)

For the jobs that are not surveyed (non-benchmark), employers fill in the gaps in survey data by using job or position evaluation techniques. There are two kinds of job evaluation: *market pricing,* and *job (content) evaluation.*

1. *Market pricing plans.* In market pricing plans, the prices of the non-benchmark jobs are estimated by interpolating or extrapolating from the available market data. The benchmark and non-benchmark prices are combined and arranged in a hierarchy of job levels.

2. *Job content evaluation plans.* In job evaluation plans, the prices of the non-benchmark jobs are assigned points that are estimated by comparing subjectively the arbitrarily chosen "contents" of the jobs as determined from their position descriptions and arranging them in a hierarchy based on complexity. (Stay with me.) The jobs are assigned a dollar amount on the assumption that there is a correlation between pay amount and job content. The results of the job content evaluation process are then reconciled with the market survey data to produce the "going rate" for that job market. They are then arranged in a hierarchy of job levels. (The most common of these "black box" plans is called the Hay plan after the company that sells it.)

The result of either system produces what is called the "going rate" for each position.

Pay Ranges

The average salary from the survey or job evaluation data for each position—or going rate—is used to set the "midpoint" of a pay range so that there is room to reward an individual employee's performance and/or longevity on the job. Typically, in professional and managerial jobs, a range for the job is established by subtracting 20 percent from the midpoint to get the minimum and adding 20 percent to get the maximum. Thus, the maximum of the range is 50 percent higher than the minimum (120 divided by 80).

Starting Salary

The starting salary is normally the minimum of the range, although depending on your previous experience, your skill in the bargaining process, and the state of the job market, you may be able to start between minimum and midpoint. Bear in mind that employers are often constrained by salary budgets and the relationship of your salary to those of incumbents in peer jobs, which limits their flexibility in offering you a higher starting salary.

Lowballing or Price Cutting

Some job hunters think they will be more successful in getting a job if they accept a lower salary than the job pays or than they were making in their previous jobs. Generally, this is not a good strategy for several reasons:

- If you take a cut, it is reflected in all your income-related benefits, so the negative impact on your standard of living is leveraged.
- This reduction hits both currently and into the future. Merit pay increases will be calculated as a percent of your lower salary and you may never catch up. Your retirement benefits will also be lower because the pension calculation and/or your contribution and that of the employer to your 401(k) plan will be smaller.
- Many employers are suspicious of job candidates who say they are willing to take a pay cut. They worry that you will leave as soon as you get a higher offer from somewhere else and they will lose you. Therefore, they may not make you an offer.

Performance Evaluation, Merit Increases

Subsequent pay changes are based on *performance* evaluation (not to be confused with *job* evaluation). Most large employers have formal procedures to assess performance and determine the size of the merit increase

---

Smaller Companies

There are nearly seven million companies with less than 25 employees and only some 20,000 with more than 500 employees. There are only 500 companies that are listed in Fortune 500. Small companies are different. As the Web site for *Inc.* magazine (www.Inc.com) says:

> Among small companies, salaries are still all over the map, mainly because compensation is driven more by the philosophy of the founders or CEOs than by hard data.

Therefore, when you get to the point of discussing pay, you are likely to be asked such questions as "What was your last salary?" "What is the minimum salary you are willing to accept? "How much do you need to live?" Your response could result in you ending up with a salary below the amount the employers are actually prepared to pay.

A better answer is "My research indicates that the appropriate range for this position is $_____ to $_____." The company may appreciate your help in setting a salary range that enables them to both hire and keep you.

---

based on the rating. They also have guidelines for the amount of pay increase for promotions.

Bonuses and Other Pay for Performance Incentives

In addition to base salary, many companies pay incentive and other bonuses in cash or stock. Normally, these incentives are paid annually, although some may be tied to performance over shorter intervals. They may be based on one or more of individual, unit, or corporate performance.

Nondiscretionary Cash Bonus Plans

Most *large companies* have cash bonus plans to motivate people to work better. Many of them use a process of setting goals, measuring performance, and paying cash bonuses based on achieving the goals. These plans are known as *nondiscretionary* because they use objective criteria. In many companies, the proportion of the bonus increases with job level and can represent a substantial part of total cash compensation.

Some things to be wary of: Make sure the goals are achievable and the measurements are clear; some are not. Check if there are provisions that disqualify you, for example, if you are not employed by the company at the bonus date (as compared to paying on a pro rata basis for the part of the year you worked for the company).

Discretionary Cash Bonus Plans

Other bonus plans are known as *discretionary* because the amount is based on the judgment of the management. Criteria and the amount generally are not set ahead of time.

Profit-Sharing Bonus Plans

Some *smaller companies*—as well as many stock brokerages and partnerships—have year-end *profit-sharing* bonuses. (These are different from the profit-sharing plans that are designed to provide retirement income.) These plans simply divide up profits among eligible employees according to some formula such as level or title or length of service rather than performance.

Commissions and Prizes

Sales compensation plans typically consist of a mix of base salary and commissions, although some may be commission only. Commissions are based on formulas relating to sales volume or profitability. They may be figured on a sliding scale that rewards you proportionately less or more than the target depending on how your actual performance compares to a goal. Sometimes extra rewards are offered to encourage the introduction of new products or services or to build market share.

The ratio of commission to base generally reflects the relative importance of the salesperson's selling skills needed to get the order, the length of the sales cycle, the technical difficulty of the product or service, and the profitability of the product. For example, if not much product knowledge is needed, the product is easy to sell, orders are placed at or near the time of the sales call, and there is a high profit margin, the balance is weighted toward commission. Many people who sell such products may be on 100 percent commission. Conversely, people selling highly technical products with long sales cycles and high rates of rejection will receive a higher portion of their cash compensation in the form of salary.

Company policy is also a factor. Two companies in the same industry can take opposite approaches. In the insurance and securities industries, some companies pay their representatives salaries only while their competitors pay commissions only. Both believe that their way is the one that will most benefit the customers or the employers. What you have to do is decide which of the alternatives fit you best.

Sales contests are prevalent. Elaborate prizes are awarded to the highest producer(s). Salespeople respond to such inducements because of their natural competitiveness. The thing to remember is that everyone has been working extra hard to get the prize but only one or two actually win. The nonwinners have not been rewarded for their extra efforts. The big winner is the employer whose compensation costs have been reduced.

Stock Bonuses

Some employers pay annual bonuses in the form of company stock as outright grants, as distinct from stock purchase or option plans. You do not have to put up any money to become an owner, but you do have to pay ordinary income tax on the value of the shares. (See the section on Asset Creation Plans that follows for information on other stock ownership plans.)

Employee Services, Programs, and Perquisites

Some employers provide subsidized services to employees that are valuable ways of augmenting cash income. These include company cafeterias, refreshments, day care centers, recreation facilities, concierge services, on-site banking, low cost loans, parking, tuition aid, transportation assistance, housing assistance, company stores, employee discounts on company products or services, company uniforms, shoppers club memberships, company sponsored activities, matching gifts and donations, and other ways of enhancing the employment relationship.

Some of these programs also are really designed to work to the advantage of the employers. Cafeterias and concierge services keep employees on the premises or at their desks. Educational assistance programs such as staff development, fees for seminars, and tuition aid increase the employees' skills and competence. Employee Assistance Plans and Information and Referral Programs enable employees to keep their minds on their jobs instead of on off-the-job concerns. Wellness programs, including health club memberships, keep employees fit and productive and reduce employers' health insurance and absenteeism costs. Telecommuting and other forms of flexible work arrangements may reduce turnover and save employers the expenses of providing office space. Nevertheless, they all effectively add to your income by saving you expenses that you might otherwise have to pay yourself.

There are also such one-shot payments as sign-on bonuses and relocation expenses (if the new job requires moving), as well as awards for long service, suggestions, and referrals of job candidates.

Payroll Deductions

As the costs of employee benefits—especially for health insurance—have risen, more employers are shifting them to employees. Noncontributory plans have been changed to require employees to pay a share of the premiums. Hospital, medical, and prescription drug deductibles and coinsurance amounts have been increased, in some cases substantially, so that more of the cost is borne by employees. Retirement plans have been switched from employer-paid defined benefit to employee-paid/company-matched defined contribution designs. (See the next section for information about 401(k) plans.)

Costs of Going to Work

The other side of the coin is that it costs money to go to work. Your take-home income is reduced if you have to pay out of your own pocket for the services and programs listed previously. There are also differences in the costs of living in various parts of the country. (Some of these are so extreme that employers have to establish regional pay differentials to offset them.) As you assess and compare job offers, factor these costs of going to work into your decision making about the offer you receive.

City, Region, and State Comparisons

The large variations in state, commuter, and/or local living costs make a significant difference in your take-home pay. You can compare living costs in various cities on such Web sites as:

http://pathfinder.com/money/depts/real_estate/bestplaces

http://houseandhome.aol.homefair.com/homefair/usr/hoodform.html ?cid=homestor

Asset Creation Plans

Employers make it possible for you to create assets by giving you ways to save and invest through payroll deduction. Many of them subsidize what employees put aside. Some of the plans are tax-sheltered.

In addition, some companies provide opportunities to own company stock through outright grant or purchase of shares or by giving employees options to purchase them at possibly favorable prices. The purpose is to increase your feeling of commitment to the success of the company because you are a shareholder and therefore keep stockholders' interests in mind. A secondary purpose is to respond to many employees' expressed desire to control their own investments instead of letting their employer do it for them.

There are several major facts to consider, including:

- There are risks attached to the rewards of investing in the stock market. Stock prices go down as well as up.
- The potential risks are compounded if you invest in company shares because both your livelihood and your savings, investments and retirement income, are tied to the fortunes of your employer.
- Most of the plans have restrictions built into them by the company or imposed by the government that limit your control of and access to your investment portfolio.
- It is not easy to be consistently successful in managing your portfolio. Consider the wide range of success or failure of professional pension

and mutual fund managers—and they spend their full time studying the markets and making investment decisions! Can you spend your full time, become fully expert in the companies and stocks, and have the intestinal fortitude you need to exceed their performance?

These issues were spectacularly demonstrated at the beginning of the twenty-first century as company failures and plummeting stock prices wiped out members' retirement savings.

That said, this section describes briefly how these asset creation plans work.

Thrift and Savings and Investment Plans

Thrift and savings and investment plans have been around for many years. They enable employees to save for retirement, often with employers matching all or part of employee contributions. They are also called *defined contribution* plans because there are formulas that define how much can be contributed by employees and added by employers.

As employers have come to realize that these defined contribution plans are less costly and risky to themselves than conventional defined benefit pension plans and as employees have increasingly felt they wanted to manage their own investments, there has been a dramatic switch in their favor. However, these defined contribution plans do not guarantee the amount and regularity of your monthly pension. What you get depends entirely on what you have saved, how much the company has matched, what withdrawals you may have made while you worked and contributed, what you did with your funds if you changed jobs, what you have invested your funds in, how the securities markets have performed, and what kind of deal you have made in buying annuities with your payout.

There are two kinds of defined contribution plans: before-tax and after-tax as defined by the tax code.

Before-Tax Dollar (401(k)) Plans

Beginning in 1979, 401(k) plans gained prominence as companies set up "before-tax dollar" plans to take advantage of the favorable income tax treatment accorded to active employees under a new section 401(k) of the Internal Revenue Code.

Savings are made in before-tax dollars. This enables you through pay-roll deduction to save and invest on a tax-sheltered basis to build a re-tirement fund. Your taxable income is reduced by the amount you contribute, which lets you reduce your current income taxes and there-fore makes your current take-home pay higher. To find out the maximum you can deduct, check sources such as tax guides or the IRS Web site. Your salary deferral contributions do not affect your Social Security pay-roll deduction taxes. Your other group benefits continue to be based on your gross pay.

However, you pay taxes on the distribution after retirement at the rate that is in effect when you receive it. This tax rate may be higher or lower than the rate at the time you put the money aside depending on your total income when you withdraw funds and the tax rates at that time.

After-Tax Dollar Plans

If you save and invest in after-tax dollars, you pay higher current taxes and therefore have a lower take-home pay. However, you do not pay taxes on the money that is distributed to you when you withdraw your funds because that would be double taxation.

Company Contributions

In many plans, the company helps you build your retirement fund by matching your savings partly or fully. Some employers contribute com-pany shares instead of cash. Considering that the typical company con-tributions range from 25 percent to 100 percent or more of what you put in, this is a real deal. Where else can you get such a large return on your investment?

Investment Accounts

The money withheld from employee paychecks or added by employers is de-posited into investment accounts that accumulate tax-free to provide funds for retirement income. Usually plans allow you to invest both your own contributions and company contributions in any or all of a variety of sep-arate funds. Your investment account grows or declines as a result of inter-est, dividends, and investment gains or losses on balances in your account.

Look for a sufficient variety of choices so that you can allocate your funds to meet your investment objectives and spread your risks. Be aware of the dangers of plans in which the company makes its contribution in its own shares. Also, be wary of rules that reduce your flexibility to manage your portfolio, such as restrictions on sale of company stock or long waiting periods before you can change your allocation or investments in your portfolio. Check who pays the administrative costs, you or the employer.

Vesting

Vesting means that you own all or part of the money in your investment account. The rate at which funds are vested depends on the design of the plan, but the sooner the better for you in case you leave the company.

Remember, by joining a thrift or savings and investment plan, you are becoming an investor on your own of your own funds. This is true whether you invest in securities or mutual funds. Do your research. Your retirement depends on it.

Profit-Sharing Plans

These are tax-deferred savings and investment plans in which the company's contribution is a percentage of annual profits. They are designed to enable you to accumulate funds for retirement. Distinguish them from profit-sharing bonuses that add to current income (see section on "Income Creation Plans").

Payroll Savings Plans

Many employers allow you to save through payroll deduction and deposit the money directly into such vehicles as Credit Unions or Government Savings Bonds. There are no tax restrictions or implications. Such plans are purely a convenience for you as a way of forcing you to put money aside before you see it in your paycheck.

Executive Deferred Compensation Plans

Some employers permit you to defer part of your salary and cash or equity bonus payments as a tax planning device for you to accumulate funds for retirement. In most plans, they are held in trust until you retire.

These are complicated plans. If you are offered this arrangement, be clear about:

The conditions under which the deferrals may be taxed before you actually receive them.

Your payment options.

The possibility that if you leave the company before the period of time specified in the plan, you leave your deferred pay with the company.

If the company declares bankruptcy, the assets of the deferred compensation plan become company assets, subject to the claims of banks and other secured creditors. You become an unsecured creditor and run the risk of losing most or all of your money.

See your tax and investment advisors before choosing to defer your compensation.

Stock Ownership

Most companies have plans that enable you to acquire company shares and thereby get a "piece of the action." Theoretically, they encourage employees to think like owners and work to increase the company's profits and supposedly the value of shares. In reality, there is often little correlation between company performance and stock prices. The "market" even punishes outstanding profit improvement if results fall below expectations.

Typically, there are three kinds of arrangements:

1. *Stock Bonus Plans.* Some employers pay annual bonuses in the form of company stock as outright grants (as distinct from stock purchase or option plans). You do not have to put up any money to exercise the award, but you do have to pay ordinary income tax on the value of the award.

2. *Stock Purchase Plans.* Some companies have a payroll deduction Employee Stock Purchase Program (ESPP) that facilitates the purchase of company stock at the current market price (which is re-set annually or at some other interval). Some plans offer a discount. They may also pay the brokers' commissions.

3. *Employee Stock Ownership Plans.* Many smaller companies have an Employee Stock Ownership Plan (ESOP) to motivate employees to think and act as owners by giving them company stock. The employer contributes company shares to a trust fund. Stocks are allocated to individual employees based on their salary level or some other formula. Employees do not contribute to the fund.

Some larger employers use ESOPs as a way of matching employee contributions to savings and investment plans. Some have even used ESOPs as a way of fending off hostile takeovers.

These are exceedingly complex plans, so make sure you get advice on the way they affect your compensation package.

Stock Options

As attractive as the prospect might be of obtaining options to buy company stock at a fixed price, be aware that these plans are extremely complicated and potentially risky.

First, recognize that your option grant takes on value only if and as the market price increases from the price set in your award.

Second, stock options are subject to many restrictions that do not apply to purchase and sale of shares on the open market.

Third, you may have to come up with the money to exercise your options. If you borrow to do so, you may find that the value of the shares you own falls below the amount you owe, that is, "goes underwater."

Fourth, the tax treatment of options depends on the kind of option you are awarded. Tax rules change from time to time.

There are many different kinds of stock options. In fact, this is one of the most creative and challenging areas of the total compensation plan. It keeps armies of compensation managers, consultants, lawyers, accountants, chief financial officers, boards of directors, Securities and Exchange Commission staffers, members of Congress and their staffs, and journalists busy.

There are numerous, often convoluted, rules and laws governing these plans. Regardless of the specific kind you are granted, when you get stock options, you become an investor. Look at options to buy your employer's shares with the same scrutiny as you would if you were to buy them outright through a broker. Study the provisions of the stock option plan and the grants you are given very carefully and consult experienced investment, legal, and tax experts for advice.

As an investor, would you invest your life savings and future earnings in the company? What portion of your assets are you willing to put at risk? This is the *acid test*.

Investment Planning Education

Some employers provide an investment planning education service, usually through a third party. Take advantage of it.

Caveat Emptor

The bottom line is that these plans work well:

When the company is successful and growing.

When stock prices are rising.

When the plans are understandable.

When there is a correlation between individual and company performance on one hand and the price of the shares on the other.

If these conditions are met, these plans may be great wealth-creating opportunities for you.

But, there are risks attached to the rewards. Your role is to make sure that you take on only the amount of risk you are comfortable with and that you have the time and are prepared to acquire enough skills to manage your financial affairs.

Meanwhile, don't forget to do your job because that is what your boss hired you to do in the first place.

Income Protection Plans

Employers provide benefit plans that protect your income if you are not able to work and your paychecks stop coming because you are disabled, unemployed, retired, or if you die. All of these plans supplement statutory programs such as Social Security old age, survivor income, disability income benefits; Workers Compensation disability income, survivor income, and accidental dismemberment benefits; and Unemployment Compensation and—where applicable—state-sponsored temporary disability income. They are designed to do so because the statutory plans generally have maximum covered incomes that are less than exempt levels of salary.

Some employers require you to contribute toward the cost of these benefits. Some allow you to buy extra protection at your own expense beyond what the company pays for. Time-Off-with-Pay plans keep you on the payroll while you are on sick leave, vacation, holiday, bereavement leave, jury or witness duty, military duty, using personal days, and on other paid leaves of absence. This section describes briefly how these income protection plans work.

Disability Income Plans

Sick leave and disability income plans provide financial protection for you while you are disabled because of injury or illness. They continue to pay you part or all of your salary from up to four sources:

1. Company-paid sick leave that pays full or partial salary for a duration of time that depends on your length of service. This plan usually augments disability income from other plans.
2. Statutory plans such as state short-term disability income (where applicable), Workers Compensation for work-related injuries or illnesses, and Social Security disability income benefits.
3. Company-sponsored short- and long-term disability income insurance benefit programs. These plans add enough to government programs to provide a total percentage of your income based on plan formulas.
4. Disability income benefits from defined benefit pension plans.

Retirement Income Plans

Retirement income plans pay you a pension for your lifetime. They are subject to many rules set by plan design or imposed by law. They supplement Social Security old age pensions.

Defined Benefit Pension Plans

Some employers, especially larger ones, pay retirement income based on your income and length of service. The formulas vary considerably but the objective generally is to provide you and your family with enough income to sustain your standard of living after retirement if you have spent a substantial part of your career with that employer. They have vesting provisions that enable you to receive a pension even if you leave the company before retirement age. (Note that many employers provide "defined contribution" plans in addition to or instead of defined benefit pension plans. See previous section.)

Survivor Income Plans

Company-sponsored retirement income plans pay pensions for all or part of the lifetime of your beneficiaries, whether you die before or after retirement. They are subject to many rules set by plan designers or imposed by law. They supplement Social Security Survivor Income and, if applicable, Workers Compensation Survivor Income payments.

These survivor income benefits represent a substantial amount of financial protection to your beneficiaries and you should take them into account in your estate planning.

Death before Retirement

If you die before you retire, pension plans typically pay your spouse an automatic 50 percent joint and survivor lifetime annuity as a monthly payment calculated on the date of your death.

Death after Retirement

Typical options you can choose to protect your survivors after you retire are:

- *Lifetime or Term Certain.* This choice guarantees a pension payment to yourself for your lifetime and to your beneficiaries for the unpaid part of the minimum 5 or 10 years if you die prior to the guaranteed duration you choose at retirement.

- *X Percent Joint and Survivor.* You receive a reduced payment for your lifetime. If you die before your beneficiary, the percentage you select of your monthly benefit is paid to your surviving spouse for his or her lifetime. For example, if you choose a 75 percent joint and survivor option, your beneficiary will receive 75 percent of your reduced benefit.

To pay for these survivor benefits, your "lifetime only" monthly pension payment is reduced actuarially. This is tantamount to a payroll deduction for a contributory life insurance premium.

Because of the complexity of these rules and choices, get advice from Human Resources and your own financial counselor so that your estate planning takes these survivor income benefits into account.

Unemployment Income

Most larger employers provide separation (severance) pay if you are terminated for reasons other than cause to provide you with income while you are unemployed. The formulas vary very widely. For this reason, ask about the separation plans at the time you receive an offer. The plans may or may not be described in the Employee Handbooks. If not, try to get the severance pay arrangements written into your offer letter. Given the volatility of employment, these are very important considerations. This may be a delicate subject, so approach it carefully (see "Negotiating the Compensation Package" in this section).

Separation (Severance) Pay

Separation payments are usually based on length of service and the level of the job. The formula for the amount may vary from one week to one month per year of service. Some plans have sliding scales. Some are totally discretionary. Some pay only two weeks in lieu of notice. Some pay nothing.

Employment Contracts

Employment contracts are a combination of terms of employment, a severance pay plan, and noncompete and nondisclosure requirements. Such contracts have increasingly been extended downward from executive to middle management levels. They are individually negotiated within the general provisions of company policy. It is worth your while to negotiate carefully so that the contract is favorable to you and not biased in favor of the employer.

Outplacement Counseling Services

Many employers provide outplacement counseling or transition services to terminated employees as a way of speeding up and professionalizing their job search, thus protecting their incomes against prolonged periods of unemployment. The services consist of:

- Coaching on job finding, interviewing, and career-changing techniques.
- Time-shared office facilities and services.
- Databases and other sources of information about employers.

They do not include marketing you to prospective employers.

Outplacement counseling services are paid for by employers. The extensiveness of the services may vary according to job level, length of service, and company practice.

Asset Protection Plans

Asset protection plans are offered to help you pay for health care, dependent care, home and automobile insurance costs, moving and other relocation expenses, and expenses relating to your death or that of a dependent.

Some employers require you to contribute toward the cost of these benefits. Some allow you to buy extra protection at your own expense beyond what the company pays for.

This section describes briefly how these asset protection plans work.

Medical Insurance Plans

Medical plans typically cover hospital, home and extended care, diagnostic, surgical, medical, prescription drug, vision, physical and mental therapy, services and supplies, and dental care expenses. All of them are very complicated so you should examine them carefully to find out exactly how they work.

There are large differences among them, however, such as the amount you have to contribute toward the insurance premiums, the deductibles and co-pay amounts, the exclusions and exceptions, and the maximums. These out-of-pocket expenses represent a large and growing part of your family budget.

If both you and your spouse or covered partner work, you may be able to choose the better plan to save one payroll deduction. Alternatively, it may pay you to subscribe to both and obtain larger benefit payments through the "Coordination of Benefits" provision.

Types of Insurance Plans
There are three main kinds of plans:

1. Indemnity plans reimburse part of reasonable and customary expenses when claimed.
2. Health Maintenance Organizations (HMOs) are group practices you become a member of and receive all your services from (or that refer you to other providers whom they select). They penalize you for using non-HMO practitioners. Often there is a Primary Care Physician to coordinate care.
3. Preferred Provider Organization Networks (PPOs) consist of participating physicians who accept prenegotiated fees from insurance carriers. There is no Primary Care Physician to coordinate care and patients may seek care from any provider in the network without a referral.

Any of them may involve managed care organizations that determine the utilization of services and the costs that will be covered.

Workers Compensation pays medical expenses if the injury or illness is work-related.

Medical Reimbursement Plans
Some employers offer medical reimbursement plans that allow you to set aside a tax-exempt part of your salary that you can use to pay for such costs. Bear in mind that whatever you do not use is forfeited at the end of the year.

Dependent Care

Some employers provide or subsidize the cost of dependent day-care facilities for their employees. Some offer reimbursement plans that allow you to set aside a tax-exempt part of your salary which you can use to pay for such costs. Bear in mind that whatever you do not use is forfeited at the end of the year by law.

Long Term Care Insurance

A relatively new group benefit is Long Term Care Insurance (LTCI) that pays for the costs of caring for elderly or ailing employees and their qualifying relatives. It typically covers many of the charges for home nursing care services, community care services, assisted living facilities and services, and licensed nursing home facilities and services.

LTCI is invaluable if you are faced with caring for an aging or ailing partner or parent or if you fall into that category yourself. Costs of long-term care can wipe out your savings or your expected inheritance and put you into debt—at which time Medicaid will take over.

This plan was characterized by Consumer Reports in October 1997 as, "one of the most complex types of insurance sold by the [insurance] industry. . . ." There are innumerable choices to make including waiting periods before benefit payments begin, the amount of dollars paid per day of care, the maximum duration of the payments, inflation protection provisions, and many other options. There are also many exclusions and exceptions. Criteria for insurability and eligibility for benefits of the individual as well as for inclusion or exclusion of any given facility or service vary from plan to plan.

For more information about Long Term Care Insurance and the facilities and services that are covered by it, go to www.princetonmanage mentconsultants.com, click on the tab "Publications & Speeches," scroll to Benefits Planning, and click on *Elder Care Advice*.

Life and Accidental Death and Dismemberment Insurance

This insurance plan pays benefits if you die or are killed (or lose hands, limbs, or eyes) accidentally, whether on or off the job. Most plans provide a minimum benefit of about one year's earnings with options to buy additional coverage at group rates. You may also be able to insure your dependents.

Workers Compensation

Workers Compensation pays death and dismemberment benefits if the accident is work-related.

Moving and Relocation Expense Reimbursement

Some larger employers pay moving and relocation expenses for new hires who are being moved to a company facility at a different location. Because such expenses are substantial, try to negotiate full or partial reimbursement as part of your offer package. Expenses that may be covered are:

- *Home or apartment finding assistance.* Helps you find suitable accommodations at your new location.
- *Pre-move home or apartment hunting trip expenses.* Pays travel and living expenses for house or apartment hunting trip to new location.
- *Home sale assistance.* Helps you sell your house quickly or purchases your house at fair market value.
- *Lease cancellation allowance.* Helps you pay lease expenses at your present location.
- *Temporary living expenses.* Pays reasonable living expenses for you at the new location while you are separated from your family because of the move.
- *En route moving expenses.* Pays reasonable expenses for you and your family while traveling from your old to your new location.
- *Incidental expense allowance.* Helps pay for many of the incidental costs that result from your relocation including temporary accommodations for you and your family at the new location.
- *Movement of household goods.* Arranges and pays for the movement of household goods.
- *Federal income tax offset.* Helps offset additional income taxes resulting from reimbursements.

Expatriate Compensation

Most employers pay employees who are transferred abroad various cost of living adjustments and subsidies as well as home leave privileges in addition to relocation expenses.

Protective Option Strategies

Some employers protect the value of employee stock options and employee owned company stock against substantial losses. If its stock has fluctuated widely or seems likely to do so, inquire if your prospective employer has Protective Option Strategies insurance.

Negotiating Your Compensation Package

Opportunities for Negotiating Compensation

At first sight, it may seem that the compensation package is a "take-it-or-leave-it" proposition. The salary level may be constrained by policy and budget. Incentive and benefits plans are predesigned and eligibility for them is predetermined.

Salary

But, dig deeper and you will find that there is plenty of room for bargaining when you get to the offer stage. Ask what the salary range is for the job, and you may be able to negotiate starting pay above the minimum, that is, entry level, rate. You can possibly make a deal for a performance review and pay increase after a shorter interval than the merit plan provides. If you think the job is underpriced, bring salary survey data to the next interview that show that the range should be increased. Ask to review the job description and see if you can add to the duties based on your experience, and thus get the job upgraded. (Position this approach as being to the employer's advantage because it receives more value by hiring you than it would a less qualified candidate.)

Incentives

Analyze the provisions of incentive plans to see what the goals, measurements, and rewards are and try to strike a bargain that will give you a bigger payment. Many bonus and commission plans are designed so that annual goals and rewards are established by mutual consent between you and your boss. Make sure that the goals are attainable and if they are not, negotiate a more feasible target. Try for a larger initial stock option grant.

Benefits

The day is long gone when it was considered inappropriate to talk about employee benefits in the hiring process. Too much of your compensation package is tied up in these indirect pay plans for you to be diffident about them. Benefits can account for as much as a third of your total compensation. As soon as you can in the interviewing process, get copies of the prospective employers' benefits booklets, employee handbooks, plan texts, and summary plan descriptions. Many of them have the legal effect of a contractual relationship and many are mandated by law. They're important.

Increasingly, costs have been switched to employees, thereby reducing their take-home pay. Ask if the employer will pay more of the employee contributions. Check waiting periods for eligibility and you may be able to get them waived. Try for a longer vacation, one that is based on your service with all prior employers so you don't have to start from the bottom. Ask about transportation and housing subsidies if costs of living and transportation are above average. Find out about ways to shelter income so that your taxes are reduced (see "Deferred Income" under "Asset Creation Plans" in this chapter).

Analyze the Offer

Compare the offer item by item with your present or previous total pay package to see if you really are getting a better deal. Some people have found that a large increase in direct pay has been more than offset by other elements that are smaller or nonexistent, or that they have to make larger contributions for the employee benefits thereby reducing their take-home pay.

Learn How to Negotiate

"Like it or not, you are a negotiator. Negotiating is a fact of life. Negotiation is a basic means of getting what you want from the other. . . . It is back-and-forth communication designed to reach an agreement when your and the other side have some interests that are shared and others that are opposed. . . . Although negotiation takes place every day, it is not easy to do well." [*Getting to Yes, Negotiating an Agreement Without Giving In*, Roger Fisher and William Ury (New York: Penguin Books, 1981).] Better learn how to be an effective negotiator. Remember also that once you reach an agreement, you have to live with each other in a workable relationship for some time to come, so seek a mutually beneficial outcome.

When you finally agree on the offer, you are making one of the most important decisions in your life. Whatever you get will affect not only your current standard of living but will influence it for the rest of your lifetime and that of your heirs.

8

Sales Plan

Lead Generation (Networking)

Willie Sutton, the notorious bank robber, was asked why he robbed banks. He answered, "Because that is where the money is."

That's a great principle for job getters to follow in networking, too. Go to places where you are likely to meet employers. Target and prioritize the networking contacts you want to make.

While at first this approach seems consistent with Willie Sutton's principle, in reality he asked the first person he met in a new town to tell him where the bank was. So actually he was networking with strangers to find his target.

Therefore, network with people who have contact with prospective employers, and with people who have contact with people who have contact with potential employers.

In other words, network with *everyone*. You just never know who your brother-in-law, neighbor, hair stylist, or chance encounter knows.

When I set up my practice in 1979, I told my hair stylist that I was starting my own consulting business and looking for corporations who would use my services. He said, "As a matter of fact, one of my customers is the executive assistant to the Chief Executive Officer of such and such company. Here's her phone number. Tell her I said to call her." I got an eight-month assignment out of that highly unlikely source.

Recently, my wife and I went to my university's alumni reception. I knew no one, but we chatted socially with various people. One of them, it turned out, was director of Human Resources for a major pharmaceutical firm. After we talked for a while, she asked me to send her information about my consulting practice. By coincidence, her husband advises start-up companies, which is where my wife is job hunting. So she too made a networking contact. That's a "twofer!"

Purposes of Networking

The first purpose of networking is word-of-mouth marketing to generate leads.

The second purpose is to turn other people into your public relations spokespersons and sales representatives. Employers prefer to hire people who are recommended by someone they trust because that adds a greater degree of certainty to the hazardous process of finding good people.

Your goal is to build relationships and a web of alliances, increase your exposure to opportunities in your industry or occupation, and get insider information about who decision makers are in the companies you would like to join.

Networking puts you in control because you don't rely on ads or recruiters. You take the initiative and stay in charge.

Use networking as a means to an end, not the end in itself. Focusing on the relationship will produce greater results than focusing on yourself or your product or service. Get to know the people you meet so that they know you and feel confident enough to refer you to their network.

Build a Database

Get a database or contact manager software package that works for you. (See Chapter 2, "Business Operations.") List everyone you know, whether or not they know your work. Enter in your database everything you know about them such as name, title, company, address, phone number, e-mail address, and facts and impressions about them. As you contact their referrals, get the same data about them, and so on.

List your work contacts ranging from people you worked with directly as well as those in other business units, departments, and divisions. Include your clients, customers, and suppliers. Sales representatives are great sources of information about what is going on and where to network.

As you go to the places where you can network, get business cards of people you meet. Write on the back what you talked about, what you committed to do, what will help you remember them, and what will help them remember you. However, be careful not to cross the line from being opportunistic to being obnoxious.

Follow through on your commitments, both to yourself and others. A good referral or piece of advice only becomes activated when you follow it up.

Be Prepared

Your first step in networking is to create a concise, positive message delivered effectively about who you are and what you have to offer others. Be memorable. Have your 15-second "elevator speech" ready and polished.

Make it easy for the people you network with to perceive the connection between what they or their contacts need and what you have to offer.

How Not to Network

First, here are some things *not* to do when you network:

- *Tip 1*
  Don't expect to get a job from the person you are talking to. Look for leads and referrals only.

  If you ask if they have a job, the answer is probably "No," and that may close off the conversation. It also puts them on the spot.

  If you ask if they personally know someone who has an opening, the answer is also likely to be "No," so you are in another dead end.

  However, if you ask only who they know who might know someone who might have an opening, you are likely to get names of people who are connected to decision makers. Then you can ask if you can use their name to contact the people they have told you about. Depending on how well you and your contact know each other, you may even be able to ask them to call their acquaintances on your behalf.

Elevator Speech Tips

In the world of venture capital, it is a maxim that an entrepreneur must be able to describe what the business is about in the length of time it takes for the elevator they are on to get from the ground floor to the venture capitalist's office. This "elevator speech" criterion is used to determine whether or not the project will be funded.

This is a great principle for a job hunter, too. You should be able to describe clearly and succinctly what you can do for an employer to anyone you talk to. Make a lasting first impression in the first 15 seconds, whether in an interview when you are asked "Tell me about yourself," while networking, or when meeting someone casually who, after getting your name, asks "What do you do?"

Your goal is to make a statement that is memorable. Keep it brief and simple. Direct it at what you *can do* for your prospects, not what you do. Tell a story that illustrates how your experience and skills solved a problem and produced a measurable result. This works in person, on the phone, and by e-mail.

For many people, this will be one of the key accomplishments from their resume or their catalog. For example, say "In my last job, one of my accomplishments was . . ." then tell about an achievement in specific concrete terms:

- Start with an action verb.
- Briefly describe the scenario or challenge.
- End with a quantitative statement, preferably in relative terms such as percent change, or a before-and-after comparison.

Leave the person you are talking to so intrigued that this elevator speech prompts a request for elaboration or for additional accomplishments. Have more of them from your catalog at the tip of your tongue so you are ready to illustrate what else you have done that can benefit an employer.

Make It Memorable

This 15-second elevator speech takes a lot more work than the conventional two-minute statement you may have heard or read about elsewhere. You have to write it, hone it, practice it, rewrite it, try it out on someone who is knowledgeable and objective, and polish it to the point that it sounds spontaneous. Excite the listener. Long is boring.

Elevator Speech Tips (continued)

Sample Elevator Speech

Here is a sample elevator speech that you can draw from your catalog of accomplishments:

> An example of something I did in my last job was to initiate quality tests at each step of a labor-intensive production line from incoming inspections to final output—this eliminated processing of faulty components and reduced labor requirements by 50 percent.

- *Tip 2*

  Don't bait and switch by getting an appointment to network and then asking for a job. However, if the contacts do have a job for you, they will let you know and they will switch the meeting into an interview. In case that happens, be prepared to seize the opportunity.

How to Network

Your Primary Contacts

Tell the people on your initial list of contacts that you are changing jobs. (Give a reasonably truthful reason such as downsizing or looking for better opportunities.) Say that you are not asking for a job or even a lead to a specific opening but are looking for leads to other people. Remind them, if necessary, about what you do and then give an example using your 15-second elevator speech.

Then go into the lead generation routine:

> Ask who they know who might know someone who might have an opening.

Your Secondary Contacts

Open by saying that a mutual friend or colleague (give name) suggested that you call them because they felt they would be able to give you some leads. Then go into the lead generation routine.

Your Tertiary Contacts

Repeat the process to create a list of tertiary contacts. Keep doing this until you connect with employers who have openings.

Be courteous. Listen to others when they speak. Find out what their needs are. Don't monopolize the conversation or interrupt.

Get to the point quickly. After you get to know someone, exchange business cards and ask permission to follow up.

Where to Network

Read your local newspapers and business periodicals for calendars of events that give you the opportunity to meet people. These can be a wide variety of organizations, both those that are and those that are not related to your occupation or industry.

Go to job clubs and other job related events. There is a very good list at the following Web site: http://www.careerjournal.com, at the bottom of the home page, "Calendar of Career Events."

Go to meetings such as Chambers of Commerce, professional societies, and industry associations. Go to job fairs.

Use social settings such as cocktail parties and alumni events, and chance contacts such as on airplanes, buses, or trains or even in checkout lines at a supermarket. However, be discrete about how you do this. Networking can be offensive if misused.

Ask for referrals from interviewers when you do not get the job. They now know about you and can give you names of other people you should contact inside and outside the company.

Working a Room

Let your personality be your guide. Some people can go into a room and before the event ends have met everyone. Others cannot make contact with more than one or two people, but they spend enough time with each to become acquainted. Either way is more effective than not meeting anyone.

A very good article about an expert room worker is on the Web at http://www.careerjournal.com/jobhunting/networking/20011221-voigt.html.

Personal or Telephone Networking

It is conventional wisdom that you should try to get an appointment for a face-to-face visit to network. Ideally, that is true, but it may be very hard to do. People are stretched to the limit trying to do their jobs, and even half an hour may be more than they can spare.

The good news, though, is that it has been shown that telemarketing is much more time-efficient than personal selling. Your goal is to get referrals and be remembered, and that can be done by telephone. The added benefit is that you save an enormous amount of time by not traveling to the appointment, sitting in the waiting room, engaging in pleasantries, getting down to business for a few minutes, and then making your exit, and going to the next calls, repeating the process, and then traveling back home.

The downside is that you may miss the relatively remote chance of making an immediate personal impression on the person you are networking with and getting an invitation to stay for a job interview. However, if the phone conversation seems to be going that way, ask for an appointment for a personal meeting.

Reciprocate

Successful networking is based on the premise that when you give something of value, the value is returned to you manyfold. Give information to your contacts as a way of being remembered and you will get something back sooner or later. You can become a source of business and professional intelligence to your contacts as long as you do not divulge confidential information.

Follow Up

Thank the people who have helped you. Let them know where you finally have landed a job and what you are doing. It is very much appreciated by the people who have helped you along the way. Offer to help them in any way you can. Who knows when they will be job hunting?

Stay in Touch

It is easy to stay in touch with your growing list of contacts by using technology. An e-mail newsletter is one possibility. It can contain the news you have picked up on your networking travels. You can then tell what progress you are making on your job search and ask for more leads. Offer to help them.

Middlepersons

There are several kinds of people who may come between you and the hiring manager. The key to understanding them is to realize that they have two roles:

1. They are intermediaries who can be your *allies and advocates* if you treat them right and ask them for help, or
2. They are *gate keepers* who can veto your chances of being interviewed or hired if you alienate them.

It makes sense to make them your allies, doesn't it?

Executive Recruiters

Executive recruiters, a.k.a. headhunters, are paid by employers to find candidates who **exactly** fit their specifications. They are not given much leeway to use their imaginations about why you should be presented even if you don't exactly fit. Nor are they marketing agents for you.

The chances are almost infinitesimal that any one executive recruiter at any given time has an assignment from a client to fill a job for which you qualify. Therefore, from your standpoint, it is a numbers game and you should do a mass mailing to get on file. If you are called by a recruiter about your interest in an opening, that is a good sign, but again, your chances are very slender.

The best source of information about headhunters is the *Directory of Executive Recruiters*, published by Kennedy Publications; see www .kennedyinfo.com/js/der.html for information. This annual publication contains information about what executive recruiters do and how they operate. It also lists the major firms and the key contacts, plus their functional, industry, and geographic specialties (if any). Regarding the essays in the book that advise you about how to get jobs or write resumes, just remember my slogan: "There is no one right way."

Employment or Personnel Agencies

Employment agencies, a.k.a. flesh peddlers, represent job hunters to employers. Their goal is primarily to find jobs for their clients the candidates, unlike the executive recruiters. The nicknames "headhunter" and "flesh peddler" help you distinguish their respective roles. There are hybrid situations in this category of middlemen.

The major distinction is that executive recruiters target executive, managerial, and professional positions. The employment agencies (with some exceptions such as sales, accounting, engineering, information technology, and nursing) cover only nonexempt jobs. They are often paid by the employer, although you may have to pay their fee depending on their policies.

The best source of information about employment agencies is the Yellow Pages.

Human Resources

One of the worst pieces of advice that you often get is "bypass Human Resources." Think about it. Why would an employer bear the expense of in-house recruiters if they didn't think it was worthwhile? The HR specialists do their job so hiring managers don't have to waste time doing the recruiting themselves. Think of HR as the purchasing department for people. Both are specialists in sourcing and screening goods and services and employees, respectively.

Hiring managers, in contrast, are specialists in their own jobs and they are often untrained in even the rudiments of interviewing. They have to make the final choice from among the best candidates who are presented to them (based on the specifications they have established in the first place), and they often need help in doing that.

But, the good news is that you do not have to choose. You can send your resume to both and see which works for you. My suggestion is that you keep both in the loop throughout.

Executive Assistants, Administrative Assistants, Secretaries, Receptionists, and Switchboard Operators

Definitely make executive assistants, administrative assistants, secretaries, receptionists, and switchboard operators your allies. This is a fundamental rule in sales. Treat them with respect, courtesy, and friendliness, find out and record their names in your database, ask them for guidance, get information about the company from them, let them know why you are calling or visiting, **Thank them!**

For executive assistants, administrative assistants, and secretaries, in particular, this tactic is far better than trying to elude them. They know as much as anyone about what is going on in a company. They can tell you when their bosses are available, and even what kind of personalities they have. They can intercede on your behalf if you ask for their help:

> When I was interviewed by the vice president of human resources of a global corporation to work directly for him, the final decision was made by his executive assistant. She told him I was the nicest of the candidates, so I got the job.

It pays to be friendly!

Sales (Interview) Appointment Action Plan

This checklist is written in reverse order so that the goal is clearly in your mind and to explain the reasons for the steps that precede each one back to the beginning.

To make a sale, you need:
to make an appointment

To make an appointment, you need:
to make a phone call

To make a phone call, you need:
a way to overcome fear of phoning:
    an achievable plan for each day
    make easy ones first each day
a list:
    network
    suspects
    prospects
a purpose for each call, such as to:
    update mailing list
    renew contact, catch up, schmooze
    network

form alliance
follow up to letter and resume
make appointment for interview
qualify prospect
cold call
a script for each purpose that focuses on benefits to the prospect
a tracking system

Telemarketing

Why Telemarket?

If people hate to receive telephone sales calls, why should you telemarket?

First of all, where the objections come from is consumers who resent being disturbed at home at dinnertime. What you are doing is Business-to-Business (B2B) telephone marketing during business hours.

The second reason to telemarket is that research has shown that this sales technique is seven times as effective as personal selling in terms of the number of prospects you can reach.

The third is that "A telephone follow-up to a direct mail offering may yield ten times the result of direct mail alone" (Dr. Gary S. Goodman, *Reach Out & Sell Someone,* Englewood Cliffs, NJ: Prentice Hall Press, 1983).

Finally, phone calls receive priority. Think of how often you have been in a meeting when the phone rang and the meeting was interrupted while you or the chairperson answered it.

Keep Your Purpose Clearly in Mind

Your purpose in calling is to get an appointment for a personal interview. That is all you should try to do by telephone. If there is no alternative, however, then agree to a telephone screening interview and end by asking for a personal meeting.

Goal Setting

Set aside a specific amount of time for telemarketing, such as one hour at a specific time each day, perhaps first thing in the morning (when you are more likely to get through).

Set a realistic target for the number of calls that you can make in any day. Ten probably is a good limit because then you won't feel overwhelmed. But have batches of 20 calls on the desk for each day so that you don't run out if you get through faster than you expected. As you become more proficient, raise your time and number goals.

Do the calls geographically because if you make appointments, you can combine the visits without wasting time en route. Use the classic line "I'm going to be in your area. . . ."

Start with and Keep the Right Attitude

The first call each day is always the hardest, so start with the easiest one on your list. Choose someone who knows you and will be pleased to hear from you. This may not even be anyone on your list, but just a friend you haven't seen for a while. It may be a fellow job seeker you have partnered with for mutual support. Whoever it is, you will get pleasure from having made the contact. Then keep going through your predetermined list in the sequence—from easier to harder, from less to more important—so you maintain momentum.

Expect Success in Every Call

Many people will actually be pleased to hear from you because you bring them solutions to their problems. Sound successful and you will be successful. Feel and show confidence that you will succeed. (The opposite is also true, unfortunately. If you lack confidence, that will betray you. It's tough to be out of work, but they don't want to hear about that. They want to know how you can benefit them.)

List your three most satisfying telemarketing calls. Analyze them for reasons they were so good and build that into your technique. Visualize that good feeling when starting to make calls.

Avoid Procrastination

There will be rejections, no question about that. That expectation may cause you to procrastinate. But they are rejecting what you are offering, not you. They just don't happen to need your services at this time. Remember instead the ones who said "Yes," and that will help you start and move you on to the next call. Keep in mind the sales slogan: "Each rejection brings you one step closer to an acceptance."

Get the Screeners on Your Side

Be courteous to the screeners, they have a job to do. More important, they will be your allies if you ask for their help. Thank them in advance for helping you.

Let them know the reason you are phoning and say that the person you are phoning expects your call, which is true because you wrote in your cover letter or left a message that you would phone.

If the screeners ask if they can help you instead, thank them for their offer to help but say you really need to talk to the person you originally requested.

If the person is not available, ask when a good time would be for you to call back. Just in case, leave your name and number too so that they can call you.

Voice Mail

This inanimate screening machine can be very frustrating. Recipients are able to ignore your message without compunction. While there is no good answer to this problem, try to get a response by piquing the interest of the person you are calling. Leave a message that includes the reason it would be worthwhile calling you back. If it is a cold call, for example, give your 15-second elevator speech and promise to tell about additional benefits you can offer as their employee. Here is a suggestion:

> Hello, Mr./Ms. [name]? This is [your name] speaking. I am calling to follow up on the resume I sent you on [date] regarding the management position in manufacturing. As I wrote, I initiated quality tests at each step of the labor intensive production line from incoming inspections to final output—this eliminated processing of faulty components and reduced labor requirements by 50 percent.
>
> I would like to tell you about some of my other achievements that would contribute to your company's success. Please call me at [your phone number]. If I don't hear from you by next Wednesday, I will be pleased to call you again that morning.

If you don't get a reply, calendar the call for a week later, and try, try again. Many employers appreciate the follow up. Open the conversation or message by saying, "I called you last Wednesday and promised I would call you back today. As I said, I would like to tell you about some of my other achievements that would contribute to your company's success."

When you get the person on the phone, be ready to move into your 15-second elevator speech and have other accomplishments ready to tell about. Then ask if that is the kind of thing they need you to do for them. If you get voice mail again, loop back to the previous message, or state some other accomplishment to further whet the appetite of the recipient.

Use a Telephone Voice

In a personal call, body language accounts for 75 percent of the communication. In a phone call, you don't have that advantage, so compensate for it by using a telephone voice.

- *Be enthusiastic.* Like the person you are calling. Create a bond between you. Be enthusiastic in a polished way.
- *Smile as you talk on the phone.* It actually comes across the wire and is infectious. Some people have a mirror in front of them to check if they are smiling. Make your voice sound light instead of heavy and stressed, especially when you are talking about getting a job offer.
- *Stand up while you are talking.* This makes you sound freer.
- *Don't rush, but get to the point fast.* Say your own name comfortably when you start the conversation. Be calm, but not casual. Don't waste the person's time.
- *Use power words.* Use the action verbs from your catalog. Weak words such as "I'd like to . . ." make you sound weak, too.
- *Listen.* You will be tempted to do all the talking. Don't. Listen instead. You will learn much more about what your prospective employer needs by asking questions and then attentively listening to the answers. Paradoxically, silence is one of the most effective parts of your telephone voice.

Script

It is essential that you have a script prepared and rehearsed to the point where you can make it sound spontaneous. Don't wing it. Write it down, polish it, practice it, refine it, critique it after each phone call, improve it, and start the cycle over again.

The script and the message are really essential; otherwise things go off base. Use the text word for word. In addition, you have something to start with and don't have to get yourself all prepped up.

How to Start the Conversation

What to say when you start the conversation is often the hardest part. The first words are the name of the person you are calling. When the person comes on the line, say his or her name with a lift in your voice as if it is a question:

Hello, Jean? Hi Jean, this is Peter. How are you today? Great.

Then move quickly into your point:

I recently sent you my resume that told about how I [elevator speech or opening sentence of cover letter mentioning name of employer]. Do you remember reading it?

I'm calling to find out whether any of my accomplishments on my resume resemble projects you are working on or challenges you're facing. Could you use contributions like these to your company's success?

[If not remembered] What sort of problems are you encountering in your (functional area)?

Can you tell more, please? Great. When I encountered that problem, here's what I did [relevant accomplishment from your catalog]. I'd love to help you fix that.

If this is not a good time for you to talk, when would be a better time to phone you, please? How's Thursday at 10:00 A.M. or 2:00 P.M.? Okay, I'll call you back at 10:00 on Thursday morning. Bye for now.

Close the Sale

Get a commitment out of every call—know the conclusion you want and get it! When you hang up the phone, have something as a result of making the contact. Get an appointment for an interview:

> Let's get together on [day] at [time] to talk about your needs and how
> I can help you. I look forward to meeting you.

If that does not work, ask for referrals just the way you do on your networking calls. Leave your phone number, e-mail address, and (if you have one) your URL for your Web site.

Strategic Interviewing

First, an interview is *not:*

An interrogation by the interviewer (although that does happen).

Purely an exchange of information (although that must take place).

A way to trap the candidate into revealing lies or personality aberrations (although that may have to happen too).

An interview *is* a sales call with a single purpose: *to get the job.*

With that objective, you can build your strategic plan to conduct the interview so well that you will get the job. The same concepts apply to a networking interview, an information interview, a screening interview, and a hiring interview.

Become an Expert in Sales Methods

An interview is so much like a sales call that you should become skilled in sales techniques. To become proficient, read books on the subject. The most popular ones are listed in www.amazon.com: click on the "Books" tab; under "Search Books" enter "sales." You can find details about the books under "Explore this Book." Look for those about Business-to-Business (B2B) and choose the one that appeals to you.

You can also take seminars in selling at community colleges and other sales training seminars.

This chapter provides some tips about how to succeed. Remember the slogan: *There is no one right way.*

The most successful salespeople are those who learn the basics but then use creativity and ingenuity to take them to the top. The same is true of the most successful interviewees.

Practice, Practice, Practice

The more work you put into the preparation phases, the greater your chances of success. You wouldn't dream of competing in a sport, acting in a play, or appearing in a piano recital without thorough preparation. This is equally necessary when it comes to interviews. Therefore, practice your interview skills. Get your sales routine down pat. Use a counselor, a friend, a video camera, a tape recorder, or a mirror to make it so smooth that it comes out naturally.

Your goals in preparing for the interview are to:

- Get fluent. If you need to learn speaking skills, join Toastmasters, take a Dale Carnegie course, or get a coach.
- Get confident.
- Get relaxed.

You'll be amazed how your mood transmits itself to the interviewer.

Now, at last, you are ready to go on interviews.

Do Due Diligence on the Employers

To be effective in the sales process, you want to know everything you can about the prospect. Ask hard questions before the interview, during it, and afterward. You are making a big decision about whether you want to devote a good part of your life to this company. Jobs that "don't work out" are in retrospect the result of the candidate not finding out enough about the employer beforehand.

Research the Prospects

Learn everything you can about prospective employers. Look up their Web sites. Read their annual and quarterly reports and 10K forms. Read about them in the premier business gossip sheets: *Business Week*, *Fortune*, *Forbes*, the *Wall Street Journal*, and *Inc.* magazine. Research investment periodicals for the inside lowdown on listed companies. Get valuable insights into the future outlook of companies and the industries they are in from stock brokers' analyses and other reference sources such as Standard and Poor's, Dun & Bradstreet, Moody's, and Value Line. Ask the reference librarian for help in finding sources about smaller companies, especially local ones.

Find out about executives in the many *Who's Who* books on the market. Dun & Bradstreet's *Reference Book of Corporate Management* gives the business biographies of 12,000 executives.

Use your network to make contact with present and former employees of the companies. They can give you the inside scoop on the company that will confirm or modify the impression that you get from the outside. Listen very carefully to them for negative comments and assess their validity by asking other sources. There are even rogue Web sites about some companies that you can search for on the Internet.

Size Up the Prospects

Many industries, companies, and occupations have their own vocabulary, their own buzzwords. You can learn them from job advertisements, periodicals, networking contacts, and keeping your ears open when you are on site or on the phone. Nonverbal communication is even more important than oral and aural. Keep your antennas out as you make calls on prospects to pick up cues as to how they function.

On the other hand, don't try to fit your prospects into boxes. They are not things. The pseudo-Jungian and pseudo-Freudian systems for categorizing a human being are too simplistic to be of any value in a dynamic interpersonal situation. Here too, there is no one right way. Use your judgment based on your own perceptions.

Understand Their Style

You want to look like one of them, sound like one of them, act like one of them. This may mean slavish conformity in some organizations and wild diversity in others, but most likely it will be somewhere in between. Be sure of what they like and are like, because if you are not in synch, you probably will be ineffective.

As a *New York Times* research study reported, "Job seekers . . . believe that hiring managers are looking for experience, but hiring managers tend to value personality over experience. . . . Resumes are less important and interviews are more important than job seekers think" (http://nytimes.com/ads/marketing/jobmarket/020502research.html).

There is an old saying, "You don't get a second chance to make a good first impression." Look the part of a successful executive, manager, or professional in your occupation. Before you go for the interview, ask about their normal dress customs. For example, they are different in a Wall Street law firm than in a Madison Avenue advertising agency. They differ even within companies. It is probably wise to err on the side of being conservative, however.

Qualify the Buyer

Sooner or later, get answers to the following questions: What are the approval processes? Who makes recommendations? Who are the decision makers? Who does the actual hiring? Is there money in the budget for the resources you need to do the job?

Find Out What They Are Looking For

The employer's basic purpose for filling a job is to solve its problems. Contrary to what many job seekers put as an objective on their resumes, employers are not looking to further your career and give you an income commensurate with your hoped-for lifestyle. They are looking for a person who can hit the ground running.

How do you find out what they are looking for? There are three ways:

1. Research, which you can do at the library, on the Internet, and from the company itself.
2. Information interviewing and networking.
3. Asking hard questions at the interview. But to do this, you have to be well-prepared with appropriate questions so that it is clear that you know your stuff. This is also an excellent opportunity to show your

stuff. You should have some idea from your research and your own experience what challenges the employer faces. Have your questions written out and make sure you ask about them as leading questions in the interview.

Find Out the Compensation Range for the Job

You need to be the right "price" for the employer. Most organizations have salary systems and budgets that they must stick to. Find out about going ranges of pay for your level of job so that you specifically answer the questions about salary requirements. You can do this research in the library, on the Internet, possibly in your professional organization, and by asking people in the field. (See Chapter 7 for more information.)

Two Purposes of Salary Questions in the Interview

Your salary is a short-hand way of pigeonholing you. Therefore, if the question of salary comes up early in the interview (or appears in the job advertisement), it is a way of screening out candidates who are above or below the range for the job.

In contrast, if the subject of compensation comes up toward the end interview, it is a "buy" signal that indicates their interest in hiring you. Then you want to have your response ready and start negotiating. (See Chapter 7.)

Prep Yourself

Psych Yourself Up

Expect success. Decide that you will leave the interview with some tangible result ranging from a job offer through an invitation to a second interview to at least a list of networking referrals. Just getting experience in interviewing is not good enough.

Anticipate Rejection

Rejection is just part of the game. But preparation reduces the odds of being rejected and conversely increases the odds in your favor.

Know How You Fit Their Needs

Your basic purpose in the interview is to demonstrate that you—and you alone—are the right candidate for the job.

Know Your Product (Yourself)

Make sure you know the contents of your catalog of achievements thoroughly. Then you can immediately cite an appropriate one when the prospect cites a need because you already have a measurable accomplishment that you can contribute.

Know How You Are an Asset to the Company

Once again, in the interview you must convey that you are the right candidate for the job. Use your cover letter and resume as the starting points for the process of selling yourself. After all, they were probably major reasons why you got in the door in the first place. Sell to your advertising.

Have many back-up accomplishments in your head so that when the employers talk about challenges *they* are facing, you can unhesitatingly cite an appropriate measurable achievement that will benefit them.

The Screening Interview

The purpose of the screening interview is to narrow the field of candidates to those few who best fit the criteria for the job. The screeners receive possibly hundreds of applications from which they have to select perhaps half a dozen to present to the hiring managers. This is a daunting task. They have to make judgments based on only two or three sets of data: the resume and cover letter, the screening interview, and a reference check.

Recruiters—whether in-house or outside—put their jobs on the line every time they send the finalists to the hiring manager. The candidates they propose have to fit the job, both initially and over the long haul, or the recruiter is eventually replaced. Remember, the screening interviewers do not create the specifications nor make the hiring decision. But they do have veto power over 95 percent of the applicants.

Your goal in the screening interview is to sell yourself to the hiring manager through the recruiters. Give them the ammunition that will persuade their clients to hire you. Make the recruiters your allies and advocates.

The Hiring Interview

The hiring managers are even more at risk than the recruiters are. Their career depends on the people they hire and manage. Your job is to reduce their risk by demonstrating that you are going to make their jobs easier and make them look good. Establish rapport and then show factually why you are the right candidate based on your accomplishments and qualities.

Consultative Selling

Consultative selling is the most effective technique to use in an interview. Think only about the prospects' needs, not your own. Use consultative selling to find out what the employer's challenges are. Say the word "you" frequently. As the old sales saw goes, "Telling ain't selling, asking is." Just telling what you do may miss the mark of what they need.

Do a Needs Analysis

Find out what they need and show your ability by asking perceptive questions. If you have done your homework, you will have a list of questions ready. The smarter your questions, the smarter you look to the interviewer. Take notes if you wish (ask permission). It impresses the employers that you are really paying attention to their needs.

Present the Solutions

As you find out the challengers facing the interviewer, relate an accomplishment from your catalog that demonstrates that you can solve them when you join the company. In other words, tell the features you offer and the benefits you bring to the employer. (Refer also to the following section for a description of assumptive closes.)

Overcome Objections

Show how what they consider weaknesses are really strengths. For example, if the interviewer says that you are overqualified, acknowledge their feelings. Then say this gives you an edge over other candidates because you will be able to produce more results more quickly.

Give Testimonials

As you tell about your accomplishments, name the company you did the work for. This is an implicit testimonial. It can also be the basis for the reference check that the prospective employers may do.

Interview the Employer

Your goal is to make sure that this employer and this job are right for you. In the interview, confirm or reverse what you found out in your market research by asking astute questions. Do your own reference check on the employer.

If their criteria or working environment are not right for you, don't take the job. You can adapt. But if you cannot transform yourself, you will not be effective. It is a sad fact that most terminations are based on interpersonal issues rather than on matters of competence. Gracefully exit the interview. But don't walk out empty handed. Get referrals, either elsewhere in the company or in other companies. You never know how you can benefit from having had an interview, so cultivate the relationship you have been establishing with the interviewer.

The Close—What It Is All For

As you reach the end of the interview, ask your key questions again to confirm that you understand the employer's needs and that they understand that you are the solution to its problems.

If the match is right, **ask for the job.** Summarize what you bring to it. Tell and show the interviewer how enthusiastic you are about working there and ask when you can start. If you are told that there are more candidates they have to interview, ask when you can expect to come back for a second interview.

Get a Commitment

All buyers have to be motivated to take action—and that applies to hiring managers too. Even if you do not get an offer on the spot, try to get a commitment for some action they will take and the date they will take it. See if you can move the process forward.

Confirm Your Interest in Writing

Your follow-up letter is not just to say thank you. It is another opportunity to demonstrate that you are the one right candidate and that they will have made a good choice in you. You can, for example, reiterate points that resonated with the interviewer or make a new point that you wish you had made in the interview that strengthens your case.

Provide References (Testimonials)

If you are asked for references toward the end of the interviews, that is a very good sign that the employer is interested in making you an offer. (If you are asked for references at the beginning of the process, ask if you can wait until you receive an offer.)

Say you will be very pleased to provide references. First, though, you would like to contact your references to let them know you have received an offer and that they will be contacted by the prospective employer. Then call them and tell them the name of the company and what the requirements of the job are. You can enumerate which of your accomplishments appealed to the interviewers. This will help them focus on the important things to say about your performance.

Note, however, that some employers have policies that they will only confirm that you were employed by them. They have adopted these rules to protect themselves against charges that they impeded you getting employment. Some companies require that all inquiries be referred to HR.

Ask for the Offer

See the next section, "How to Get the Job by Asking for It," for details on how to ask for and get a job offer. Get the offer in writing. It is like a contract and deserves a formal statement of agreement.

Evaluating the Offer

When you get the offer, ask for time to evaluate it. You do not need to, and should not, give your answer immediately. Say that you need time to think about it and will get back to them by a specific date. The employer may pressure you for a commitment right away, but try to avoid a spontaneous response unless you have already discussed the details and the letter is a formality.

There are several reasons to ask for time. You may have other offers in hand or pending, and need time to compare them. In the latter case, you can use this offer to precipitate offers from other employers you are negotiating with (see the section, "How to Get the Job by Asking for It").

You should go through the offer with a fine tooth comb with respect to its general terms and the compensation package (see Chapter 7). This is your best shot at getting the best deal and there may not be any other opportunities. Compare the terms offered to your previous job or the other offers to make sure that you get everything you had bargained for—or wish you had bargained for.

Depending on your level and the nature of the offer, such as an employment contract, you ought to get professional advice from someone knowledgeable. If an executive recruiter or outplacement counselor is involved in the process, consult your advisor. If there is an employment contract, your lawyer should examine it.

Make a counter offer if that is appropriate. The negotiations are not finished until both parties have signed off.

How to Get the Job by Asking for It

As a job seeker, you may see an interview as an interrogation or exchange of information. It's neither. Interviews are sales calls. And, as any sales pro knows, you only get the sale by asking for it.

You aren't begging for a handout when you ask for a job. You're offering prospective employers your experience and ability to contribute to their goals. If employers don't need what you're offering, they won't buy. However, if they do need your skills—or if you can create the need—you'll get the job.

It may surprise you to learn employers like to hear candidates say "I'd like to work here." Dick Stone, a recruiting manager, says, "I like it when [candidates] give me the feeling they like us. A little flattery goes a long way. Often the missing part in the interview is the commitment from the candidate to the firm."

Sounds easy, but for most job hunters, it isn't. Asking for the job in lieu of silently waiting for an offer is the hardest part. This step is what salespeople call "closing" the sale.

Anyone can learn to apply the tricks of the sales trade to a job interview and close a sale. Following these nine steps will help you ask for the job—and get it.

Prepare for the Interview

Learn what your prospect needs. Research the employer, formally and informally. If you're answering an advertisement, go beyond its sparse facts to learn as much as you can about the organization.

Determine which of your skills, traits, or experiences the employer needs. Then you can tailor your credentials to your research findings.

Plan your interview and rehearse your message. Make sure your pitch is easily understandable. This means converting your skills and experience into terms employers will immediately recognize as useful. If you're confused about your benefit to the organization, the interviewer also will be confused and there won't be a job for you. Make your presentation persuasive and believable.

Learn about the Interviewer

When you enter the interview, start by learning everything you can about the interviewer. Forget labels and generalizations that categorize personality types. Concentrate on that particular individual.

Put yourself in his or her shoes. Fear and greed are usually at work. A recruiter is taking a risk in recommending a candidate. The hiring manager is taking a bigger chance in choosing a candidate. If they make the wrong choice, at best, time and money are wasted. At worst, a bad choice could jeopardize the recruiter's or manager's job or even the success of the organization. So it's up to you, the candidate, to show the decision to hire you will be a good one.

If you turn out to be as terrific as you say, you bring success not only to yourself but to the people who hired you. Be positive and present good news. Help the interviewer relax and see you as someone who's going to solve his or her problems.

Use Consultative Selling

The type of selling that works best is called *consultative selling*. This isn't high-pressure selling. Remember the old saw in sales: "Telling ain't selling, asking is." By asking the right questions, you help the employer come to the inevitable conclusion you're the right choice. You identify the problems and show you're the person to solve them. You learn the organization's weaknesses and demonstrate how you can provide the solution.

This technique can create demand. Many times, it leads to the employer exclaiming, "That's just what we need here!"

Motivate Yourself

The desire to close—to ask for and get the offer—is essential. It can be scary to be so bold. Most job hunters aren't used to it, but it can be done with practice. You just have to psych yourself up.

Sell yourself first. Expect success and think lucky, and you'll create desire from within. Get rid of negative thoughts and problems before you enter the interview. Be confident and courageous. It takes audacity to ask for the job.

When Judith Gelb of Lambertville, New Jersey, was seeking a job in international sales, she sold herself on the idea she was a hot candidate. Next, she lined up interviews. "The fact that I was in demand made me more appealing to employers and precipitated offers," she says. "They can smell when you're being sought after." When she had two offers pending, she was up front about it. "I made it clear I had two other offers. The employers got worried about the risk of losing a high-potential candidate," says Ms. Gelb. "They quickly made offers. I controlled my destiny."

Many salespeople take comfort in knowing they can't win them all. And you'll encounter many employers who don't need your talents at this moment. (To put it in salesman's terms, for example: I don't need a car right now. But I do need a computer, so it'll be hard to persuade me to buy a car now. Maybe later. Unless you have a really good deal for me now.)

There's a 98 percent chance of being told "no." However, you have a 2 percent chance of being told "yes." By following these steps, you'll boost your chance for success. The best thing to do is take a chance and try to close the deal. The probability you'll hear "yes" will be higher than if you don't ask.

Know When to Close

When should you try to close? All the time. Keep trying throughout the interview in small ways. These are called "trial closings." For example, when you learn the employer has a problem you've solved in your previous job, explain how you solved it. Then ask, "Would this help you here?" The answer will likely be "yes." Do this whenever the opportunity arises. Hearing "yes" along the way makes it easier and less frightening to ask for a "yes" when the time is right for the big one.

Close when the interviewer is ready. Listen for signs of interest, look for body language, and sense when there's an opportunity to close. Then ask for the offer.

Some candidates talk so much during interviews that they talk themselves out of a job they've already landed. Or worse, they keep selling after they've made the sale. Then they're dead. Listen and give the interviewer a chance to hire you.

Silence is an amazingly powerful tool in closing. If you don't say anything, the interviewer may feel compelled to fill the void and tell you something vital. Do this discretely. Too many silences can be awkward. Pace yourself with the interviewer.

Try These Closes

There are many so-called "closes." Several of them work particularly well in job interviews.

The Choice Close

This technique is useful when you are setting up an appointment for an interview. Ask, "Is 9:30 A.M. or 2 P.M. better for you?" This presupposes the interviewer will see you. Just asking, "May I come in to see you?" may result in a "no" answer.

It also works when you're asking for the job: "When do I start, Monday or Wednesday?" This may seem aggressive, but it shows you're ready and eager to work for that employer.

Third-Party Endorsements

When explaining an accomplishment that will help the prospective employer, mention the employer you did it for. "At XYZ company, I . . ." This gives you credibility and adds the strength of that employer's name to the story. Then ask, "Will this help you solve your problem here, too?"

Assumptive Close

This is one of the best closes. You simply talk and act as if you're already working for the interviewer's organization. Use "we" and "us" in your conversation. Describe the situations in which you can see yourself working and accomplishing goals. Become part of the team even before you've been hired. Identify with the interviewer and the organization.

When you follow this strategy, the employer feels more comfortable with you than if he or she has to make a deliberate decision to extend an offer. When you assume you'll get the job, the only question remaining is, "When do I start, Monday or Wednesday?"

A word of caution: Don't appear too eager. You need to maintain your professionalism.

Overcome Objections

One stumbling block for many candidates is the inevitable objection: "You're over-/under-qualified, too old/young," and so on. There are hundreds of reasons given why candidates aren't right for the job. Many are just excuses or stalls to avoid the risk of hiring someone.

Turn these objections into opportunities to strengthen your candidacy. Acknowledge the objection. "You feel I'm overqualified. That's possibly true." Then turn the weakness into a strength: "However, that means I'll start being productive for you that much faster. As I've mentioned, I solved this problem at XYZ company." Make a list of standard objections that apply to you or that you encounter and work out the answers.

Overcoming objections is an art unto itself. The key is to remember that patience and persistence pay off. Don't take no for an answer. Try one more time. The secret to closing is to keep trying.

Sum Up and Ask for the Job

When it is the appropriate time, summarize. Say what you have to offer based on your accomplishments. Salespeople call these "features." Show how the features will benefit the employer. Keep it simple and brief. Stick to basics. Prepare one dramatic sentence on why you're the person for the job. Remind the interviewer how you've contributed at your previous employer and reiterate how you'll contribute to the success of the prospective one.

Confirm the Close

Repeat the terms of the offer as you've discussed it. Ask for clarification of any terms not fully described or understood. Each time you close, ask the interviewer, "Do you have any questions?" When you've been completely clear about how you'll help the employer—then and only then—close.

Be sure to thank the interviewer at the end. Write the words "thank you" in your follow-up letter, too, and repeat the statement of benefits you used to close. Also add the other features and benefits you wished you'd expressed during the interview. The thank-you packs a punch. As Mr. Stone says, "You don't often get thank-you letters. They mean a lot."

Asking for the job intimidates most of us. Fortunately, these techniques can make it easier to close the deal and get the job. Practice these tips and you'll soon grow comfortable with these methods and use them automatically.

9

Customer Relations Management

Once you have landed the one customer you have been hunting for, that is, your new employer, your challenge is to satisfy its needs. This means switching to a "customer relations management" model. While you were job hunting, your philosophy was "put the customer first." This slogan is as or more valid now that you are at work. Do the best you can for the company and the company will do the best it can to keep and "grow" you.

> Hordes of consultants, coaches, and other gurus of various stripes have been studying the question of why new managers fail, and their unanimous conclusion is that personal chemistry and cultural compatibility—the soft, people skills stuff that makes up that old black magic called fit—are all-important. The failure to build good relationships with peers and subordinates is the culprit an overwhelming 82% of the time. (*Fortune*, June 22, 1998, p. 160)

Build Relationships

You have gained invaluable experience in the networking process to land your job. Now use it to succeed on the job. Forge good relationships from the start. Learn who the influencers are, both those on the organization chart and those who are the informal leaders.

Watch Politics

As the new kid on the block, you will be scrutinized by many people who want to take your measure. You may have been hired to do a job that a disappointed inside candidate had wanted. You may be seen as an ally or an enemy even before you actually begin the job. Your reputation will most likely have gone before you. Keep your guard up without making politics your agenda at the expense of your achievements.

Listen to What They Want

The article in *Fortune* went on to say:

> . . . most managers who make up the . . . 40% failure rate start to go off the rails in the very first few weeks in the new job. How? By not asking enough questions of their bosses, peers, and underlings to know what the critical few objectives are—or by not listening carefully enough to the answers. . . . Many successful people, unfortunately, think they already know everything. This is where failure begins. (p. 162)

Deliver What You Sold and Keep Track of Your New Accomplishments

When you get the job and know who the players are and what you are supposed to do, hit the ground running. Make your employer's number 1 priority your number 1 priority. Deliver what you have promised. Make sure that your actions confirm the wisdom of their decision to hire you.

Start racking up accomplishments as quickly as possible—and add them to your catalog as you go. You can use them to document that you have earned merit pay increases. If it happens that you leave the job, you can start to look for another one without having to go through the process of creating your inventory all over again.

Appendix

Cover Letters and Resumes

These cover letters and resumes were prepared for and with clients over the past 20 years. Therefore, many of them have dates that extend back into the last century. However, the earliest are just as relevant as those that were created this year.

All names of people, employers, and educational institutions have been disguised to respect the privacy of the job seekers.

The cover letters and resumes range over a wide variety of occupations and job levels. You can use them as models to help you develop your own versions. You should not copy them because you want to create cover letters and resumes that reflect your unique experience and background.

JOHN S. MILLER
327 Magna Gates Court
Cranbury, NJ 08512
609-555-1234

name   date
title
company
address
city, state zip

Dear name:

As Chief Operating Officer, I reversed a $1 million loss to a $600,000 profit in the first year and doubled revenues from $2.6 million to $5.2 million in 18 months.

As head of mergers and acquisitions and business development for the enterprise subsidiary of a multibillion dollar, multinational firm, I targeted the 50 largest telemarketers in the country for acquisition. I brought 10 of them—ranging from $4 million to $75 million in price—to the table in only 15 months.

If you would like to know more about my accomplishments in a wide diversity of industries and roles, please read my attached resume.

In addition to a finely-honed sense of business and sense of urgency, I can bring the following record to your operation:

> Building and motivating strong management and sales teams,

> Creating strategic plans and bringing them to reality,

> Turning around failing corporations and focusing their businesses for future growth and profitability,

> Strengthening banking and investor relations,

> Integrating acquisitions into parent operations and making and keeping them both profitable.

I have the flexibility and adaptability that enable me to size up and run an operation from day one.

I wish to form a long-term affiliation with a team that wishes to aggressively expand its company's profitability - and have fun while doing it. I would be happy to discuss how my abilities can contribute to the success of your firm. In a week, I will call your office to set an appointment for us to get together.

Yours sincerely,

JOHN S. MILLER

327 Magna Court   Telephone
Cranbury, NJ 08512   609-555-1234

CAREER SUMMARY

Chief Operating Officer with a record of merging and acquiring businesses and turning around troubled companies to achieve sustained profitability.

BUSINESS ACCOMPLISHMENTS

BELL CANADA ENTERPRISES INFORMATION SERVICES   1988 to date
Head of Mergers & Acquisitions and Business Development

Targeted 50 largest telemarketers in country for acquisition. Brought 10 to the table over 15 months ranging in price from $4 million to $75 million.

Targeted cable operator for acquisition - brought $100 million deal to table.

Brought largest 900 phone marketing program company ($20 million revenues) to table for acquisition.

STERN & JOHNSON, INC.   1986 to 1988
Chief Operating Officer

Doubled revenues from $2.6 million to $5.2 million in 18 months. Reversed $1 million loss to $600,000 profit in first year.

Repositioned company to take advantage of changes in tax laws and markets. Instituted add-on and cross-sale tactics.

Set up marketing and sales campaign:

> Targeted wealthy individuals in selective mailing lists to attend estate planning seminars and provide new business.

> Used joint ventures with private banks to obtain referrals.

Turned pension administration cost center into a profit center that yielded $1 million in revenues annually.

Trimmed expenses by staff reductions, streamlined procedures, and productivity gains - saved $600,000 annually.

John S. Miller   page 2

BANNON FINANCIAL CORPORATION   1984 to 1986
Vice President - The Bannon Financial Services Group
Vice President and Board Member - Freeman Credit Corporation

Created profits of $7 million that returned the entire Bannon Financial
Corporation to profitability.

Acquired Transworld Services Corporation for $28 million gross, recaptured $7
million cash in one day thereby reducing purchase price to $21 million net.

Turned company around from having had five years of worsening losses to
achieving $1.1 million profit in 15 months.

Wrote three-year turnaround plan for Freeman Credit Corporation. Repositioned
company to serve large financial institutions.

Negotiated with financial institutions to obtain favorable lease terms of $2.5
million for a period of five years.

LANDER MANUFACTURING CO. INC.   1983 to 1984
Director Financial Systems

JOHN S. MILLER CONSULTING AND FINANCIAL SERVICES   1978 to 1983
Principal

OLSON EQUITY CORPORATION   1968 to 1978
Controller

EDUCATION

C.P.A., 1981, State of New York
M.B.A., 1979, Columbia University Graduate School of Business, major, finance
M.B.A., 1973, Columbia University Graduate School of Business, major,
accounting
    Honors: Beta Gamma Sigma (Phi Beta Kappa)
B.A., 1968, Pace University, major, biology and chemistry

Honors: Listed in Who's Who Worldwide Registry, 1991.

PERSONAL

Born: New York City, January 31, 1947, married, 2 sons
Hobbies and interests: Community service, soccer and Little League coach,
fishing, gardening

THOMAS J. BROWN, Ph.D.
46 Crest Lane
Princeton, NJ 08540
609-555-1234

date

name
title
institution
address
city

Dear

In less than two years as President and Chief Executive Officer, I turned around a struggling career-oriented college—both academically and financially—so that it kept its accreditation as well as increased its enrollment and retention of both traditional and nontraditional students.

As Deputy Director of the Delaware Council of Technological Science, I raised over $400 million in seven years. At Pace University, I obtained first time ever grant moneys for members of the humanities faculty.

In addition to my academic leadership abilities, I have also been instrumental in developing university-industry partnerships in high-technology research.

If you need a CEO who has both the educational and business skills to make your college flourish in these difficult times, you may wish to read about more of my accomplishments in my attached resume.

I am a highly creative, energetic, quality-oriented, entrepreneurial, and motivated academic administrator. I combine thinking and doing in a way that turns vision and ideas into effective action and programs. And I have a talent for bringing the best out of the people who work with and for me.

I would be very pleased to meet with you to discuss how my record of achievement can contribute to the needs of your institution. I will call you in a week to set a time when we can get together.

Yours sincerely,

enclosure

THOMAS J. BROWN, Ph.D

46 Crest Lane
Princeton, NJ 08540

Bus: 212-555-1324
Res: 609-555-1234

CAREER SUMMARY

Chief Executive Officer and strategic planner with a record of developing and revitalizing public and private institutions through fund-raising and program innovation.

PROFESSIONAL ACCOMPLISHMENTS

ARTHUR COHEN COLLEGE   1992 to date
Director of Development

Developed fund-raising initiatives linking innovative private college to national efforts in public schools with support from the American Scholastic Development Institute.

Identified corporations, private foundations, and government agencies to target proposals for the college's endowment, scholarship aid, and building funds.

PENNSYLVANIA DEPARTMENT OF EDUCATION   1992
Director of Resource Development

Created a new public and private fund-raising program for the state designed to look beyond state staffs for innovation and beyond taxes for financial resources.

Organized a proposal team comprising Department of Education managers, Pennsylvania State University faculty, and Philadelphia Institute of Politics experts to obtain funding from the federal Eisenhower National Program for Mathematics and Science Education.

TECHNICAL DEVELOPMENT INSTITUTE (formerly CLP Institute) 1989 to 1991
President and Chief Executive Officer

Turned around prestigious industry-supported technical college; redefined its mission, revitalized curriculum, organized faculty with 14 months—prevented loss of accreditation.

Won support of industry—specifically Northern Laboratories and Bellcad—to donate over $200,000 of equipment for upgrading the college's computer laboratories.

Revived Industrial Advisory Committee by recruiting IGB, Tillman Research Center, and Norfield National Laboratory as members—encouraged active participation in all aspects of college program.

Thomas Brown, Ph.D.   page 2

DELAWARE COUNCIL OF TECHNOLOGICAL SCIENCE   1982 to 1989
Deputy Director

Created a new agency to improve collaboration between Delaware's industries
and its research universities to enhance economic development—raised more
than $400 million in seven years.

DELAWARE DEPARTMENT OF HIGHER EDUCATION   1980 to 1982
Special Assistant to the Chancellor

Initiated study to develop university-industry high-tech research
partnerships—led to creation by the Governor of the Commission on Science and
Technology.

PACE UNIVERSITY   1977 to 1980
Assistant Director, Office of Research and Project Administration

Developed and improved the grants preparation process for humanities faculty
(many of whom had never received federal sponsorship)—obtained $5 million
from National Endowment for the Humanities.

BICENTENNIAL YOUTH DEBATES   1976 to 1977
Director of Research and Evaluation

Published six articles in nine months in both professional and popular media
describing this National Endowment for the Humanities project and its relation to
the history of the American Revolution.

AMERICAN REVOLUTION BICENTENNIAL ADMINISTRATION   1972 to 1975
Program Officer

Coordinated work of 20 historians to produce, *Above Ground Archeology* - U.S.
Government Printing Office distributed 200,000 copies.

EDUCATION

B.A., 1967, Hofstra University, major: history
Ph.D., 1972, Pennsylvania State University, history
Honors: National Defense Education Act, Title IV Fellow

MEMBERSHIPS

National Society of Fund-raising Executives
Council for Advancement and Support of Education

Mitchell W. Kramer
103 Powell Avenue
Princeton Junction, NJ 08550
609-555-1234

date

name
title
company
address
city, state zip

Dear name:

As Vice President Marketing, Business Development and Sales, I turned around the company's long-term sales and profit decline. For example:

> I analyzed existing customer base to determine the profile of best buyers and focussed on highest potential prospects—grew sales by $1 million in first year.

> I created three new CD ROM and six new print products—produced $1.5 million in annual sales growth.

How did I accomplish these things? Leadership.

I hired the best people, people who are independent thinkers, who have strong personalities. Then I formed them into a team and encouraged them to take the lead and to achieve our business goals.

I strove for results and completion and success. I kept the team focussed on the goal - to find out what customers really needed specifically, and then satisfy them. We sweated the details that produced the sales and profits.

I get to know and am concerned about the people who work with me as individuals and their success in the project. I am unselfish about giving credit. The result of this kind of leadership is success and loyalty. My team works hard for me because it does not want to disappoint me.

Once I am convinced we have a good thing, I have the courage to make it happen - even if there is opposition. I take a hard line if that is what it takes. The results are there to see in my resume.

If you would like my kind of business smarts working to grow your business, we need to get together. In a week, I will call your office to set a date to see how we can work to our mutual benefit.

Yours sincerely,

MITCHELL W. KRAMER

103 Powell Avenue   Telephone
Princeton Junction, NJ 08550   609-555-1234

CAREER SUMMARY

Profits and sales producing marketing, business development, and sales executive with special expertise in information industry.

PROFESSIONAL ACCOMPLISHMENTS

DATATECH INFORMATION SERVICES GROUP - Hillman Publishing 1990 to 1993
Vice President Marketing, Business Development and Reprint Sales

Turned around company's long term sales and profit decline:

Eliminated marginal and duplicate products - saved $250,000 and increased sales by $600,000 in first year;

Instituted formal planning and market research function - created first five year plan for acquisitions, addition of electronic delivery of information services (on-line, CD ROM, tape), competitive analysis, and routinized visits by officers to customers.

Involved market and outside experts in development process:

added three new CD ROM and six new print products for information technology industries - produced $1.5 million in annual sales growth;

added three on-line services for library market - contributed $100,000 in six months;

Analyzed existing customer base to determine profile of best buyers, focussed on highest potential prospects, instituted direct mail and telemarketing - grew sales by $1 million in first year.

Initiated public relations campaign emphasizing company's technical expertise, created advertising program, developed collateral pieces to replace consignment process of selling.

Reorganized and upgraded Reprint Sales department, clearly defined tasks and goals - increased sales by 21%.

Set up Sales Support group to provide steady stream of qualified prospects to sales force - grew new sales by $1 million a year.

Mitchell W. Kramer   page 2

FELLOW MARKETING SERVICES - Fellow & Bradshaw Corporation
                                                                  1973 to 1990
Vice President - Marketing   1986 to 1990

Upgraded target market from middle managers to senior marketing and sales
executives; developed and introduced new service that increased average order
size from $10,000 to $25,000 and sales by 8% in first year.

Vice President - Niche Marketing and Development   1984 to 1986

Headed up team to integrate newly acquired companies and leverage their
specialists with company's own full line sales force - grew sales by 15% and cut
marketing costs by 20%.

Director - Product Management   1981 to 1984

Responded to customer demand by introducing *Enhanced Fellow's Market
Identifiers*, a new prospecting and direct mail database product - obtained 40%
premium prices, achieved first year sales of $1.2 million; it was the most
successful product in FMS's history and at $10 million, is now the core business
for the division.

Senior Product Manger   1979 to 1981

Negotiated agreement to put first ever business file on Dialog - annual
contribution exceeds $10 million.

District Sales Manager   1975 to 1979

Developed major brokerage and insurance clients - they produced $2 million sales
a year of quota of $5 million; finished first in country, received Presidential
Citation for four years.

Account Executive   1973 to 1975
Won "Rookie Sales Contest."

THE GANDOLF COMPANY (advertising agency)   1970 to 1973
Account Executive

Secured Bookman, the city's largest saving bank, as a client, produced $50,000 in
revenues.

EDUCATION

B.S., 1970, Miami University, major Communications
University of Connecticut, Executive Education in marketing and planning.

PERSONAL

Born February 8, 1948, Queens, NY; married, three children

Daniel Kane
308 Harris Circle
New Vernon, NJ 07976
973-555-1234, daniel.kane@tmail.com

name   date
title
company
address
city, state zip

Dear name:

International executive with a record of multimillion dollar industrial deal-making,
mergers and acquisitions, marketing, business development, engineering, finance, and
planning - does that sound like the kind of talent you need to grow your company's sales
and profits?

If so, you should read my attached record of getting results.

In addition to my ability to find, negotiate and execute large scale business opportunities
that leverage my knowledge of new technologies, I can offer you the following capabilities:

- versatility and adaptability in working and/or living with people of many
  nationalities and cultures including Bahrain, Japan, Korea, Philippines,
  Singapore, South Africa, Sweden, and Taiwan, as well as Texas and New York;

- success at persuading governments, economic development agencies,
  investors, lawyers, key customers, partners, alliance members, and licensees
  to work together in order to initiate and bring major projects to completion;

- participative management, leadership and interpersonal skills with history of
  identifying, diagnosing, and solving organizational, people, and team-building
  problems;

- ability to hit the ground running, make the tough decisions, and produce
  results early and on a sustained basis;

- record of leading large and small projects that come in on time and on budget;

- strong written and oral communication skills, effective public speaker with
  ability to think on my feet and handle difficult questions;

- solid integrity, honesty, and trustworthiness.

If your company needs an international marketing and sales executive with a demonstrated
record of creating and building profit-making opportunities, I would be pleased to get
together with you to discuss how I can contribute to your success. I will contact your office
on [date] to set up an appointment at a mutually convenient time.

Yours sincerely,

Daniel Kane

308 Harris Circle, New Vernon, NJ 07976   973-555-1234, daniel.kan@tmail.com

CAREER SUMMARY

Senior executive in marketing, business development, engineering, finance, and planning with a record of initiating and completing multi-million deals throughout the world.

PROFESSIONAL ACCOMPLISHMENTS

FRANKLIN GASES   1998 to date
Key Customer Executive   1999 to date

Implemented corporate decision to re-invent company from a geographically-based to a global lines-of-business, customer-oriented organization structure. The challenge is to meet the needs of key customers by choosing "the optimum investments in big plants, ensuring that they fit Franklin's growth strategy, and delivering the projects at agreed returns on investment."

As one of first "Key Customer Executives" reporting to Chief Executive Officer, convinced Franklin's executive team to endorse our selection of six global key customers to be handled by Global Key Customer Executives, and a dozen "zonal" key customers.

Vice President Global Markets Sector   1998 to 1999

Completed first-of-its kind comprehensive analysis of potential demand for industrial gases from each of three giant global market sectors: metals, chemicals and petroleum. Result: projected demand for both "air gases" (oxygen, nitrogen, argon) - Franklin's traditional strength - and "synthesis gases" derived from hydrocarbons.

Assessed industry trends, underlying drivers and likely impact of competing technologies and prospective environmental legislation throughout the world. Developed easily updated, interactive spreadsheets for each facet of each market sector by country.

METROTEX, INC.   1983 to 1998
Manager, Business Development, Metrotex Global Gas and Power   1994 to 1998

Conceived, negotiated and aggressively promoted a "syngas hub" to both Singapore Sanitation Company and Senko. Result: both companies signed long-term contracts suitable for project financing, with Singapore Synergy (a 50/50 joint venture between Metrotex and Kessler), that will build, own and operate a $200 million gasification facility to supply crucial gases to each customer starting September 2000.

Daniel Kane   page 2

Metrotex (cont'd.)

Spearheaded business development projects that licensed proprietary Integrated Gasification Combined Cycle technology. In first two years of deregulation of Japan's electric power industry, won intensively competitive Independent Power Producer bidding. Coupled with newly-developed alliances with contractors and key vendors, this resulted in two large power generation projects exceeding 300 megawatts in size and $600 million in capital cost, and in power prices about half of pre-deregulation rates. In four years, achieved 50-fold increase in revenue commitments for Metrotex gasification technology in Japan to $40 million.

Licensed two projects and laid groundwork for a third. Sold and performed ten paid feasibility studies - work that had previously been done at no charge - generating $1.5 million in revenues. Exton signed an unprecedented global umbrella licensing agreement with Metrotex that has already produced revenue commitments exceeding $50 million, dwarfing previous revenues from any single customer.

Won an important gasification licensing opportunity with Samson-BP, a joint venture between a leading Korean chaebol and a dominant player in the global acetyls business. Results included over $2 million in revenue and an enhanced relationship with a global key customer.

Director, Affiliate Analysis Group, Executive Department	1991 to 1993
Manager, International Finance, Finance Department	1987 to 1990
Staff Coordinator, Strategic Planning Department	1983 to 1986

Pacific Petroleum Corporation	**1968 to 1982**
Manager of Marketing (Tokyo)	1980 to 1982
Analyst - Planning & Economics Department (New York)	1979 to 1980
Senior Project Engineer (Houston, Yokohama)	1975 to 1979
Project Coordinator (Bahrain, New York)	1974 to 1975
Engineer (Bahrain, South Africa, Philippines, USA)	1969 to 1973

EDUCATION

M.B.A, Ithaca College, major International Business	1983
M.S., Mechanical Engineering, New York University	1968
B.S., Mechanical Engineering, New York University	1967

PERSONAL

Born 1945, Washington, PA, married with four children

Hobbies and interests: community leadership positions in USA and abroad; golf, squash, tennis, swimming, gardening, photography and reading

SHARON WILLIAMS
2150 Sunrise Highway
Princeton Junction, NJ 08550-1201
609-555-1234

name   date
title
company
address
city, state zip

Dear name:

As Vice President of Marketing for a multi-branch credit union, I redirected a planned name change strategy and persuaded management to retain and broaden the use of its existing well-established name instead of replacing it. This enabled the credit union to keep its original members' loyalty *and* open it to non-company sponsors.

As Senior Account Executive for an advertising research agency, I mounted an intensive marketing and sales campaign to land a Fortune 100 company as a client. I obtained a contract that was four times the average size for agency.

If you would like to know more about my accomplishments, please read my attached resume. It also shows that I have a unique combination of business, academic and legal expertise that all contribute to my achievements in marketing management.

In addition to my broad-based experience, my strengths include:

> written and oral communication,
>
> conceptualizing, planning, organizing, and evaluating programs,
>
> problem solving, negotiating, and arbitrating,
>
> establishing priorities, working under pressure, setting and meeting deadlines and budgets,
>
> hands-on knowledge of desk top publishing and other computer applications.

I am sure that my record and capabilities in marketing and public relations can contribute to the growth and profitability of your organization. I would be pleased to meet with you to discuss our mutual interests and will call you next week to set a time when we can get together.

Yours sincerely,

SHARON WILLIAMS

2150 Sunrise Highway
Princeton Junction, NJ 08550-1201

Telephone
609-555-1234

CAREER SUMMARY

Broad-based marketing executive and advisor with track record of achieving success for employers and clients.

BUSINESS ACCOMPLISHMENTS

BANNON & CANGLEY, INC.   Advertising research firm   1989 to date
Senior Account Executive

Mounted intensive marketing campaign to land Fortune 100 company: used cold calls, direct marketing, telemarketing, and formal presentation to obtain request for proposal; prepared response - obtained contract that was four times the average size for firm.

Directed customization of research for this client - determined that one-page, four color version was twice as cost-efficient and achieved 20% higher communication level than two-page spread.

Researched ad copy, uncovered ambiguities in readers' minds - advertising agency clarified and pin-pointed message, heightened impact.

PARKER COMMUNITY FEDERAL UNION   1987 to 1988
Vice President of Marketing

Used market research to redirect strategy of planned name change; convinced management to retain and broaden use of existing well-established name instead of replacing it. Enabled credit union to keep original members' loyalty _and_ open it to non-company groups.

Established a targeted program to attract new employee groups as members using direct mail, personal presentations and open houses - signed up five new employee groups as members.

Instituted various research methods of obtaining feedback from membership (customers), received 20% response rate (most highly positive) that showed need to increase awareness of full range of services. Created quarterly newsletter - increased cross-selling.

Targeted a direct mail campaign for credit accounts to selected segment of membership: worked with agency to develop direct mail piece, worked with VISA to establish method for tracking results - increased credit accounts by 30%.

Received Golden Ace Award from Credit Executives Society and first place Golden Hawk award from Advertising News for best logo design.

UNIVERSITY OF ILLINOIS
COLLEGE OF BUSINESS ADMINISTRATION 1986 to 1987
Adjunct Professor of Marketing; Consultant

First woman marketing professor to be appointed, first MBA adjunct in marketing department.

MARKETING PARTNERS 1984 to 1986
Marketing Analyst

During pre-opening of hospital recovery center, developed marketing campaign: evaluated market, defined niche, created logo, brain stormed names, wrote and designed brochure - achieved 80% occupancy rate in second month.

SIBEN & KENSETH 1982 to 1984
Litigation Manager

MARKO CORPORATION 1978 to 1982
Public Affairs Research Analyst 1982
Contractor Administrator 1981 to 1982
Legal Assistant 1978 to 1980

FAHEY, APPLE & CRENSHAW 1973 to 1978
Paralegal

PROFESSIONAL AFFILIATIONS

United Marketing Association
Pennsylvania Communications Advertising And Marketing Association

EDUCATION

Masters of Management in Marketing, 1981, Freeman Graduate School of Management,
Purdue University

Bachelor of Arts, 1973, Columbia University, major, German, minor, Political Science

Working knowledge of German, French, Spanish

PERSONAL

Born Chicago, September 20, 1951, married, two children
Hobbies and interests: travel, adoption support group, swimming

JESSICA M. MONAHAN
1188 Bruno Avenue
Willingboro, NJ 08046
609-555-1234

date

name
title
company
address
city, state zip

Dear name:

Not only was a marketing strategy that I initiated (to consolidate a product group for display) accepted by management of the unit I worked in, when it had produced a 10% increase in sales, it was extended throughout the retail chain.

I developed a merchandise presentation for silk dresses that was so strong that it increased that line's share from 9% to 13% of the total better dress business.

My success in retailing has been based on my ability to marshal the full spectrum of marketing activities to boost sales. If you would like to read more of my accomplishments as a marketer, please see my attached resume.

In addition to a flair for marketing and sales, I have a track record as a manager who achieves increases in employee productivity, reductions in turnover, and improvements in managerial performance through attention to the people side of the business. My other characteristics include:

leadership, initiative, take charge attitude, self-motivation,

determination, perseverance,

professionalism, honesty, loyalty, commitment, thoroughness, high energy level, hard work,

cooperation, team play, flexibility, dependability, enthusiasm,

creativity, problem solving, results orientation, completion of assignments on time and within budget - and then some.

I would be pleased to meet with you to discuss how my achievements and capabilities can contribute to the success of your organization. I will call your office in a week to set a date to get together.

Yours sincerely,

JESSICA M. MONAHAN

1188 Bruno Avenue
Willingboro, NJ 08046

Telephone
609-555-1234

CAREER SUMMARY

Marketing manager with record of accomplishment in profit-producing strategies and promotions based on effective market research.

MARKETING ACCOMPLISHMENTS

Marketing Strategy

Instituted marketing strategy to consolidate a product group for display, persuaded management to implement it - increased sales by 10%, strategy was extended throughout chain.

Developed marketing plan to communicate Lyme disease awareness and tick identification knowledge to parents and children as the primary targets.

Market Research

Analyzed sales trends and projections, identified hot items - propelled sales increase of 40%.

Researched and analyzed business trends, purchased line of holiday dresses - achieved 95% sell-through in three weeks.

Sales Promotion

Persuaded management to relocate Women's Plus size sportswear to prominent location - increased sales by 20%.

Set up promotional tables in dress department to create multiple sales of Easter items - sold 98% of stock.

Developed strong merchandise presentation for silk dresses - increased share from 9% to 13% of better dress business.

Restructured department layout to capitalize on special sale of down coats - achieved number two rank in eight unit department store chain.

Designed and wrote promotional brochure for Children's Time Program of mental health agency.

Jessica Monahan   page 2

Management

Devised employee productivity and retention strategy - result, decreased
employee turnover by 40% and absenteeism by 20%.

Created and implemented a training program for assistant manager -
incumbent promoted to department manager level in three months.

Used listening and problem solving techniques to salvage problem
department manager - increased productivity 75% immediately.

CAREER HISTORY

STONY BROOK HOSPITAL   1991
Marketing and Public Relations Intern

KID CO.   1989 to 1991
Assistant Store Manager

JEFFRIE'S CLOTHIER   1984 to 1989
Department Manager

WHITMAN'S   1981 to 1984
Department Manager
Assistant Buyer

EDUCATION

Bachelor of Science, major - Marketing, 1981, Alfred University

Master of Business Administration, concentration - Marketing, New Jersey
College of Textiles & Science

PERSONAL

Born New Brunswick, NJ, October 26, 1957

Associations: Zeta Phi Beta Sorority, member   1989 to date

Hobbies and interests: Community Guidance Center of Mercer County,
Children's Time Program, volunteer; tennis, biking

JOHN K. DONNER
332 Atlantic Avenue
South Brunswick, NJ 08852-9792
908-555-1234

name   date
title
company
address
city, state zip

Dear name:

You may need a Business Development Officer who sees and seizes profit opportunities in what others consider problems.

    As the Assistant Vice President - Business Development for a hospital, I saw a need for off-street parking in our residential location, overcame management doubts, acquired the land, and built a revenue-producing visitor parking facility.

If you wish to learn more about my profit-contributing accomplishments, please read my attached resume.

I have a track record of creating innovative <u>and</u> practical solutions to financial, tax, accounting, and insurance problems. My auditing background with Marlan Agency taught me to be a fast learner in almost any situation in virtually every kind of profit and non-profit operation. I have applied these skills as I have subsequently progressed in my business management career.

In addition to my business skills, my strengths include:

    a dedication to efficiency in operations,

    a talent for identifying, delegating to, and growing promotable people,

    a nose for finding the real problems and solving them so they stay fixed,

    courage in tackling the tough ones and persistence in bringing them to successful conclusion,

    a determination to get things done.

I would be pleased to meet with you to discuss how my experience and abilities can contribute to the success of your operation. If I may, I will call your office to set up an appointment at a mutually convenient time. I look forward to meeting you.

Yours sincerely,

JOHN K. DONNER, CPA

332 Atlantic Avenue   Telephone
South Brunswick, NJ 08852   908-555-1234

CAREER SUMMARY

Chief Financial Officer with strong profit-making and business development track record.

BUSINESS ACCOMPLISHMENTS

VITELLO BUSINESS BROKERS, Union NJ   1990 to date
Business Consultant

Provided services to sellers and buyers of businesses by valuing and determining appropriate terms of sale.

DALE ENTERPRISES INC.   1987 to 1990
Affiliate of The Hospital Center at Hollis, NJ
Assistant Vice President - Business Development

Designed and implemented reorganization that turned urgent care center's loss into a $98,300 profit in first year.

Initiated in-house temporary nurse agency - reduced expenditures on outside services by 12%.

Set up home health care joint venture - achieved 30% profit margin.

Created child care center for nurses' children - attracted and retained scarce nurses and other employees, reduced turnover by 25%.

Acquired land in residential area surrounding hospital to develop visitor parking facility - overcame severe shortage of parking space and produced revenues from parking charges.

Developed Employee Assistance Program (EAP) as a profit center.

ADVENTURE WORLD, Jackson, NJ   1977 to 1987
Director of Finance

Directed financial aspects of company turnaround from a loss position to 9.8% profit.

Negotiated business interruption insurance settlement - obtained payment of $1.8 million compared to original offer of $50,000.

John K. Donner   **page 2**

ADVENTURE WORLD (cont'd.)

Identified hidden provision in tax laws that enabled company to avoid $150,000 property taxes annually.

Segregated seasonal workforce from permanent full time employees for unemployment insurance purposes - took advantage of UIC cap to save $200,000 a year in payroll taxes.

Developed creative pricing policies that cut sales taxes by $100,000 per annum.

Directed computerization of daily reporting and order entry system - streamlined scheduling to meet weekly and seasonal patterns.

Hired and trained subordinates who were subsequently promoted: one to Corporate CFO of Adventure World and another to CFO of a company subsidiary.

THE BROOKHAMPTON FARMING COMPANY, Valencia, CA   1971 to 1977
Corporate Treasurer   1975 to 1977

Designed and installed self insured property, liability, and workers' compensation programs - saved $500,000 annually.

Controller, Wizard Mountain subsidiary   1971 to 1974

Centralized purchasing departments to achieve substantial savings.

MARLAN AGENCY, Los Angeles CA   1965 to 1971
Audit Senior

PERSONAL

B.S., University of Southern California, 1965, major accounting

Certified Public Accountant, California and New Jersey

Affiliations:

      Trustee, Freehold Hospital
      President, Freehold Rotary Club
      Board of Directors, Western Monmouth Chamber of Commerce

FRANK MUMFORD
8 Keiser Place
Belle Mead, NJ 08502
908-555-1234

date

name
title
company
address
city, state zip

Dear name:

To be successful, a Business Development Planner at your company needs experience with databases and Electronic Data Interchange (EDI), needs to perform Purchase Order System (POS) analysis, needs to implement POS customer data requirements, and needs to train users to become effective very quickly.

> I installed our custom pricing and inventory software at customer locations and trained their staffs to use the EDI. This enabled them to generate their own quotations based on the pricing profiles we created in the database.

> I took over from sales force day-to-day activities of quotations order entry, expediting, and managing accounts receivables - reduced office time of sales staff from 3 days a week to 1.5; brought past due rate down from 9.0% to 0.9%.

> I also created a call tracking program to show clients amount of time spent for them by the sales support team, to monitor open calls, and to track response times. This demonstrated that actual average response time was 3 hours compared to clients' perception of over 4 hours and enabled department to cut response time even further by signaling need to return calls promptly.

To be successful, a Business Development Planner at your company needs exposure to one or more of such business disciplines as Sales Support, Distribution, Marketing, Finance, Order Management, and Logistics.

As shown on my attached resume, I have personal experience in all of them.

name   - 2   date

To be successful, a Business Development Planner at the J&J Consumer Sector
needs the ability to learn J&J and customer system applications to highlight
integration opportunities, standardize category review formats and to assess,
design and procure potential or new applications.

> As a Supervisor of the Sales & Support Department of a value
> added reseller, I always have had to learn my customers'
> systems applications and technology quickly to make sure that
> whatever hardware or software I sell them really fit into their
> systems and formats and really improved their efficiency.

To be successful, a Business Development Planner at the J&J Consumer Sector
needs to be an excellent representative of the team on sector projects and be able
to communicate IS issues and solutions. He also needs to make the best use and
deployment of technology among all parties so that the technically sophisticated
as well as the merely computer literate can fully understand and use the
solutions.

> I created a quarterly report for a $10 million Fortune 500
> national account customer that highlighted major projects and
> problems and showed graphically the distribution of types and
> amounts of products used. This helped the customer
> standardize on products, and permitted the purchasing
> department to obtain better prices for service and parts.

If you need someone in your department who can be really successful in hitting
the ground running in ensuring effective interaction between IS and users, we
should get together. I will call your office in a week to set up a time when we
can discuss how my abilities can contribute to your companies' success.

Yours sincerely,

Frank Mumford

enclosure

FRANK MUMFORD
8 Keiser Place, Belle Mead, NJ 08502   908-555-1234

CAREER SUMMARY

Information technology sales and support manager with a record of solving clients problems and increasing employer's sales and profits.

PROFESSIONAL ACCOMPLISHMENTS

MILAN COMPANY   1987 to date
Manager Sales & Support Department

Sales

Conducted active campaign of cold calling and new lead generation for sales force - exceeded $600,000 sales quota by 50%.

Proposed $70,000 486 PC-based local area network (LAN) to replace mid-range computer - cut annual maintenance cost from $15,000 to $3,000 and gave customer faster and more flexible operating platform.

Scheduled vendors and coordinated collection of demo equipment for day-long product fair - sales force met 100+ new prospects and made contact with 20% of them for project follow-up.

Configured 125 node network for client consisting of less expensive third-party products supported by the company - improved performance of system and saved customer 25%.

Supplied major national account with 60 laptop computers, fully configured, within one month and within budget in spite of shortages of some items.

Second-sourced hard drives for network servers during a period of shortage, found alternative configurations that gave better performance than original specifications.

Support

Created call tracking program to show clients amount of time spent for them by sales support team, also monitored open calls and tracked response times - demonstrated that actual average response time was 3 hours compared to clients' perception of over 4 hours and enabled department to cut response even further by signaling need to return calls promptly.

Recaptured a competitive bid for 400 printers lost because of price by guaranteeing 3-day delivery when winner could not deliver on time after all - won customer back.

Frank Mumford   page 2

Milan Company (cont'd.)

Took over from sales force day-to-day activities of quotations order entry,
expediting, and managing accounts receivables - reduced office time of
sales staff from 3 days a week to 1.5; brought past due rate down from 9.0%
to 0.9%.

Installed our custom pricing and inventory software at customer locations
and trained their staffs to use the Electronic Data Interchange (EDI) -
enabled them to generate own quotations based on pricing profiles we
created in database.

Established pricing and inventory software in company office for use by
sales and service representatives - let them support all clients quickly and
accurately.

Created quarterly report for a $10 million Fortune 500 national account
customer that highlighted major projects and problems, showed graphically
the distribution of types and amounts of products used - helped customer
standardize on products, permitted purchasing department to obtain better
prices for service and parts.

Persuaded company to purchase and install security system following
disappearance of merchandise - demonstrated that cost would be offset by
savings in thefts and in insurance premiums.

GREINER ORGANIZATION   1986 to 1987
Phone Interviewer

Conducted public opinion and market polls, dealt directly with top business
executives in major corporations.

EDUCATION

B.A., 1986, Amherst College, major Communication, especially public and
mass communication

Courses in management, computer education, marketing and sales

Awards: Atlantic Employee Honor Roll

PERSONAL

Born June 10, 1965, Plainfield, NJ, married

Hobbies and interests: fly fishing, motor cycling

TIMOTHY PETERS
5018 Jackson Street
Princeton, NJ 08540
609-555-1234

date

name
title
company
address
city, state zip

Dear name:

Most market analysts can crunch lots of numbers and produce lots of reports. Most of them can use one or another kind of PC software reasonably effectively.

What I do is use my head to make the numbers tell the story that leads management to the right decisions. And I am a virtuoso on the personal computer.

There is more. I am a very fast study. I have had numerous positions in a wide variety of industries where I have had to hit the ground running and produce useful results quickly.

I have applied this unbeatable combination to enable management to maximize returns on its financial, sales, and marketing resources.

I have been able to do this is because I have obtained such a solid grounding in the fundamentals of planning, budgeting, control, and reporting at the best companies and consultancies. I also offer highly-developed interpersonal skills and the flexibility to work well in teams or on my own.

If you would like to know more about my accomplishments and how they can contribute to the success of your firm, please read my attached resume. If you would like to know more about me, let's get together. I will call your office to set up an appointment at your convenience.

Yours sincerely,

enclosure

TIMOTHY PETERS

5018 Jackson Street   Telephone
Princeton, NJ 08540   609-555-1234

CAREER SUMMARY

Financial and market analyst with record of providing decision-making, profit-producing information to management. Especially effective in use of spread sheet, database, graphics, word processing, local area network (LAN), and project control software.

PROFESSIONAL ACCOMPLISHMENTS

BARTELS FINANCIAL ANALYSIS CONSULTING   1991 to date
Principal

ABC Pharmaceutical Co.   1992 to 1993

Analyzed sales figures, doctor call statistics, and travel expense reports - determined specific costs per representative and identified ways to optimize allocation of sales resources.

Defined most appropriate screens to display IMS data - demonstrated significant trends that enabled company to maximize return on sales investment.

Chandler-Marks Company   1991 to 1992

Performed feasibility studies for new products and markets that evaluated impact of global influences on sales projections.

Produced forecasts, strategic plans, and sales and marketing analyses that identified major developments - enabled management to capitalize on business dynamics and get ahead of the competition.

ADELLO SYSTEMS, INC.   1989 to 1991
Senior Financial Analyst

Designed and developed integrated Lotus 1-2-3 system to generate marketing proposals that gave customers choices - demonstrated company's customer-orientation and increased yield on proposals.

Created templates to automatically generate standard forms for clients - reduced production time from 125 hours a year to 1 hour and eliminated error-proneness of old system.

Timothy Peters   page 2

<u>**VELLICO BUSINESS SYSTEMS**</u>   1988 to 1989
Consultant

Developed time lines for five mainframe-based systems on <u>Workbench</u> -
accelerated completion time.

<u>**KAPLAN FEDERAL SAVINGS AND LOAN**</u>   1986 to 1988
Information Services Planning Analyst

Created and implemented a tracking system on *Symphony* that monitored,
analyzed, and controlled a $2.5 million project against budget.

VISUAL SCIENCES CORPORATION
Project Control Manager

Initiated and installed a project management system to report on variances
in dollars and labor hours in major construction project.

<u>**NORTHSTART STEAMSHIP LINES**</u>   1984 to 1985
Senior Financial Analyst

<u>**AMERICAN TESTING SERVICE**</u>   1978 to 1983
Budget Analyst

EDUCATION

B.A., 1975, Hampton University

M.B.A., Princeton University, 20 credits in finance and marketing

STEVEN HARRINGTON
8046 Hopewell Road
Princeton, NJ 08540
bus 609-555-1234; res 609-555-1234

date

name
title
company
address
city, state, zip

Dear name:

Lots of people have experience in market research. Lots of other people have experience in health care.

I am one of the relatively few people who has substantial experience in both.

For 11 years, I was a statistician in the Pennsylvania Medical Assistance and Health Services division of the Department of Human Services. I forecast demographic changes in AdelAid-eligible populations. I conducted in-depth analyses of hospital patient data. I produced quality control and financial reports for review by governing bodies.

Subsequently, I worked as a freelance telephone interviewer for market research firms in the Princeton area.

My work has centered on my analytical skills and my attention to detail. I make sure things are right. One of my personal interests is writing - I write articles for newsletters for organizations I belong to.

As you will see on my attached resume, I have an MBA in marketing management and research, a BBA in economics, and am currently taking courses in medical records management.

What this all adds up to for you is that I have the unique combination of talent and experience that fit your needs in the market research analyst position. I look forward to meeting you to discuss how we can get together to our mutual benefit.

Yours sincerely,

STEVEN HARRINGTON
8046 Hopewell Road
Princeton, NJ 08540
bus 609-555-1234; res 609-555-1234

date

name
title
company
address
city, state zip

Dear name:

Your company may need a market research analyst who has a history of
achievement as a statistician in both the private and public sectors:

> I worked at Carson Inc. as a Senior Statistical Analyst where I
> analyzed and verified financial statements submitted by competing
> insurance companies for use in rating carriers.

> I worked at the Division of Medical Assistance and Health Services
> in the Pennsylvania Department of Human Services where I prepared
> in-depth analyses of hospital admission rates, average lengths of stay,
> and utilization rates. I also forecast demographic changes and
> nursing home charge inflation rates.

> I worked at the Department of Labor as Senior Statistical Analyst
> where I developed a method to forecast trends in the state by
> economic regions. I also maintained the database relating to
> commercial construction projects.

As you will see on my attached resume, I have an MBA in marketing
management and research, a BBA in economics, and am currently taking
courses in medical records management.

What this all adds up to for you is that I have the unique combination of
talent and experience that fit your needs in market research analyst
positions. I look forward to meeting you to discuss how we can get together
to our mutual benefit. If I may, I will call your office to set up a convenient
time to get together.

Yours sincerely,

STEVEN HARRINGTON

8046 Hopewell Road   bus 609-555-1234
Princeton, NJ 08540   res 609-555-1234

CAREER SUMMARY

Statistician with in-depth experience in health care delivery and market research.

PROFESSIONAL ACCOMPLISHMENTS

CARSON INC.   1989
Senior Statistical Analyst

Analyzed and verified financial statements submitted by property-casualty insurance companies for use in rating carriers.

MULLINS STATISTCAL AGENCIES   1988 to 1989
Freelance Telephone Interviewer

Conducted market research surveys; coded responses.

STATE OF PENNSYLVANIA   1974 to 1987
Department of Human Services   1978 to 1987
Statistician, Division of Medical Assistance and Health Services

Forecast and monitored Medicaid-eligible population changes; forecast inflation rate for nursing home rate-setting.

Prepared in-depth analyses of hospital admission rates, average lengths of stay, and utilization rates for Professional Standards Review Organizations.

Prepared quality control reports.

Prepared financial reports for submission to Federal government and other Adel-Aid bureaus.

Department of Labor, *Senior Statistical Analyst*   1974 to 1978

Developed a method to forecast retail trade trends in state by economic regions.

Maintained data base relating to commercial construction projects throughout Pennsylvania.

PROFESSIONAL ASSOCIATIONS

American Health Information Management Association
American Society for Public Opinion Research
Delaware Valley Geographers Association
Society for American Baseball Research

EDUCATION

Suffolk County Community College, 1992-1993, medical records
management courses.

M.B.A., 1980, Ithaca College, marketing management and research, GPA
3.5

B.B.A., 1973, New York University; major: economics; minor: geography;
GPA 3.0
Memorial Award in Economics.

PERSONAL

Born June 11, 1950, single.

Hobbies and interests: baseball research, bicycling, writing.

JOANN FITZGERALD
129 Olivia Court
Lawrenceville, NJ 08648
609-555-1234

name   date
title
company
address
city

Dear Name:

In preparing direct mail advertising, success demands creativity and effectiveness in reaching the consumer. I can demonstrate my record of results-producing creativity.

In managing a direct mail operation, success demands skill in motivating creative people. I can demonstrate my record of motivating <u>and</u> growing creative people.

In making advertising make money, success demands a deep and first hand understanding of the importance of the bottom line. I can demonstrate my record of success as an entrepreneur.

If you would like to learn more about my accomplishments in marketing management for some of the country's biggest and most successful retailers and direct mail marketers, please read my attached resume.

In addition to my professional capabilities, my strengths include:

> an ability to learn complex material very quickly - would you believe insurance,

> a facility to convert the complexity into simplicity so that it is immediately grasped and appreciated by all readers,

> a flair for coming up with ideas - the <u>right</u> ideas,

> an all-round experience in direct marketing including research, product development, targeting and segmentation, sales promotion, collateral, product testing, report writing, and tracking,

> an energy level that enabled me to thrive in an aggressive, fast-paced, deadline-oriented environment that included 15 products and 40 individual mailing dates a year.

If you need a high-potential, results-producing direct marketing and advertising executive, we should get together. In a week, I will call you to set a time to meet to discuss how my successes can contribute to your sales and profit growth.

Yours sincerely,

JOANN FITZGERALD

129 Olivia Court   Telephone
Lawrenceville, NJ 08648   609-555-1234

CAREER SUMMARY

Results and profit producing marketing communication executive with heavy emphasis on direct mail, consumer advertising and promotions.

BUSINESS ACCOMPLISHMENTS

TIMELESS, INC.   1988 to date
Owner

Started up ladies casual sportswear retail store, wrote business plan, secured financing. First year sales exceeded $250 per square foot compared to $175 industry average.

CARBONARO FINANCIAL SERVICES   1979 to 1988
Vice President, Sales Promotion and Creative Services   1984 to 1988

Developed quarterly national sales contests for targeted products - produced increases ranging from 35% to 94% over previous years.

Conceived bi-monthly field publication distributed to 1200 employees in telemarketing, direct mail, and field sales; featured successful sales techniques and results, recognized accomplishments - opened communication, improved sales force effectiveness.

Provided creative promotional mix - doubled volume of sales leads in first year.

Devised and produced annual meetings and recognition and awards ceremonies using full audio-visual support.

Managed creative process and production of 3,000 pieces of advertising - achieved record premium income of $107 million from the direct response program.

Direct Response Marketing Director   1979 to 1983

Developed and implemented a series of direct response programs that:

> built policy-owner marketing profits by 17% from prior year,

> increased present value of profits on accident insurance by 32%, hospital insurance by 28%, and life insurance by 27% over prior year.

Conducted package tests in which 7 out of 9 "control packages" were beaten - generated significant incremental profits.

JOANN FITZGERALD   page 2

Carbonaro (cont'.d)

Developed three new insurance products - generated over $400,000 in first-year-issued premiums.

MARVIN TILE   1977 to 1979
Assistant National Advertising Manager

Managed $10 million in-house advertising program.

Created television commercials including script writing, story-boards, product mix, talent, and production for placement in 25 markets - enabled company to open one new store per week.

Initiated seasonal promotional incentive contests - motivated sales force to increase sales of floor tile by 30% over prior year.

Managed a weekly newspaper advertising program covering 200 publications.

PROSCAPES HOME CENTERS   1970 to 1977
Director of Advertising & Public Relations   1972 to 1977

Implemented zoned circulation concept for newspaper inserts to target retail trading area - minimized wasted circulation and reduced printing costs by 10%.

Devised a co-op advertising program with major name brand suppliers - reduced expenditures by $100,000 annually.

Store Manager   1970 to 1972

DOWLING COLLEGE   1969
College Registrar

SUFFOLK COUNTY COMMUNITY COLLEGE   1967 to 1968
Admissions Counselor and Registrar

PERSONAL

Bachelor of Education, 1965, University of New Mexico
Master of Education, 1966, Tulane University
Merit Award for Sales Promotion, 1985, Orlando Advertising League

Born January 12, 1947, married, two children

FRANCIS LONGO
303 Cavel Avenue
Lawrenceville, NJ 08648
609-555-1234

date

name
title
company
address
city, state zip

Dear name:

As an All American gymnast in college, the secret of my success was a rare combination of hard work at quickly learning new routines, intense competitiveness, a fresh approach, and unwavering dedication to teamwork.

As a business-building Sales Manager and representative in industry, the secret of my success has been a rare combination of quickly learning new businesses and products, intense competitiveness, a fresh approach, and unwavering dedication to teamwork - *plus* a sixth sense in discovering where the prospects or clients are and what their needs are.

My style is consultative selling: I find out what their hot buttons are, what they know and what they need my expertise for, and how I can ease their workload and problems. I am on the clients' payroll as far as they are concerned.

You can see the results of this empathetic, trust-building approach on my attached resume. Now, I would like to contribute my skills as a top-flight producer to the benefit of your company.

Let's get together and discuss how my sales abilities can help you build your business. I will call you on [date] at [time] to make an appointment for when it is convenient for us to meet.

Yours sincerely,

enclosure

FRANCIS LONGO

303 Cavel Avenue, Lawrenceville, NJ 08648   **Telephone 609-555-1234**

CAREER SUMMARY

Sales Manager and Account Executive with a record of starting up new lines and multiplying sales of existing lines - profitably.

PROFESSIONAL ACCOMPLISHMENTS

SALES MANAGER   1991 to date
Kramer Industries, Inc.

Brought in $700,000 of new business for start up company.

ACCOUNT EXECUTIVE   1990 to 1991
Aspec, Inc.

Learned new business from bottom up working in factory for first three months.

Grew my largest account's volume by 28% in nine months.

Developed over $700,000 in new business in two years, grew my territory from zero to 16% of total company volume.

ACCOUNT MANAGER   1988 to 1990
Oakdale Paper Company, Inc.

Built 34 new accounts in addition to growing existing sales volume - generated $380,000 new business in second year, a 5% increase in total company volume.

SALES REPRESENTATIVE   1986 to 1988
Bohemia Paper Company, Inc.

Solicited and developed 27 new accounts which generated over $200,000 in sales.

EDUCATION

B.S., 1985, Florida State University; major, horticulture; minor, business administration.
    Four year full tuition gymnastics scholarship - Division I All American

MARIA SANCHEZ
1099 Morris Place
Princeton, NJ 08540
609-555-1234

date

name
title
company
address
city, state zip

Dear name:

If you opened a new specialty retail store on a side street during a recession in a town where there were already three firmly-established competitors, what is likely to happen?

Not when I did it.

Instead, I built volume from zero to $98,000 in the first year and $150,000 the second - and the biggest of the competitors went Chapter 11 and blamed it on me!

If the town then decides to tear up your side street for six months during the busiest time of year, and the recession continues, what happens?

Not when I run the store.

Instead, I went out and targeted customers for custom work and built a following at seminar and conference centers - and kept sales equal to last year.

If every store in the block is complaining about poor sales and several of them go out of business, what do you do?

Not when I am involved.

I became block captain for the merchants' association, signed up all the stores and developed block promotional activities - and brought traffic past the construction barriers to all of us.

If you would like to know more about my accomplishments, please read my attached resume. I look forward to hearing favorably from you.

Yours sincerely,

MARIA SANCHEZ

1099 Morris Place   bus 609-555-1234
Princeton, NJ 08540   res 609-555-1234

CAREER SUMMARY

Retail store manager with record of opening store and building volume and profits during prolonged recession.

PROFESSIONAL ACCOMPLISHMENTS

XYZ OUTLET STORE   1990 to date
Store Manager

Opened new manufacturer's outlet store to sell first quality T-shirts and other clothing to college and high school students. Managed store without supervision; handles purchasing, merchandising, design of sales items, sales promotion and advertising, loss-prevention, sales and service. Set and achieved sales and profit goals.

Provided customers with value merchandise = price + quality + service:

> personally greeted each individual entering store, complimented them on their appearance, welcomed browsing, listened to their stories, displayed wares helpfully, remembered previous visits - landed them as customers.

Built volume from zero to $98,000 in first full year and $150,000 in second year in spite of recession, strong competition, and out-of-the-way location; maintained $150,000 level in third year in spite of total reconstruction of street:

> handed out premiums such as "welcome back" gift to returning university students;

> sponsored Seaver Soccer Association team, Marathon, Rutgers University Telethon for annual giving campaign, community events, high school teams;

> targeted Rutgers University Alumni at annual reunions using advertising and direct mail campaign, built volume during three day event from zero to $3,000 in first year and $5,000 in current year;

> solicited custom-design T-shirt work from specific colleges in university;

> obtained and retained repeat business from seminars and conferences at local hotel and educational institutions; many people come back as individual customers.

These techniques have proved so successful that my much larger competitors have come to the store to see how they can use my methods.

Maria Sanchez   page 2

As block captain for Alltown Merchants' Association with responsibility for
uniting all store keepers, I did the following:

>   overcame skepticism, promoted mutual benefits of joint action and
>   friendship - signed up 100% of merchants, including seven new ones,
>   in my section of the downtown business district;
>
>   ran promotional events during key holidays, university activities,
>   National Governors' Conference, Old Fashioned Days, window
>   decorating week competition, etc.; and
>
>   demonstrated value of cooperation by referring prospects to competitors
>   when my store did not have requested merchandise.

SELF EMPLOYMENT   1989 to 1990
Counselor to Members of Hispanic Community

RUTGERS UNIVERSITY   1980 to 1989
Assistant to Director of Graduate Admissions   1984 to 1989
Expediter in Purchasing Department   1981 to 1984
General Assistant in Procurement Department   1980 to 1981

PERSONAL

B.A., 1964, American School of Business, Ecuador

Full time course work, School of Business Administration, Hofstra University

Hobbies and interests: community relations, government relations publicity,
writing, classical folk music.

KENNETH J. BAXTER
895 Wiley Street
Boca Raton, FL 33434
407-555-1234

date

name
title
company
address
city, state zip

Dear name:

As District Sales Manager, I revitalized under-developed relationships with major food and non-food retailers and distributors; sold programs directly to corporate purchasing managers; pruned small unprofitable customers. That is how I added $1.75 million in new business to grow total sales by 22% in four years during a recession.

Formerly, as Sales Supervisor, I overcame obstacles of a previously abandoned market, lost shelf space, and an inexperienced, high-turnover sales force. I increased my sales area from 7 to 10 routes and average volume per route by 57% to $5,500 a week in the space of six years.

How did I accomplish these things? Leadership and salesmanship.

I build sales forces and get them productive. I hire the right people, train them well, communicate to them, motivate them, and give them enough freedom to make and beat their goals.

In addition, I have a real sense of what our customers want and need to succeed. I know that I need them and they don't need me, so I help them as their partner to improve their competi/tiveness and profitability. What I learn, I communicate to the sales force so that they implement the strategies and goals precisely.

In addition to being a top-rated sales executive who has never missed a bonus, I am persistent, patient, perceptive, honest, reliable, and self-motivated. I use a soft sell approach that really works. I am first of all a businessman who adds value and grows profits. The results are there to see in my resume.

I have just relocated to Florida. If you would like this kind of business smarts working to grow your business, we need to get together. In a week, I will call your office to set a date to see how we can work to our mutual benefit.

Yours sincerely,

KENNETH J. BAXTER

895 Wiley Street, Boca Raton, FL 33434   **407-555-1234**

CAREER SUMMARY

Sales Manager with a history of aggressive penetration and expansion using leadership skills to achieve goals.

PROFESSIONAL ACCOMPLISHMENTS

FOODCO, INC.   1975 to 1994

DISTRICT MANAGER (Customer Relations)   1989 to 1994

Revitalized under-developed relationships with major food and non-food retailers and distributors; sold programs directly to corporate purchasing managers; pruned small unprofitable customers thus adding $1.75 million in new businesses to grow total sales by 22% in four years during a recession.

DISTRICT MANAGER (Route Sales Development)   1983 to 1989

Infiltrated adjacent states without benefit of advertising in fiercely competitive market; set up national account system by selling major food chains - grew business from 20 routes to 30, and sales from $5.7 million to $8.3 million, or 46%.

SALES SUPERVISOR   1977 to 1983

Overcame obstacles of a previously abandoned market, lost shelf space, and an inexperienced, high-turnover sales force by careful recruitment and training, motivation, teamwork and freedom - increased sales area from 7 to 10 routes and average volume per route by 57% to $5,500 a week.

ROUTE SALES REPRESENTATIVE   1975 to 1977

Built three routes from scratch in highly competitive virgin territory based on service, quality and cooperative advertising - brought each from under $1,000 a week to $4,000.

EDUCATION

Bachelor of Science 1975, Florida State University

PERSONAL

Born Scranton, Pa., June 24, 1953, married.

Hobbies and interests: tennis, golf, skiing, sailing, spectator sports.

Nadia Davies

28 Porter Road
West Windsor, NJ 08550
Home 609-555-1234, Work 609-555-1234
ndavies@tmail.com

name   date
title
company
address
city, state zip

Dear name:

"Nadia is truly an inspiration to all who work with her. She possesses the necessary traits of a winner while being a most enjoyable person to be professionally associated with. ... When she goes into gear, very few can compete with her." That's what my General Agent wrote when he presented me with the President's Club Award.

Following my highly successful career as a broker and agent for Milton Owens, I set up my own agency and built annual property and casualty premiums from scratch to $1 million in 10 years. I continued to grow my life and health sales at the same time.

I am now ready to return to full time employment and to turn my record of building a profitable book of business to improving the success of [company name]. In addition to my sales skills, I will bring you:

> expertise in client relations,
>
> an excellent history of providing senior level executive sales support,
>
> a strong marketing background, and
>
> a proven ability to plan and implement instructional programs.

I am motivated, energetic, highly committed and ready to work. On [date] at [time], I will call you to set up an appointment to discuss how we can work to our mutual benefit.

Sincerely,

P.S.   If you can't wait until I call you, please contact me at home 609-555-1234 or at work 609-555-1234, or e-mail me at ndavies@tmail.com.

Nadia Davies

28 Porter Road
West Windsor, NJ 08550
Home 609-555-1234, Work 609-555-1234
ndavies@tmail.com

CAREER SUMMARY

Full service insurance broker-agent with a record of building sales through ability to create and implement new concepts, initiative and persistence, and results-producing consultative selling.

PROFESSIONAL ACCOMPLISHMENTS

Arkin Davies Insurance Agency   1982 to date
Owner

Needs Analysis

An "orphan policyholder" had an $8,000 life insurance policy on a 9-year old son, which was purchased at his birth. While discussing the child's policy, I recommended that the parents obtain a financial needs analysis. Result: increased child's policy to $100 000, opened a growth mutual fund policy on the child as well as for his sister with automatic monthly contributions for their college education, wrote a $300,000 life policy on the father, and wrote a $4,300 monthly disability income policy on the mother.

Consolidating Mortgages

Every Tuesday morning, I made a list of all the mortgage transactions in the courthouse, got the telephone numbers, and called for appointments. In speaking with a wife about a $15,000 mortgage addition, I discovered it was a loan for a business renovation. Result: consolidated the husband's personal and business mortgages into a single $500,000 mortgage, and wrote the commercial property, workers' compensation, and group health insurances, while simultaneously reducing total premiums. Consequently, I was asked to do the same thing for three other businesses that were owned by the family.

Prospecting/Cold Calling/Referrals

Utilized the crisscross, church, and school directories to compile a mailing list to which I systematically sent direct mail on a weekly basis. Result: got a 3% response and closed 1% to 2% of the original number.

Nadia Davies   page 2

Cold called those who didn't respond to the letters we mailed to them. As a result of a call, a manager who was happy that I called bought a disability policy for herself, a life insurance policy on her husband, a large insurance policy on a daughter who was joining the Navy, and an insurance policy on another daughter who was engaged to be married. Through referrals from her, I wrote several policies on her colleagues and their families.

Combined Group and Property & Casualty Policies

While discussing medical coverage in an automobile insurance policy, the client, who was the owner of a business mentioned that the group health insurance policy might be changing soon. Result: I provided a very competitive quotation on the group plan as well as on the business owners and workers' compensation policies and saved the client a total of 50% of premiums. This enabled him to purchase the D&O coverage that he had been thinking about.

Strategic Shift

When automobile insurance carriers began leaving the state, I had to shift my prospecting to homeowner and umbrella coverages. I took advantage of company promotional programs to combine homeowners, auto and umbrella policies. Result: Kept agency's total premium volume at a high level.

Milton Owens Agency   1977 to 1982
Broker, Full Time Agent

Addition of Property & Casualty License

As a Life and Health agent, I also wanted to obtain Property and Casualty (P&C) licenses. In spite of my manager's fear that his sales people would slack off on life insurance sales if they could sell property and casualty policies, I made a decision to get the licenses. As my results started coming in, the manager offered P&C throughout the office and promoted me to P&C manager.

I qualified for numerous President's Honor Club awards.

LICENSES

Life and Health
Property and Casualty
National Association of Security Dealers, Series 63

EDUCATION

B.A., Drew University   1978
Foreign Languages: Arabic, Armenian

ARNOLD LAGARA

33 Pamlico Avenue, Franklin Park, NJ 08823   **908-555-1234**

CAREER SUMMARY

Group insurance account representative and agent with a record of building business by providing best coverage at lowest cost from best markets.

PROFESSIONAL ACCOMPLISHMENTS

MITCHELL & DAVIS   1990 to date
Account Representative

Underwriting

In spite of complete absence of claims history for a group of 200 employees of a spin-off and the refusal by 20 carriers to bid, obtained quotation from three carriers within two months - result, selected Travelers and earned $25,000 commission revenues for agency.

Obtained minimum premium coverage for a group of permanent *part time* employees not normally insured; solicited 12 carriers - result, obtained one quotation which produced $4,000 commission income.

With numerous U.S. subsidiaries of Japanese companies, converted plans to managed care dual option - results, saved clients 15 to 20% of their premiums.

Consolidated insurance coverage for two subsidiaries of Japanese companies - results, enabled client to avoid community rating and to save 50% in premiums; later added Los Angeles office for a saving of 50%.

Claims Administration

Persuaded carrier to re-instate an employee inadvertently left off billing statements for three years - result, when employee was hospitalized the following week for quadruple by-pass surgery, the claim was honored.

Negotiated with insurer to pay a $3,000 claim that it had denied as not reasonable and customary - result, averted losing account.

Sales and Service

Marketed and participated in sale of new account, the Town of Salisbury, Connecticut, covering all employees including union members - result, generated $500,000 annual premiums.

Sold existing clients additional lines of coverage such as group major medical, student accident, interscholastic sports, and group travel, while working with them to renew policies.

Arnold Lagara   page 2

FAIRVIEW AGENCY   1987 to 1989
Group Marketing Administrator

Trained brokers how to properly approach prospects, reduced turnaround time
for response to requests for proposals, increased contact with clients - result,
increased sales and retained 100% of existing clients.

CHASE AGENCY   1986 to 1987
Administrative Assistant

EDMUND LIFE ASSURANCE   1981 to 1985
Insurance Agent

Met company sales goals - result, won several agency sales contests and
attended sales conferences.

SELF-EMPLOYED   1978 to 1981
Insurance Broker

RICHARDS LIFE INSURANCE COMPANY   1974 to 1978
Agent

HAMLIN ALDO & COMPANY   1969 to 1974
Stock Record Keeper

BRAUN GUARANTY TRUST   1965 to 1969
Bookkeeper

PERSONAL

Born Mt. Vernon, New York, November 17, 1940; married

Ithaca College, two years toward business degree in management and
accounting

Hobbies and interests: golf, bridge, tennis, travel, reading, Masons

ROBERT STEWART
P.O. Box 32
North Brunswick, NJ 08902
908-555-1234

date

name
title
company
address
city, state zip

Dear name:

If you need a Service Director who can really make a difference in your dealerships, you need me. I have the hands-on experience and the record of business-building and profit-making accomplishment as a Service Director, Shop Foreman, Assistant Parts Manager, and Warranty Investigator, that Infiniti requires of its successful Service Directors.

I turned around a service department from a monthly loss averaging $10,000 to a break even position after three months and a monthly profit of as much as $20,000 within 18 months. I increased the dealer's customer satisfaction index from bottom 20% in the district to the top 20%. As a result, we were named *Product Feedback Dealer* by the manufacturer and participated in pilot programs and surveys, evaluated product weaknesses, and proposed methods of repair.

I have the analytical skills to spot problem areas, the technical skills to help managers and employees to fix them and achieve excellence, the financial skills to direct attention to the bottom line, the negotiating abilities to achieve goals while keeping the good relationships, and the sales know-how to get the customers in the door - and keep them! I win by communicating to my employees and by training them how to be smarter; and I teach new technicians at the vo-tech school.

Because I have been on the receiving end, I know how Service Directors can really help improve performance in the service and parts operations.

For more information about my accomplishments, please see my attached resume.

I would appreciate the opportunity to meet you personally to discuss how my capabilities can contribute to the success of Infiniti. In a week, I will call you to set up an appointment at a mutually convenient time.

Yours sincerely,

ROBERT STEWART

P.O. Box 32, North Brunswick, NJ 08902   **908-555-1234**

CAREER SUMMARY

Profit-making Service Director for Automobile Dealerships.

PROFESSIONAL ACCOMPLISHMENTS

Carson Motors   1979 to date
Service Director   1981 to date
Shop Foreman   1979 to 1981

Turned around service department from monthly loss averaging $10,000 to a break even position after three months and monthly profit of as much as $20,000 within 18 months. Increased dealer's customer satisfaction index from bottom 20% in district to top 20%.

Named *Product Feedback Dealer* by manufacturer; participated in pilot programs and surveys, evaluated product weaknesses, and proposed methods of repair.

SALES

Converted dealership from being sales-driven to becoming service-driven. Aggressively solicited service business using direct mail, manufacturer's recalls, and telephone sales.
Result - some days, over 75% of cars in shop came from other dealers.

Notified customers by telephone of repairs not included in warranty and offered discount if they booked at dealership - increased retention rate from under 40% to over 70%.

Found many sources for cooperative advertising with suppliers - cut dealer's advertising cost by 72 cents to 28 cents of every dollar spent to obtain service business.

Conducted monthly customer awareness meetings, quarterly car care clinics and semi-annual ladies' nights to promote friendly relations between customers and service staff.

PRODUCTIVITY

Created labor and parts pricing guide for technicians - eliminated their waiting for prices and disruption of countermen's work, increased productivity from 55% of available time to 88%.

Instituted repair order control system so that any job could be identified as to location, technician, and advisor - eliminated confusion and constant enquiring about status.

Overcame reluctance of technicians to use computerized diagnosis equipment - reduced average number of times a car was in for same repair from three to one.

Robert Stewart   page 2

FINANCE

Negotiated with insurance companies to raise set rate from $32.00 an hour to $52.00 - reduced customers' out-of-pocket charges from $26.00 to $6.00 an hour.

Reduced receivables from as high as 120 days to under 30 days.

Reviewed cost analyses to find savings in semi-fixed expenses - saved $1,200 a month and cut expenses to 12% of sales compared to standard ratio of 14%.

HUMAN RESOURCES

Initiated Honesty Policy in shop: any unneeded repairs on cars were subject to immediate dismissal; spot checking performance and implementing policy resulted in total compliance.

Set up system of posting weekly productivity rank of each technician - encouraged employees to strive to be high on list and avoid being at bottom.

Developed new incentive pay plan which rewarded customer service advisors based on combination of Customer Satisfaction Index and repair work sales results.

Open Road Auto   1972 to 1979
Shop Foreman/assistant Parts Manager

ACE Appraisal, Inc.   1989 to date
President

Investigated warranty claims from dealers to ensure manufacturers' integrity. Consulted with manufacturers to evaluate warranty claims. Administered warranty claims and made recommendations based on investigations.

Suffolk Vocational Technical School   1978 to 1981
Instructor

EDUCATION

Nassau County Community College, Business Management courses
ASE National Automotive Industry Certification
Vo-Tech Teaching Certificate, State of Pennsylvania

PERSONAL

Born May 27, 1956, married, two children

Hobbies and interests: motorcycling, motorcycle and car racing (spectator now, participant in previous times), golf.

PETER JONES
422 Crescent Circle
Lawrenceville, NJ 08648
609-555-1234

date

name
title
company
address
city, state zip

Dear name:

"Super Emergency Road Service" - what does that mean?

It means that someone is in trouble, is probably upset, and needs help NOW!

It means that the 3A member has to be cared for, calmed down, and reassured that help is on the way. It means that the telephone counselor gets all the facts right, no matter how complex. It means that the right help is dispatched and gets there promptly. It means that the service provided is always top quality, and is kept that way by representatives who monitor and motivate the providers.

It means super customer *satisfaction*.

As an operations and customer service executive in the Parker Hotels, I know what 3A expects. That is why the hotels in my region always exceeded the Four Diamond ratings standards. Here are some examples of the kinds of things that I have frequently done that exactly fit your needs.

My concierge received a call at 11:00 a.m. to take care of a last minute change in travel plans and to provide a rental car and a new airline ticket by noon. He made the reservations, the car was at the door, and the guest on his way to the airport with his ticket taking him to the new destination - very pleased with the service. This is how I will train 3A telephone counselors to provide super customer service.

At 2:30 in the morning, a frantic wife called the switchboard saying that her husband did not call home as promised. He had recently had a heart attack, the line was busy when she phoned the room, messages were not responded to. The switchboard operator roused the Assistant Manager and the Security Officer and dispatched them to the room. The door was double locked and chained, and no one answered the knock. My people got the door unlocked and cut the chain, only to find that the guest had taken sleeping medication and could hardly be awakened. They roused the man, called the wife and got him to talk to her. Another customer satisfied with super service. This is how I will train dispatchers.

name   - 2 -   date

As Regional Director of Rooms Division, I had to ensure that my
six hotels maintained or exceeded the quality standards that won
us Four Star ratings. My role was to train my managers so well
that they took pride in their customer service and could handle
whatever came up. When the earthquake hit San Francisco in
1989, Parker Union Square was faced with having to take care of
its guests in a crisis as well as caring for the many people in the
vicinity who had to be helped. The hotel staff rose to the crisis
and provided extraordinary service to customers - and won many
friends for the hotel and the Parker chain. This is how I will
manage the field representatives to monitor and motivate the 3A
garages to provide super customer service.

You need someone with a vision for great potential for the future growth. I
took a hotel from a hole in the ground, scoped the market, built the business
plan, got the vendors and the bank lined up, set up the computer systems,
and built the site to a volume of $12 million in 18 months with minimal
supervision from headquarters.

The opportunity you have for the Business Unit Manager very much appeals
to me - and I am sure, my credentials are just what you are looking for. I
will call you in a week to set up an interview where we can discuss how my
strengths will help you build the kind of Five Star service you want to offer
3A members.

Yours sincerely,

Peter Jones

PETER JONES
422 Crescent Circle
Lawrenceville, NJ 08648
609-555-1234

QUALIFICATIONS

- Quickly Identifying and Resolving Problems to Improve Customer Service
- Profitably Managing All Aspects of a Full-Service Up-Scale Hotel
- Effectively Increasing Revenues Using Strong Marketing Strategies
- Successfully and Consistently Meeting and Exceeding Annual Sales Forecasts
- Efficiently Managing a Multi-Million Dollar Annual Operating Budget
- Implementing Operating Efficiencies to Reduce Labor and Operating Costs
- Controlling and Monitoring Hotel Assets Worth As Much as $130 Million
- Maximizing Occupancy Using Total Quality Management Programs
- Directing Reservations, Front Office, Concierge, Security and Housekeeping
- Negotiating Contracts and Working Closely with Vendors and Suppliers
- Using Positive Personnel Skills to Oversee Management and Staff

EXPERIENCE

CONSULTANT   1991 - Present
Franklin, Morgan & Kane, Sacramento, California

Utilized proven business management and marketing skills to create strategic action plans for private clients.

Successfully developed specific marketing avenues that increased a client's sales 100%.

EXECUTIVE ASSISTANT MANAGER (Rooms Division)   1989 - 1991
Parker Regency Sacramento, Sacramento, California

Selected to plan, organize, and direct all phases of hotel start-up operations for the new 500 room hotel.

Utilized strong human resources background to recruit, hire, train and schedule all department management and staff-level employees.

Implemented creative sales and marketing techniques to reach the pre-opening sales forecasts of $9 million.

Developed and initiated operating strategies to control costs and increase hotel efficiency.

Simultaneously served as a Regional Rooms Executive for Parker Hotel's Northern California division providing operating strategies for 13 properties resulting in annual sales of $120 million and profits of $85 million.

Peter Jones   **page 2**

EXECUTIVE ASSISTANT MANAGER (Rooms Division)   1987 - 1988
Parker Regency Oakland, Oakland, California

Improved profits 6% by analyzing operations; creating and implementing cost efficient management techniques; and increasing the room rates 15%.

Actively participated in community events and City Council activities and developed marketing and advertising strategies to increase the image of the hotel to potential guests.

EXECUTIVE ASSISTANT MANAGER (Rooms Division)   1985 - 1987
REGIONAL ROOMS EXECUTIVE
Parker Regency on Capitol Hill, Washington, D.C.

Improved the 834 room property's customer service rating from 88% to 97%.

Successfully increased net profits to $16.1 million using positive customer service techniques, ability to resolve problems, and critical staffing skills.

Recruited, hired, trained, supervised, and motivated as many as 230 employees including department managers and supervisory - level employees.

Interacted closely and negotiated new contracts with a wide range of vendors, suppliers, and service contractors.

Provided extensive industry expertise to also serve as the Regional Rooms Executive overseeing six of the company's major properties including the Parker Richmond and the Parker New York.

Improved employee development; implemented new management systems; and developed stronger operating programs.

EXECUTIVE ASSISTANT MANAGER (Rooms Division)   1981 - 1985
Parker Arlington at Key Bridge, Arlington, Virginia

Maintained maximum occupancy while managing a $1.5 million renovation project for 300 room facility.

Controlled a $6.2 million operating budget; increased profits to $4.8 million.

Honored by corporate office for achieving the company's highest overall profits and the company's best customer satisfaction ratings.

EDUCATION

B.S., Business & Hotel Management, Stanford University

GRETA MARKS, D.V.M.
7 Andover Road
Princeton NJ 08540
609-555-1234

date

name
title
company
address
city, state zip

Dear name:

You may need a veterinarian on your staff who has an unusual combination of practical experience with large animals, research achievements in animal reproduction, and success in running the business end of veterinary medicine.

As a veterinarian, I have succeeded in solo practice working with and performing surgery on large animals and small ruminants. In fact, I have demonstrated my versatility and ingenuity by gaining expertise with llamas - a field that has very little literature. Simultaneously, I have become highly effective as a business manager by developing my interpersonal and communication skills.

But, as a former broad-spectrum researcher, I now feel it is time to get into the kinds of veterinary work that will use my intellectual talents. I want to apply my problem identification and solution abilities to work related to such areas as herd health and maintenance, food animal production systems, food safety, animal related public health, teaching, or clinical research and development.

In addition to the professional and academic accomplishments shown on my resume, I am highly self-motivated, perceptive and energetic. I have worked with people at all levels and occupations.

I believe that these capabilities can make a significant contribution to your organization. I would be very pleased if you and I could get together to discuss how my record of achievement can contribute to your needs. If I may, I will call your office to set up an appointment to meet at a convenient time. Many thanks.

Yours sincerely,

GRETA MARKS, D.V.M.

7 Andover Road   bus. 609-555-1234
Princeton, NJ 08540   res. 609-555-1234

CAREER SUMMARY

Large animal veterinarian with strengths in research and animal
reproduction.

PROFESSIONAL ACCOMPLISHMENTS

ANIMAL MEDICAL ASSOCIATES   1987 to date
Sole Proprietor

Started and built private practice in large animals including small
ruminants: horses, llamas, sheep, goats, cows and pigs.

NATIONAL ZOOLOGICAL PARK, Charlottesville, VA   1982 to 1983
Veterinary Extern
  Supervisor: Janet Michaels, D.V.M.

METROPOLITAN ZOO, Ontario, Canada   1982
Veterinary Extern
  Supervisor: Jay Kessler, D.V.M.

ACADEMIC ACCOMPLISHMENTS

**UNIVERSITY OF VIRGINIA, SCHOOL OF VETERINARY
MEDICINE**   1985 to 1986
Resident in Theriogenology

**UNIVERSITY OF VERMONT COLLEGE OF VETERINARY
MEDICINE**   1984 to 1985
Clinical Instructor in Ambulatory Medicine

**COLUMBIA UNIVERSITY, COLLEGE OF VETERINARY
MEDICINE**   1983 to 1984
Intern in Ambulatory Medicine

HOUSTON ZOOLOGICAL GARDEN   1981
Research Fellow in Avian Metatology and Hematozoa
  Supervisors: Gordon Miller, M.D., Ph.D., and Angela Fahey, D.V.M.

**ROYAL ROTTERDAM ZOOLOGICAL AND BOTANICAL
GARDEN**   1980
Research Fellow in Avian Hematozoa and Veterinary Extern,
  Supervisor: Owen Kaplan, D.V.M., Ph.D.

GRETA MARKS, D.V.M.   page 2

DALLAS CITY ZOO   1979 to 1980
Research Fellow in Avian Hematozoa and Veterinary Extern
   Supervisor: Maggie Jones, D.V.M., Ph.D.

GEORGETOWN UNIVERSITY   1978 to 1979

Research Technician in Cardiac Physiology,
Supervisor: Alex Page, M.D.   1979
Research Technician in Urologic Oncology,
Supervisor: Anthony Maher, M.D.   1978

PROFESSIONAL AFFILIATIONS

Delaware Veterinary Medical Association, Executive Board Member, 1991
Delaware Equine Advisory Board, Alternate Delegate, 1990 to date
Delaware Veterinary Medical Advisory Committee, Member 1987 to date

American Association of Bovine Practitioners
American Association of Sheep and Goat Practitioners
American Association of Equine Practitioners
American Veterinary Medical Association

Licenses: Illinois, Indiana, New Jersey, New York
Board eligible next year in theriogenology

EDUCATION

A.B. 1979, Brandeis University, *magna cum laude*, major, anthropology

D.V.M. 1983, Cornell University, School of Veterinary Medicine

Phi Zeta, Omicron Chapter, Cornell University, 1983

American Association of University Women
Outstanding Senior Woman, Cornell University, 1983

Landreth Research Fellowship Grant, Primary Investigator, Dallas City Zoo,
1979 to 1980

PERSONAL

Born Washington, D.C., December 22, 1957, married, one boy and one girl

Hobbies and interests: antique restoration, decorative painting and design,
guitar, gardening, swimming

NICHOLAS SULLIVAN

397 Church Street   bus. 908-555-1234
Plainsboro, NJ 08536   res. 609-555-1234

CAREER SUMMARY

Pharmacologist with unique combination of marketing, clinical, research, managerial, and teaching experience in industry, hospital, and academic settings.

PROFESSIONAL ACCOMPLISHMENTS

MEYER & KINKEL   1991 to date
Manager, Medical Development

Provided medical input to and review of promotional, educational, marketing, and public relations materials to ensure compliance with regulatory and corporate requirements.

Conducted training classes and created and updated training manuals relating to pharmaceutical products and developments.

Contributed scientific and practical knowledge for use in marketing plans and campaigns and in advertisements.

Ensured coordination of research and marketing objectives for post-marketing clinical/phase IV and V studies.

Developed pharmacoeconomic studies of drugs in developmental stages to ensure their marketability.

FAIRFAX MEDICAL & MENTAL HEALTH CENTER   1989 to 1991
Director of Clinical Pharmacy Services
Assistant Director of Pharmacy

Managed pharmacy department of this 750 bed hospital; ran home infusion therapy program.

Developed quality assurance and par stock drugs programs; expanded unit dose system of drug distribution.

Created and installed multi-disciplinary monitoring of Adverse Drug Reaction program.

Developed Drug Use Evaluation (DUE) program used in upgrading quality assurance, drug-use policies, educational programs, and medical staff credentialing.

Nicholas Sullivan   page 2

LINDEN HOSPITAL CENTER   1988 to 1989
Assistant Director of Clinical Pharmacy Services
Acting Assistant Director of Inpatient Pharmacy

Established pharmacy-based cost containment program on drug costs and
usage at this 1,250 bed hospital.

Developed guidelines for the Pharmacy and Therapeutics (P&T) committee
to select a primary H-2 antagonist for the drug formulary as well as for
streamlining the formulary for nonsteroidal anti-inflammatory agents -
incorporated these activities into the pharmacy department's quality
assurance program.

ST. JAME'S/HILLMAN HOSPITAL CENTER   1987
CAROLINA MEMORIAL HOSPITAL
Critical Care Clinical Pharmacist

TEACHING POSITIONS

STANFORD UNIVERSITY COLLEGE OF PHARMACY AND   1988
ALLIED HEALTH PROFESSIONS
Clinical Pharmacy Preceptor

CONNECTICUT COLLEGE OF PHARMACY AND HEALTH   1987
SCIENCES
Assistant Professor of Clinical Pharmacy

UNIVERSITY OF MINNESOTA   1986 to 1987
Post-Pharm. D. Fellowship, cardiovascular pharmacotherapy

INTERNSHIPS

CVP PHARMACY, St. Paul, Minnesota   1984 to 1986
Community Pharmacy Intern

FISHER MEDICAL CENTER   1982 to 1984
Hospital Pharmacy Intern

JACOB HOSPITAL, Faribault, Minnesota   1982
Hospital Pharmacy Intern

ASSOCIATIONS

American Society of Hospital Pharmacists
New York State Council of Pharmacists

Nicholas Sullivan   page 3

EDUCATION

B.S. Pharmacy, University of Tennessee College of Pharmacy   1984

Pharm. D., University of Tennessee College of Pharmacy   1986

ASHP Foundation Anticoagulant Clinic Traineeship Program   1988
    Medical College of New Jersey Hospitals and Hunter Holmes
    McGuire Veteran's Administration Medical Center, Morristown

Licensed Pharmacist: North Carolina, New York, Florida

Honors: South Vine & Frank Tagamet Investigators Award   1988

SELECTED PRESENTATIONS

RESEARCH PROJECTS

PUBLICATIONS

CHARLES DUPUY
16 Canton Street
Hightstown, New Jersey 08520
609-555-1234; dupuy@tmal.com

date

name
title
company
address
city, state ZIP

Dear name:

[John Doe suggested that I contact you for advice regarding my job search.]

As senior engineer in spacecraft systems I had direct responsibility for planning and implementing the final integration and testing of spacecraft. I developed schedules, lead teams, organized operations, and communicated status to the customers.

As a self-employed engineering consultant, I planned and implemented the expansion of lab capacity for test throughput from less than 3 systems per week to more than 15 per week.

For more examples of my accomplishments, please read my attached resume.

In addition to my engineering achievements, I can offer the following abilities:

skill in negotiations and fact finding techniques,

knowledge of the theories, manufacture, and applications of advanced composite materials, heat transfer components, and drive mechanisms,

design experience with electronic packaging components that would function in such demanding environments as outer space,

manufacturing experience in electronics, NC machining (using both laser and conventional tooling), and final assembly, and

extensive background in both government and commercial industries.

I would appreciate the opportunity to meet with you to discuss how my achievements and abilities can contribute to the success of your firm. If I may, I will call you next week to set a mutually convenient time to get together.

Yours sincerely,

enclosure

CHARLES DUPUY

16 Canton Street, Hightstown, NJ 08520 609-555-1234, dupuy@tmail.com

CAREER SUMMARY

Creative and energetic engineering and systems professional, with demonstrated leadership and organizational skills. Accomplished negotiator with diverse experience in manufacturing, design, and subcontract management. Successful track record of meeting all technical and performance objectives.

PROFESSIONAL ACCOMPLISHMENTS

SELF-EMPLOYED   1997 to date
Engineering Consultant

Planned and implemented the expansion of lab capacity for test throughput from less than 3 systems per week to more than 15 per week.

Developed computer programs that reduced the time to test data from 2.5 hours to less than 0.25 hours.

Carefully monitored system performance as company transitioned from prototype assembly to full-scale production by setting and maintaining strict quality standards. Reduced defect rate of catheter temperature sensors by 80%.

Expanded the role of the test organization for a company as it introduced its iris identification product to market.

DANFIELD JOHNSON/ASTRO SPACE, East Windsor, NJ   1990 - 1997
Senior Engineer - Spacecraft Mechanical Systems

Completed assembly and delivery of the GE-2 spacecraft on schedule, and the GE-3 spacecraft three weeks ahead of schedule.

Resolved a critical alignment issue on GE-3 spacecraft while identifying and implementing work-arounds that allowed deployment tests to proceed on schedule instead of falling behind.

Worked closely with the engineering teams from the launch vehicle manufacturers to identify and resolve interface issues inherent in launching spacecraft.

Charles Dupuy   page 2

Mechanical Design Engineer   1993 - 1996

Developed a combined procedure enabling the testing of multiple
components for the Intelsat program, saved over $300,000.

Spearheaded an investigation into alternative materials for the new "A2100"
spacecraft design, reduced weight and improved efficiency.

Identified and used commonalty across programs to reduce nonrecurring
engineering costs, then combined operations within the manufacturing flow,
reduced costs further.

Subcontract Manager   1990 - 1993

Negotiated cost savings of up to 15% through the use of fact-finding
missions, and design and manufacturing reviews.

MANSFIELD ELECTRIC COMPANY, Valley Forge, PA   1998 - 1990
Manufacturing Management Program

Increased production of circuit boards by more than 500% by adding staff,
coordinating deliveries, and streamlining throughput using Just In Time
management.

EDUCATION

M.S. Systems Engineering, University of Connecticut   1996
B.S. Mechanical Engineering, California Institute of Technology   1988
GE Advanced Courses in Engineering
Manufacturing Leadership Curriculum
EIT Certified, New York State

SKILLS

MRP, MRP II, ISO 9000, SPC, CPI
UNIX, Windows (95 and NT), MacOS, FORTRAN, I*DEAS, Interleaf
Microsoft and Claris software packages

HONORS

Deans List, CalTech
Phi Theta Kappa Honor Society
CalTech Engineering Science Medal and Scholarship
Plant Engineers Award

JAMES T. MATUZA

22 Richmond Avenue   609-555-1234
Mount Laurel NJ 08054   908-555-1234

CAREER SUMMARY

Results-producing engineering professional with more than 14 years of experience in telecommunications and electrical design and management at both field and corporate levels.

BUSINESS ACCOMPLISHMENTS

ADAMS TELECOMMUNICATIONS GROUP   1978 to date
Engineering Consultants to Bell Operating Companies:

Eastern Bell, Newark, NJ   1985 to date
Electrical Protection Engineering Consultant

Developed, modified, implemented, and interpreted Eastern Bell's practices and procedures pertaining to the electrical protection of the telephone network.

Designed, implemented and supervised installation of high voltage protection systems for power company substation customers of the communications network.

> Redesigned and improved existing high voltage isolation hardware at power utility substations - increased quality, and cut maintenance and downtime; achieved significant savings.

Provided technical expertise to Eastern Bell claims representatives and attorneys in claims against the company for electrically-related cases of alleged shock, personal injury, or property damage.

> Analytical reports used to settle claims - saved $35,000 to $50,000 annually.

> Expert witness and court testimony resulted in favorable settlements in two cases totaling $500,000.

> Prepared and presented seminars on electrical protection to new claims representatives on how to deal with initial or routine claims without Engineering department participation.

Directed field managers and technicians in the determination and resolution of a wide variety of noise and power-related problems (including bonding and grounding) affecting the telephone network.

Computerized and standardized procedures between power utilities and telephone company regarding voltage upgrades and modifications on joint-use utility pole lines - improved productivity.

JAMES T. MATUZA

Eastern Bell, Trenton, NJ   1985 to date
Outside Plant Engineering Consultant

Designed and implemented engineering work orders for construction of copper and fiber optic cable networks, digital and light wave transmission systems (SLC-96, DS1, DS3), and pole line and conduit systems.

Western Telephone, Oakland, CA   1980 to 1982
Senior Project Engineering Consultant

Am-South, Statesville and Lenoir, NC   1978 to 1980
Consultant

CANADIAN TELEGRAPH COMPANY, LTD., Canada   1976 to 1978
Outside Plant Engineer

EDUCATION

Bachelor of Electrical Engineering, 1976, Montreal Technical College, Canada

Bachelor of Science, 1974, major engineering, Vancouver University, Canada

Evan P. Turco
66 Paige Lane
Princeton, NJ 08540-8406
908-555-1234

date

name
title
company
address
city, state ZIP

Dear name:

An insatiable drive to beat yesterday, break the rules, press the limits, target perfection, create new solutions, analyze and master all aspects of the system, identify and solve problems, turn around operations, and thereby produce profits - does this sound like what you need in your Operations Manager?

If so, please read my attached resume to see some of the results of my efforts for a high tech company. In addition to my technical and professional skills, I bring:

> the application of common sense to solve problems;

> an inventor's approach to production and inventory management;

> a strong ability to lead people and develop teamwork within and among departments;

> a capacity to orchestrate work under pressure; and

> a desire to be more than ready to rise to new and more diverse challenges.

I am a self-starter and buck stopper.

It's not the creating of major improvements or the solving of major problems that matter most to me - they are prompted by major identifiable needs. It's the daily incremental improvements, the constant drive for perfection, the polishing of the system, and the harmony of the team that I am most proud of.

If I may, I will call you in a week to set up an appointment to discuss how my unusual combination of skills and traits can contribute to the success of your company.

Yours sincerely,

EVAN P. TURCO

66 Paige Lane, Princeton, NJ 08540-8406   Telephone 908-555-1234

CAREER SUMMARY

Profit-making, hands-on production manager with a record of ingenious solutions that advanced the state of the art.

PROFESSIONAL ACCOMPLISHMENTS

OPERATIONS MANAGER   1970 to date
Exton Microfilm Corporation

Took over loose operation, analyzed every stage of production, established uniform written procedures and tighter quality control standards, cross-trained all employees to be versatile - result, in five years, increased production speed by 300%, cut chemical costs by 50%, reduced material consumption by 20%, and cut failure rate from 15% to less than 0.1%, even with the more demanding standards.

Identified printer design flaw that caused slippage, developed test master to verify the cause, devised two resolutions that were used in tandem - result, obtained absolute assurance.

Created diagnosis procedures, increased silver recovery yield, developed pollution control methods, and created automatic shut off with alarm.

Identified and selected best suppliers based on each of quality, price and delivery; benchmarked each criterion and then got winning bidder to agree to accept all three top standards. Remained involved with supplier on an on-going basis to continually upgrade its production methods and quality.

Set up systems of purchasing standards, automatic inventory control, just in time (JIT) delivery of supplies, and volume discounts.

Started up operations in Bermuda, trained two entry level employees to be self-sustaining in less than a week.

RECORDING TECHNICIAN   1968 to 1970
J. Miller Recording Studio

REPAIRMAN   1965 to 1967
Northern Television Repair

EVAN P. TURCO   page 2

EDUCATION

Electronics Technician, 1968, Jamestown County Technical Institute

PERSONAL

Born November 13, 1947, married

Hobbies and interests: golf, fishing, biking, hiking; furniture design and construction, home remodeling, cooking, gardening; automobiles, model airplanes, still and video photography, audio systems, tropical fish; community history, community service.

JAY PARNELL, JR.
442 Simko Avenue
Hopewell, New Jersey 08525
609-555-1234

date

name
title
company
address
city, state ZIP

Dear name:

Imagine a systems test engineering supervisor with excellent people skills <u>and</u> excellent technical skills <u>and</u> excellent business skills <u>and</u> a dedication to Total Quality Management.

This is the unbeatable combination I can bring to your firm.

I have the in-depth knowledge of software and hardware from the bottom up, the natural aptitude to lead and train people, the determination to produce top quality from the customers' viewpoint, and the newly-acquired education in business that makes the right things happen.

And I have three Exemplary Awards from rSystems to prove it.

My management style is to enable employees to feel pride in their work and reward them for their achievements. I take initiative, and can plan and run a project from conception to completion.

If [your company needs] [you have clients who need] [you know people who might need] a systems engineering supervisor who has a demonstrated track record in applications and diagnostics software for PCs, you may wish to look over my resume which list some of my accomplishments.

I would be very pleased if you and I could get together briefly to discuss how my record of achievement can contribute to the needs of your [company] [clients] [contacts or people they might know]. If I may, I will call your office to set up an appointment to get together at a convenient time. Many thanks.

Yours sincerely,

enclosure

JAY PARNELL, JR.

442 Simco Avenue   Telephone
Hopewell New Jersey 08525   609-555-1234

OBJECTIVE

Total Quality Management supervisory position in development of
applications and diagnostics software for personal computers and work
stations.

PROFESSIONAL ACCOMPLISHMENTS

rSYSTEMS CORPORATION   1976 to 1992

Systems Test Engineer   1989 to 1992

Led PW316 PC support team, applied TQM (Total Quality Management) principles - increased system yields from 75% to 91%.

Member of "Perfect PC" team which presented ideas that resulted in
the highest Mean Time Before Failure of any product developed at
location.

Trained manufacturing personnel on test procedures for products under
development.

Associate Test Engineer   1986 to 1989

Supervised assembly and testing center employees - received
Achievement Award for setting up a PC configuration and test center
for special customer order.

Supervised project that automated PROM/PAL programming
department - reduced manpower by 33% and almost eliminated
handling time for parts.

Received Achievement Award for providing support for developing test
diagnostics for startup of Air Force Desktop III contract.

Technician Specialist   1979 to 1986

Senior Technician   1976 to 1979

BAILEY'S DEPARTMENT STORE   1973 to 1976

Department Manager

Managed 35 employees while attending college full time.

Jay Parnell, Jr.   page 2

EDUCATION

Associate of Applied Science in Business, 1993, Nassau Community
College; major Principles of Management, Total Quality Management
(TQM).

Associate of Applied Science in Data Processing, 1991, Nassau Community
College; major Microcomputers.

Diploma Technical Electronics, 1976, Norwalk Career Institute; major V-7
circuits and systems.

Expert in Borland Turbo C and Microsoft C, proficient in Pascal, Assembler,
Windows, Word, and DOS.

Awards: Received three rSystems Exemplary Awards in recognition of
achieving strategic goals.

PERSONAL

Born March 9, 1955, Passaic, New Jersey, married, 2 children.

Associations: Treasurer, Nassau Community College Business Club.

Hobbies and interests: fishing, woodworking, race car mechanics.

PATRICK LINSEY

24 Couch Street, Robbinsville, NJ 08691   609-555-1234; linsey@tmail.com

CAREER SUMMARY

Quality assurance supervisor and analytical chemist with a record of improving quality and cutting costs.

PROFESSIONAL ACCOMPLISHMENTS

JACKSON Corp., Jamesburg, NJ   1989 to 1999
Analytical Chemist II   1997 to 1999

Coordinated installation of batch expander and developed and implemented recipes/SOPs, which enabled "Global Standardized" testing. Result - project saved $89,000 a year.

Investigated, purchased and installed numerous instruments including several automated HP GC Chemstation systems that improved efficiency and flexibility of analyses. Modified and/or developed new GC analytical methods that enhanced analytical capabilities.

QA Supervisor   1989 to 1997

Developed and led staff of 9 technicians into a more efficient, self-managed work team of 7 with one of the best safety records in BASF. Result - $93,000 a year labor savings. With my guidance, several members have been promoted to new responsibilities.

Co-directed the focus of QA testing from in-process/finished materials to a more cost-effective reliance on raw material/in-process testing. Result - improved first-time-out prime from 95 to 98% thereby saving approximately $1 million a year.

Significantly contributed to our business group achieving ISO 9002 certification within a 6 month time frame.

Developed ISO 9002, Standard Operating Procedures and other related documentation that enhanced analytical and physical testing precision and accuracy.

Trained ISO 9000 auditor/lead auditor for various sites. Assisted production in identifying quality problems.

Amhold Engineering Corp., Harrison, NJ   1979 to 1989
Chemist

Redesigned and improved cylinder conditioning. Result - more stable and higher quality ultra low ppm specialty gas mixtures.

Trained and supervised new and rotating employees.

Maintained high customer satisfaction by skillfully troubleshooting "in-house" problems and communicating effectively with customers.

Patrick Linsey   page 2

Cornell University   1978 to 1979
Teaching Assistant in Analytical and General Chemistry labs

COMPUTER SKILLS

SAP, HTML language, Web Design, Netscape Navigator, Windows NT, WordPerfect, Word, Excel, MS Mail, Lotus Notes, PowerPoint, Access, Explorer.

TECHNICAL SKILLS

Analytical Instruments/ASTM Methods, including: GC, UV/IR, AA, FPD, FID, IR specific, Chemiluminescents, Epitaxial Reactor, Ultrasonic, Flexural Strength, Compressive Resistance, and R-Value.

Process equipment/testing, including: vacuum molding and batch expansion, foam structure, laboratory scale processing equipment.

Statistical Process Control (SPC).

ISO 9000 system: standards, documentation and auditing.

Technical writing and presentations.

EDUCATION

M.S. Chemistry, 1985, Cornell University. Concentration in Inorganic and Analytical Chemistry. Worked on electrochemical properties of Lanthanides.

B.S. Chemistry, 1977, New York University.

PERSONAL

Born Teaneck, NJ, October 9, 1955, single.

Hobbies and interests: Toastmasters public speaking, hiking, camping, skiing, traveling, photography.

JOHN K. DONNER
332 Atlantic Avenue
South Brunswick, NJ 08852-9792
908-555-1234

date

name
title
company
address
city, state zip

Dear name:

You may need a Chief Financial Officer who sees and seizes profit opportunities in what others consider problems. For example:

I refused to accept an initial offer of $50,000 business interruption insurance settlement and negotiated a payment of $1.8 million.

If you wish to learn more about my profit-contributing accomplishments, please read my attached resume.

I have a track record of creating innovative and practical solutions to financial, tax, accounting, and insurance problems. My auditing background with Marlan Agency taught me to be a fast learner in almost any situation in virtually every kind of profit and non-profit operation. I have applied these skills as I have subsequently progressed in my financial management career.

In addition to my professional skills, my strengths include:

a dedication to efficiency in operations,

a talent for identifying, delegating to, and growing promotable people,

a nose for finding the real problems and solving them so they stay fixed,

courage in tackling the tough ones and persistence in bringing them to successful conclusion,

a determination to get things done.

I would be pleased to meet with you to discuss how my experience and abilities can contribute to the success of your operation. If I may, I will call your office to set up an appointment at a mutually convenient time. I look forward to meeting you.

Yours sincerely,

JOHN K. DONNER, CPA

332 Atlantic Avenue
South Brunswick, NJ 08852-9792

Telephone
908-555-1234

CAREER SUMMARY

Business Development executive with strong profit-making and financial track record.

BUSINESS ACCOMPLISHMENTS

VITELLO BROKERS, Union, NJ   1990 to date
Business Consultant

Provided services to sellers and buyers of businesses by valuing and determining appropriate terms of sale.

DALE ENTERPRISES INC.   1987 to 1990
Affiliate of The Hospital Center at Hollis, NJ
Assistant Vice President - Business Development

Designed and implemented reorganization that turned urgent care center's loss into a $98,300 profit in first year.

Initiated in-house temporary nurse agency - reduced expenditures on outside services by 12%.

Set up home health care joint venture - achieved 30% profit margin.

Created child care center for nurses' children - attracted and retained scarce nurses and other employees, reduced turnover by 10%.

Acquired land in residential area surrounding hospital to develop visitor parking facility - overcame severe shortage of parking space and produced revenues from parking charges.

Developed Employee Assistance Program (EAP) as a profit center.

ADVENTURE WORLD, Jackson, NJ   1977 to 1987
Director of Finance

Directed financial aspects of company turnaround from a loss position to 9.8% profit.

Negotiated business interruption insurance settlement - obtained payment of $1.8 million compared to original offer of $50,000.

John K. Donner   page 2

Adventure World (cont'd.)

Identified hidden provision in tax laws that enabled company to avoid
$150,000 property taxes annually.

Segregated seasonal workforce from permanent full time employees for
unemployment insurance purposes - took advantage of UIC cap to save
$200,000 a year in payroll taxes.

Developed creative pricing policies that cut sales taxes by $100,000 per
annum.

Directed computerization of daily reporting and order entry system -
streamlined scheduling to meet weekly and seasonal patterns.

Hired and trained subordinates who were subsequently promoted: one to
Corporate CFO of Adventure World and another to CFO of a company
subsidiary.

THE BROOKHAVEN COMPANY, Valencia, CA   1971 to 1977
Corporate Treasurer   1975 to 1977

Designed and installed self insured property, liability, and workers'
compensation programs - saved $500,000 annually.

Controller, Wizard Mountain subsidiary   1971 to 1974

Centralized purchasing departments to achieve substantial savings.

MARLAN AGENCY, Los Angeles, CA   1965 to 1971
Audit Senior

PERSONAL

B.S. University of Southern California, 1965, major accounting

Certified Public Accountant, California and New Jersey

Affiliations:

> Trustee, Freehold Hospital
> President, Freehold Rotary Club
> Board of Directors, Western Monmouth Chamber of Commerce

DALE GLEASON, CPA

25 Maryhaven Court
Belle Mead, New Jersey 08502
908-555-1234

date

name
title
company
address
city

Dear name:

As Vice President Finance and Administration of a United States subsidiary of a multi-national company, I arranged for the transfer of loans to the United Kingdom parent and the conversion of U.S. debt into equity funding. This move avoided domestic tax liabilities and saved $100,000 annually in cash outlays.

As Chief Financial Officer of an engineering firm, I established a management system for a joint venture project - including comprehensive costing and profit formulas. This achievement allowed the partners to receive progress payments instead of having to wait until completion of a project to obtain their profits.

If you would like to read about more of my profit-creating, productivity-increasing accomplishments, please read my attached resume.

In addition to my business acumen, I can offer strong managerial skills both as a participative leader and team player. I use my creativity, dedication and sound judgment to identify problems and come up with very practical solutions. I get my ideas across clearly and persuasively so that the right decisions are made promptly.

I would be pleased to meet with you to discuss how my experience and abilities can contribute to the success of your organization. If I may, I will call your office to set up an appointment at a mutually convenient time. I look forward to meeting you.

Yours sincerely,

DALE GLEASON, CPA

25 Maryhaven Court
Belle Mead, New Jersey 08502

Telephone
908-555-1234

CAREER SUMMARY

Chief financial and administration officer with a record of contributing to the profitability and efficiency of my employers.

BUSINESS ACCOMPLISHMENTS

CHIEF FINANCIAL OFFICER   1990 to date
Broom Construction, Inc.

Restructured company debt to improve balance sheet - prevented loss of capacity rating from State of New Jersey and allowed company to continue government work.

Initiated and implemented computerized job costing system - enabled management to know costs of each project for first time and made it feasible for company to manage large scale projects.

Standardized end-of-month record keeping procedures and policies - eliminated delays and provided timely and accurate operating and financial statements.

Established joint venture project management system including comprehensive costing and profit formulas - allowed partners to receive progress payments instead of having to wait until completion of project.

Directed physical inventory of fixed assets - uncovered $450,000 of unlisted resources.

VICE PRESIDENT FINANCE AND ADMINISTRATION   1980 to 1989
Vincente Consulting Services

Arranged for transfer of borrowing to United Kingdom parent company and conversion of United States subsidiary's debt into equity funding - avoided tax liabilities and saved $100,000 annually in cash outlays.

Reduced receivables from over 10 weeks to six weeks - increased cash flow by $100,000 a month.

Transferred management of company pension fund to outside administrator - raised return on investment from 8% to 12%.

Dale Gleason   page 2

CONTROLLER-SECRETARY   1976 to 1980
Gilbert Corporation

Prepared manual of accounting policies and procedures for field operations -
facilitated firm's growth from $4 million to $25 million in four years.

ACCOUNTING MANAGER   1974 to 1976
Noel-Joseph, Inc.

Headed credit negotiations with major supplier, managed cash and reduced
debt from $850,000 to $240,000, thereby keeping company in business.

OFFICER MANAGER   1969 to 1974
Fleck Tire and Rubber Co., Retail Stores Division

Oversaw program to evaluate computerization of consolidation of regional
accounts, instead recommended elimination of four regional offices.

EDUCATION

B.S. 1973, Purdue University, major accounting, honors graduate
Enrolled currently in MBA program at Wharton

Certified Public Accountant, 1988

American Institute of Certified Public Accountants, member
New Jersey Society of Certified Public Accountants, member

PERSONAL

Born November 1939, Rahway, NJ, married, one child

Hobbies and interests: private pilot, freshwater fishing, photography

STANLEY MICHAELSON
83 Vincent Place
Princeton, NJ 08540
609-555-1234

date

name
title
company
address
city, state zip

Dear name:

As Pension Administrator in an actuarial consulting firm, I redesigned benefit determination work sheets using spreadsheet software to encompass all prior plan formulas - a vulnerable client appreciated computer generated work sheets so much it remained a client and increased its business with the firm.

I also accepted "impossible" deadline for a study to be sent to a client's Board of Directors relating to compliance with the Tax Reform Act of 1986. I produced the report in two weeks compared to a normal six weeks and the Board adopted my proposal.

If you would like to read more of my accomplishments, and learn about my record in maintaining top billable rates, please read my attached resume.

In addition to my technical know-how, I can offer the following:

I develop and maintain excellent client relationships that result in retention and growth of clients ranging in size from local hospitals to global corporations;

I can be either a team player or work autonomously;

I am detail oriented but I see the total picture and use my ingenuity and "futurist" talents to solve problems in simple and workable ways;

I have excellent written and oral communication skills that make it possible for my clients to understand complex subjects;

I give my subordinates a clear understanding of the task and then give them lots of leeway to complete their work.

I am conscientious and reliable.

I would be pleased to meet with you to discuss how my capabilities can contribute to the success of your operation. If I may, I will call your office in about a week to set up an appointment.

Yours sincerely,

STANLEY MICHAELSON

83 Vincent Place
Princeton NJ 08540

Telephone
609-555-1234

CAREER SUMMARY

Pension administrator with track record of reducing employer pension costs, cutting turnaround times, improving service to and increasing rapport with clients, and thereby raising billable revenues.

BUSINESS ACCOMPLISHMENTS

DANIEL J. RYAN & ASSOCIATES

1990 to date

Pension Administrator

Redesigned benefit determination work sheets using spreadsheet software to encompass all prior plan formulas - vulnerable client appreciated computer generated work sheets so much it remained a client and increased business.

Accepted "impossible" deadline for a study to be sent to client's Board of Directors relating to compliance with Tax Reform Act of 1986 - produced report in two weeks compared to normal six weeks; Board adopted proposal.

Maintained excellent rapport with client based on quality of service and work performed - more than tripled billings from previous year.

Cleaned up data base for pension plan covering union members by opening up communication and cooperation with client - resulting report and purchase of annuities by insurance carrier eliminated $300,000 liability.

Proposed study so client could avoid pension plan contribution; applied mandatory test at highest allowable interest rate to reduce present value of benefits - eliminated employer contribution.

Used ingenuity to identify participants entitled to lump sum distribution from a terminating pension plan: instead of paying Social Security Administration a search fee, sent claims forms to client to distribute with pay checks - reduced PBGC premium, speeded up termination process and recovered surplus assets.

Maintained highest billable rate in entire pension department.

Stanley Michaelson   page 2

GALVAN CONSULTANTS, INC.   1985 to 1990
Senior Actuarial Assistant   1989 to 1990
Actuarial Assistant   1985 to 1989

Initiated set up of PC spreadsheet software to download liability data from
mainframe computer and asset information from trust statements -
replacement of manual system saved 25% processing time.

Prepared actuarial valuation for two new acquisitions in one week versus
normal turnaround of six to eight weeks.

Projected benefits streams for each of next 50 years for current pensioners
and present workforce with respect to alternative proposed pension formulas
- by using PC spreadsheets, was able to complete study that would have cost
too much to do manually.

Increased billable hours each year to reach 109% compared to about 90%
norm - received promotion.

MYERS ACTUARIAL SERVICES   1984 to 1985
Mathematician

PERSONAL

Born Elizabeth, NJ, August 18, 1961, single

B.A. 1983, Georgia Southern, major economics, <u>summa cum laude</u>, Phi Beta
Kappa

Passed actuarial examinations #100, 110, and 140 plus EA-2

Hobbies and interests: bicycling, cooking, softball, teaching English to
Speakers of Other Languages (ESOL).

CHRISTOPHER CATERA

62 Ferrante Avenue   bus 212-555-1234
Plainsboro, NJ 08536   res 609-555-1234

CAREER SUMMARY

Investment and credit analyst with a track record of profit-making and loss-avoiding analyses in oil and gas industry debt financing.

BUSINESS ACCOMPLISHMENTS

FREEDOM TRUST COMPANY   1982 to date
Vice President

Equity and High Yield Debt Research

Solicited lead manager mandate for initial public offering, conducted valuation analysis, determined offering price, provided information to management for road show and to investors for their analysis - all units were profitably sold at offering price.

Determined that company's publicly traded equities were overvalued but that junk bond yield was adequate - trading desk took position and made a market that produced a profit in 10 months.

Equity Investment Analyses for Fisher Capital Corporation

Conducted technical and management evaluations of several investment opportunities brought to bank - recommended against purchase because shares failed to meet the bank's return criteria.

Mergers, Acquisitions and Leveraged Buy Outs

Directed due diligence, asset review, valuation, and preparation of bid for $5.6 billion leveraged buy out of exploration and production subsidiary - showed that parts were more worth than sum of whole and divisions were sold individually at more than bid for total.

Developed off-balance sheet restructuring of properties - demonstrated that direct sale was more profitable; bank was hired to help sell company in two pieces for about 8% more than original concept.

Performed valuation of oil and gas assets for redemption offer by management to dissident shareholders; showed that, although current value of assets was significantly lower than offer, potential was much higher - shareholders were persuaded to retain investment.

Credit Analysis

Conducted engineering, technical and financial analysis for $2.5 billion defensive credit facility, recommended participation as co-lead bank - loan paid off within four years.

Overcame difficulty due to pricing in syndicating loan for £700 million United Kingdom oil company - loan performing well.

Christopher Catera   page 2

Freedom Trust Company (cont'.d)

Monitored closely $260 million non-recourse loan to Norwegian producer during the precipitous drop in oil prices in 1986 - kept project from defaulting and loan was paid off completely.

Recommended strongly against accepting request to lead $350 million acquisition financing loan - loan made by major competitor subsequently defaulted.

VINCENTE PETROLEUM CONSULTANTS, INC.   1980 to 1982
Founding Principal and Vice President

MERIDIAN ENERGY COMPANY   1975 to 1980
Senior Reservoir Engineer   1977 to 1980
Reservoir Engineer   1975 to 1977

CORNELL UNIVERSITY   1973 to 1975
Research Assistant

PELTCO, INC.   1969 to 1973
Gas Projects Engineer   1971 to 1973
Plant Engineer   1969-1971

CORNELL UNIVERSITY   1968 to 1969
Research Assistant

OIL AND NATURAL COMMISSION, India   1966 to 1968
Field Engineer

EDUCATION

B.S.	1966	Indian School of Mines	Petroleum Engineering
M.S.	1969	Cornell University	Petroleum Engineering
M.S.	1975	Cornell University	Chemical Engineering
Ph.D.	1978	Cornell University	Chemical Engineering

Associations: Society of Professional Engineers, American Institute of Chemical Engineers

PERSONAL

Born June 16, 1941, married

Hobbies and interests: travel, reading, cooking, gardening

MATTHEW DAVIS
14 Joan Street
Princeton, NJ 08540
609-555-1234

name   date
title
company
address
city

Dear name:

As Assistant Controller of a division of a global corporation, I created a realistic goal setting and work measurement system for the company that raised productivity while reducing annual overtime expenditures by 64% from $1.1 million to $450,000.

I also converted a manual system of raw material purchase orders to an on-line paperless computerized system that automatically tied in with receiving, accounts payable, and month end accruals. As a result, the company saved $65,000 a year in payroll costs alone.

If you would like to read more of my cost-cutting and productivity-improving accomplishments, please see my attached resume.

Having come up the hard way by getting my BBA, MBA, CPA, and Computer Science certificate at night, I know the value of hard work, self-motivation and dedication. I am very goal and results-oriented, using my problem-identification and solution skills to come up with creative yet practical answers.

Besides my accounting and finance skills, my strengths include:

persuasiveness in getting people to buy into ideas by listening to their points of view and showing how the changes meet their needs and self-interests,

sound judgement and sense of priority based on real experience,

ability to work with all levels from clerks to CEOs,

teamwork, enthusiasm, communication skills, and flexibility.

I would be pleased to meet with you to discuss how my experience and abilities can contribute to the success of your operation. If I may, I will call your office to set up an appointment at a mutually convenient time. I look forward to meeting you.

Sincerely,

MATTHEW DAVIS

14 Joan Street   bus 212-555-1234
Princeton, NJ 08540   res 609-555-1234

CAREER SUMMARY

Controller with strong record of computerizing accounting functions, cutting costs and increasing productivity.

BUSINESS ACCOMPLISHMENTS

MORGAN JAMES CORPORATION   1986 to date
Assistant Controller

Created realistic goal setting and work measurement system - maintained or raised productivity and reduced annual overtime expenditures from $1.1 million to $450,000 (64%).

Introduced debtor and creditor analyses for accounts payable and receivable - reduced days outstanding from 55 to 47 on world-wide basis, improved cash flow and saved $80,000 a year.

Replaced manual procedures for consolidating 15 foreign subsidiary accounts with menu-driven system - cut staff 50% and time from 7.5 to 2.5 days - saved $75,000 a year.

Superseded labor-intensive accounts payable system with on-line data enquiry computer program - avoided duplicate payments and took advantage of prompt payment discounts - saved $100,000 in workforce costs.

Converted manual raw material purchase order to on-line paperless computerized system - improved tracking of purchase orders, automatically tied in with warehouse receiving, accounts payable invoices and month end accruals. Saved $65,000 a year in payroll alone.

Analyzed workers compensation insurance policies - decreased annual premium from $325,000 to $175,000 (46%).

Set up automated bank reconciliation program bank to compare to paid voucher file downloaded from mainframe computer to PC screens - cut costs by $30,000 a year.

Discovered overbilling by electrical utility - recovered $250,000 for company.

COOPER & ANGELO   1978 to 1986
Manager - General Accounting

Persuaded Vice President Finance to stretch normal invoice payment cycle from 30 days to 40 days, gained acceptance of change from vendors - reduced cash utilization at banks by $950,000.

Matthew Davis

Cooper & Angelo (cont'd.)

Used in-house personnel to prepare tax returns, limited public accountants to reviewing results - reduced CPA fees from $110,000 to $20,000 a year.

Developed inventory of fixed assets totaling $42 million, enhanced controls and removed non-existent assets from subsidiary ledger - cut insurance premium by 10%.

Put together prospectus for eventual sale of company to BASF - results helped owners get maximum value for company.

GILLIO INC. (Corporate Offices)   1974 to 1978
Manager of Financial Accounting and Research

Researched, designed and implemented computerized Corporate and Divisional charts of accounts, adapted commercial software package - provided on-line, up-to-date reports to management.

Segregated entire accounts of a product line into a pro forma free-standing company - data used as a basis to win anti-trust suit.

LIVINGSTON & SEACREST   1966 to 1974
Audit Supervisor

Audited Forbes 500 clients.

CARMELLA & OAKLEY (Corporate Offices)   1964 to 1966
Senior Accountant

PERSONAL

Born Yonkers, New York, May 17, 1939, married, three children.

B.B.A. 1966, Purdue University, major accounting - with honors
M.B.A. 1968, Purdue University, major accounting and finance
C.P.A. 1968, States of New York and New Jersey
Certificate in Computer Science, 1981, Purdue University

Professional Associations: Member of: AICPA; New York State Society of CPAs; New Jersey State Society of CPAs; National Association of Accountants.

Hobbies and interests: tennis, fitness, reading.

ANDREA SIMMONS
62 Pamela Terrace
Lawrenceville NJ 08648
609-555-1234

date

name
title
company
address
city, state ZIP

Dear name:

As Controller of a $6.5 million general insurance agency, I went beyond crunching numbers to help manage the twelve-fold increase in the agency's profit in eight years. I was more than the financial officer; with my knowledge of insurance, I was a contributing member of the management team.

I put my knowledge of computers to advantage by completely automating the agency's business. In fact, by finding and using the right software package, I enabled the owners to acquire two other agencies for 37.5% less than the asking price.

I provided management with analyses and reports that showed them where to concentrate their efforts for maximum profitability. On a day-to-day basis, I was able to run the entire accounting operation with only one clerk.

If you would like to know about more of my accomplishments, please read my attached resume.

In addition to my financial, computer, and insurance know-how, I am able to offer a spirit of cooperativeness, an ability to listen and respond to the needs and preferences of management and employees, a knack for communicating and training, and an attitude of hard work and smart work combined.

In about a week, I will call your office to set a date to get together to discuss how my achievements can contribute to the growth and profitability of your agency. I look forward to meeting you personally.

Yours sincerely,

ANDREA SIMMONS

62 Pamela Terrace
Lawrenceville, NJ 08648

Telephone
609-555-1234

CAREER SUMMARY

Controller of independent full service property-casualty insurance agency with a track record of contributing to profits and computerizing the business.

BUSINESS ACCOMPLISHMENTS

Lansing Agency   1974 to date

CONTROLLER   1983 to date
BOOKKEEPER   1976 to 1983
ASSISTANT TO BOOKKEEPER   1974 to 1976

Provided financial support during acquisition of two agencies: analyzed financial background, generated scenarios to determine purchase price, projected cash flow needed to offset costs over term of purchase - cut price from $1.2 million to $750,000.

Initiated executive committee meetings to improve communications, set goals, monitor results, and identify and resolve business problems.

Allocated income and expenses to sub-agencies - demonstrated that the acquisitions were in fact very profitable.

Developed revenue history and comparisons, projected revenues, compared estimated actuals with forecast - enabled management for first time to analyze and target problems and areas of opportunity.

Converted sales production reports to management control reports, monitored production and commission volumes to identify trends - targeted shifts in personal and commercial lines.

Created transaction journals to track new business and cancellations, analyzed production reports - enabled management to take corrective action offsetting declines in sales.

Managed general ledger, provided up-to-date financial reports - decreased outside accountant's annual fees by 50%.

Provided accurate, concise, consistent data each month that allowed timely evaluation of financial position - cut time needed to produce audited financial statements from 5 days to 0.5 days.

Andrea Simmons   page 2

Lansing Agency (cont'd.)

Determined computer needs, canvassed vendors, obtained quotations, arranged purchase of single and multi-user equipment and software.

Installed new computer hardware and software dedicated for insurance agency use, updated software, reorganized hard drive to optimize disk space, performed frequent backups - twice saved business when disk crashed.

Computerized manual accounting system - simplified accounting function, made entries on an instantaneous basis.

Automated accounts receivable, oversaw client accounts and monthly statements - provided customer service representatives information to increase and accelerate collections.

Automated budgeting and forecasting to provide greater line item control - eliminated time-consuming and error-prone manual system.

PROFESSIONAL ORGANIZATIONS

Professional Insurance Agents
Independent Insurance Agents of New Jersey
National Users of Agena Systems

PERSONAL

Born New York City, 1937, single, four adult sons

B.A. Liberal Arts, 1958, Columbia University
A.S. Computer Science, 1987, Suffolk Valley Community College

Hobbies and interests: miniatures, doll houses, music

FRANK MUMFORD
8 Keiser Place
Belle Mead, NJ 08502
908-555-1234

date

name
title
company
address
city, state zip

Dear name:

How do you get your Information Systems department to become "customer-oriented" and "entrepreneurial" *within* your company?

One way is to re-engineer your staff to become client-based and think in terms of business-building and profit-creation. This is not easy. After all, the people in IS were usually hired and trained to do what they were told and to work to budgets.

A more effective way is to hire someone like me who has been client-oriented and profit-focused in a *vendor*-customer relationship at a value-added reseller. During the last seven years, I have made a lot of my customers happy because I have found out their needs and given them quality, price, promptness, and know-how. For example:

> I proposed $70,000 486 PC-based local area network (LAN) to replace mid-range computer - cut annual maintenance cost from $15,000 to $3,000 and gave customer faster and more flexible operating platform.

> I supplied a major national account with 60 laptop computers, fully configured, within one month and within budget in spite of shortages of some items.

Please see my attached resume for more examples of my achievements in making sure that my customers received top value in hardware, software and connectivity - all the while fielding a hundred help-desk calls a day and not losing my cool.

If you need someone in your department who can hit the ground running in ensuring effective interaction between IS and users, we should get together. I will call your office in a week to set up a time when we can discuss how my abilities can contribute to your success.

Yours sincerely,

FRANK MUMFORD

8 Keiser Place, Belle Mead, NJ 08502   908-555-1234

CAREER SUMMARY

Information technology sales and support manager with a record of solving clients' problems and increasing employer's sales and profits.

PROFESSIONAL ACCOMPLISHMENTS

MILAN COMPANY   1987 to date
Manager Sales & Support Department

Sales

Conducted active campaign of cold calling and new lead generation for sales force - exceeded $600,000 sales quota by 50%.

Proposed $70,000 486 PC-based local area network (LAN) to replace mid-range computer - cut annual maintenance cost from $15,000 to $3,000 and gave customer faster and more flexible operating platform.

Scheduled vendors and coordinated collection of demo equipment for day-long product fair - sales force met 100+ new prospects and made contact with 20% of them for project follow-up.

Configured 125 node network for client consisting of less expensive third-party products supported by the company - improved performance of system and saved customer 25%.

Supplied major national account with 60 laptop computers, fully configured, within one month and within budget in spite of shortages of some items.

Second-sourced hard drives for network servers during a period of shortage, found alternative configurations that gave better performance than original specifications.

Support

Created call tracking program to show clients amount of time spent for them by sales support team, also monitored open calls and tracked response times - demonstrated that actual average response time was 3 hours compared to clients' perception of over 4 hours and enabled department to cut response even further by signaling need to return calls promptly.

Recaptured a competitive bid for 400 printers lost because of price by guaranteeing 3-day delivery when winner could not deliver on time after all - won customer back.

Frank Mumford   page 2

Milan Company (cont'd.)

Took over from sales force day-to-day activities of quotations order entry, expediting, and managing accounts receivables - reduced office time of sales staff from 3 days a week to 1.5; brought past due rate down from 9.0% to 0.9%.

Installed our custom pricing and inventory software at customer locations and trained their staffs to use the Electronic Data Interchange (EDI) - enabled them to generate own quotations based on pricing profiles we created in database.

Established pricing and inventory software in company office for use by sales and service representatives - let them support all clients quickly and accurately.

Created quarterly report for a $10 million Fortune 500 national account customer that highlighted major projects and problems, showed graphically the distribution of types and amounts of products used - helped customer standardize on products, permitted purchasing department to obtain better prices for service and parts.

Persuaded company to purchase and install security system following disappearance of merchandise - demonstrated that cost would be offset by savings in thefts and in insurance premiums.

GREINER ORGANIZATION   1986 to 1987
Phone Interviewer

Conducted public opinion and market polls, dealt directly with top business executives in major corporations.

EDUCATION

B.A., 1986, Amherst College, major Communication, especially public and mass communication

Courses in management, computer education, marketing and sales

Awards: Atlantic Employee Honor Roll

PERSONAL

Born June 10, 1965, Plainfield, NJ, married

Hobbies and interests: fly fishing, motor cycling

JOSEPH BETHEL
707 Harbor Road
Pennington, NJ 08534
609-555-1234

date

name
title
company
address
city, state zip

Dear name:

As Project Manager of a computer systems development team, I provided the leadership needed to create and launch a new software product for commercial sale that achieved $150,000 revenues in its first year. And this was in the consulting division of a Big Six CPA firm that normally did not develop software for commercial sale.

If you need a Project Manager who has the unusual combination of abilities needed for the full range of accomplishments from conceptualization through design, quality control from day one, implementation, documentation, and marketing, you may wish to read more about my achievements in my attached resume.

In addition to my commercial sense and managerial skills, my strengths include:

> in-depth technical knowledge of IBM AS/400 and other mid-range computers, as well as personal computers,

> ability to organize people and tasks and deal with crises to get things done - right, on time, and within budget,

> interpersonal skills that produce results with employees, colleagues, vendors, and clients and customers,

> a trans-Atlantic career that even involved directing a United States based project team from the United Kingdom,

> oral and written communication facility that enhances the capabilities of both technical staff and users,

> ability to satisfy customers in ways that bring them back for repeat business.

I would be pleased to meet with you to discuss how my experience and abilities can contribute to the success of your operation. If I may, I will call your office to set up an appointment at a mutually convenient time. I look forward to meeting you.

Yours sincerely,

JOSEPH BETHEL

707 Harbor Road   Telephone
Pennington, NJ 08534   609-555-1234

CAREER SUMMARY

Computer software development project manager with record of creating innovative, profit-making software packages for mini- and personal computers.

BUSINESS ACCOMPLISHMENTS

DELOITTE & TOUCHE   1977 to date

Software Development Project Manager   1989 to date
Software Systems Assistant Manager   1986 to 1989
Software Development Project Junior Manager   1982 to 1986
Senior Programmer Analyst   1980 to 1982
Computer Specialist   1978 to 1980
Programmer   1977 to 1978

Project Management

Orchestrated launch and rollout of new software package, coordinated external and internal technical, printing, packaging, distribution, sales, shipping, telephone hot line for user support - product launched on time, achieved national press coverage

Supervised United States-based project team from United Kingdom, supervised programmers, allocated times, monitored costs, and controlled budgets - saved firm $65,000 in management salary in U.S.

Supervised programmers throughout coding, testing and execution, ensured quality and consistency - program error-free after 12 months of field use in about 100 assignments.

Marketing

Coordinated team that launched newly-developed PC software product for commercial sale for first time in firm, made sales presentations to small and large groups of prospects - achieved first year sales of $120,000.

Designed and authored marketing materials that enabled firm to sell in-house midrange computer software product in commercial markets - added revenues of $150,000 from new buyers.

JOSEPH BETHEL   page 2

Software Development, Systems Design

Assessed technical feasibility of converting software from COBOL on
mainframe to RPG on minicomputers.

Reviewed user/software interface for PC-based software package,
incorporated user needs into design.

Specified link between new user-interface PC software and existing program
- made it possible for generalists to use software instead of needing
computer specialists.

Designed system components for minicomputer software and identified
repeatable modules - reduced coding errors by 25%, increased programmers'
productivity by 30%, reduced future maintenance overhead.

Software Development, Quality Control

Implemented quality control concepts and requirements from initial
development to final documentation stages - reduced errors in final product
and thereby cut support calls by 10%.

Implementation, User Reference Manual

Converted computer reference manual to user manual - enabled buyers to
use software without assistance of computer specialists, shortened learning
time by 25%, reduced support calls by 20%.

Implementation, Training Course and Materials

Designed and wrote training modules for three-day classroom training course
- trained 75% of purchasers thereby raising revenues by $75,000.

Adapted existing introductory classroom tutorial for self-study training -
reduced in-house training costs by 50%.

VARIOUS EMPLOYERS   1972 to 1977
Sales Representative

PERSONAL

Education: Newcastle Polytechnic College, major business.
Born August 14, 1951, Southport, England, married, two sons.
Hobbies and interests: Sports, Little League baseball manager, music,
reading, travel.

JASON CREGAN
82 Chestnut Lane
Plainsboro, New Jersey 08536
609-555-1234; cregan@tmail.com

date

name
title
company
address
city, state zip

Dear name:

If you need a local and wide area network professional who has a great record of producing high quality results and who is a Certified Cisco Network Professional, you need me.

For example, I configured a Virtual Private Network with high speed broad bandwidth servers using Cisco routers and switches through the Internet that replaced a dial up 800 remote access system. The results were that remote users and telecommuters could access office computer resources at same speed as if they were located on site.

If you would like to know more about my accomplishments, please read my attached resume.

In addition to my technical skills, I offer the following strengths:

> I always adapt well to new work situations with a great deal of energy, drive and initiative.

> I like taking on new challenges, getting things started and seeing them through to the very end.

> I have strong analytic and problem solving abilities.

> I have the capacity to simultaneously learn very rapidly, process a great deal of information, and organize and categorize it.

> I am a skilled communicator and trainer, both orally and in writing.

> I work well with others, but am also effective in getting work done independently.
> I'm a self starter, can set my goals, or take assigned goals and complete them.

In about a week, I will call your office to set a date to get together to discuss how my achievements can contribute to the growth and profitability of your company. I look forward to meeting you personally.

Yours sincerely,

JASON CREGAN

82 Chestnut Lane, Plainsboro, NJ 08536   609-555-1234, cregan@tmail.com

CAREER SUMMARY

Local and Wide Area Network professional with a record of increasing productivity, speeding up communication, reducing costs, meeting deadlines, and enabling companies to achieve their business goals.

SKILL AREAS

Cisco Certified Network Professional, Cisco Certified Network Associate, Cisco Certified Design
Professional, Cisco Certified Design Associate, Microsoft Certified Systems Engineer NT 4.0, Microsoft Certified Professional + InternetNovell Certified NetWare Engineer 3.x and 4.1

PROFESSIONAL ACCOMPLISHMENTS

Stevenson Technology and Infrastructure Group   1997 to 2000
Assistant Vice President

Initiated project to identify which employees were using multiple network protocols (TCP/IP, IPX, and/or NetBEUI) and which one they needed; eliminate unneeded protocols - result: speeded up their client machines to enhance productivity

To make it possible to eliminate surplus protocols, rebuilt individual PCs from scrap parts - results: gave employees new PCs with no downtime and at no cost to company at a time of budget restraints.

Configured Virtual Private Network with high speed broad bandwidth servers using Cisco routers and switches through Internet that replaced dial up 800 remote access system - results:

> remote users and telecommuters could access office computer resources at same speed as if they were located on site

> provided unlimited simultaneous connections, eliminated busy signals on remote access system

Trained and directed outside contractors to perform this upgrade, reconfigured hundreds of laptop computers so they could work both at and away from the office.

Identified need for new company policy to avoid unauthorized use of client PCs as servers and to correctly configure computers that can be so used and to change network infrastructure - results: reduced bandwidth needs and speed up network and productivity.

Jason Cregan   page 2

Stevenson Technology (cont'd.)

Reduced size of employees' e-mailboxes on shared server hard drives by moving archives to own disks - results: avoided mail server running out of space (which prevented employees from sending e-mail), increased efficiency of mail server, relieved pressure on mail system administrator, and avoided having to buy additional hard drives.

Installed emulator program that enabled program developers to use the network to access mainframe computers from their Windows-based PCs via TCP/IP - result: programmers met tight deadlines to make the Domestic Order Management System operational.

Directed, set up and documented a system for tracking *Stevenson On Line* "hits," validating them, and analyzing them to get statistics and produce reports that told about its use by high wealth customers, technical effectiveness of site, and the use of the site by brokers - result: justified the return on investment in money and time for developing the on-line brokerage service.

Dynasty Capital & Co.   1996 to 1997
Programmer Analyst

Assembled a complex multi-platform, multi-protocol network, comprising Unix servers, MAC, Windows 3.1 and Microsoft Windows NT software, and Novell Netware: results: enabled reporters to collaborate and to send rapidly breaking developments to news wires more quickly, thus enhancing company's reputation for timeliness in a time-critical business.

Desmond Technologies International   1994 to 1995
Technology Trainer

August Food Corporation/ABC Supermarkets   1987 to 1994
Retail Automation Specialist

EDUCATION

B.A. 1987, University of Maryland

PERSONAL

Born 1963, Perth Amboy, New Jersey, single

Hobbies and interests: Skiing, New England contra dancing, history

LOUISE M. SHIELDS
332 Barclay Avenue
Yardley, PA 19067
215-555-1234

date

name
title
company
address
city, state zip

Dear name:

As Assistant to the Executive Director of a world-wide educational institution, I conceived, developed, organized and ran its first annual conference that attracted 80 of the 150 member colleges - and signed up new members. On my own initiative, I also organized the office, created desk top publishing capabilities, installed database management software, and instituted computerized accounting.

As Assistant to the President of a biomedical development company, I managed the entire office and acted on his behalf in relations with stockholders, directors, clients, government agency representatives, and suppliers.

If your Chief Executive Officer requires an Administrative Assistant who can anticipate needs and wishes, tactfully handle all levels of contacts from members of the Board of Directors and senior executives to clients, vendors and co-workers, and apply a strongly developed business sense, you may wish to read my resume for further information.

In addition to my professional attitude and appearance, I am well organized, highly motivated, hard working, dedicated, loyal, and honest in the "old world" sense. I have well developed written and oral communication skills.

I would be very pleased to meet you to discuss how my capabilities can be applied to the needs of your CEO. Please call me at my home after business hours to set up a date for us to get together.

Yours sincerely,

enclosure

LOUISE M. SHIELDS

332 Barclay Avenue   Telephone
Yardley, PA 19067   215-555-1234

BACKGROUND SUMMARY

Administrative Assistant with strong inter-personal, organizational, communication, financial, and computer skills.

BUSINESS ACCOMPLISHMENTS

ASSISTANT TO THE EXECUTIVE DIRECTOR   1988 to date
Center for International Studies, Yardley, PA

Conceived, developed, organized and ran first annual conference - result, attracted 80 of the 150 member colleges and signed up new members.

Organized second annual conference; overcame participants' concerns about traveling during wartime and about budget constraints - result, attendance increased 20% from first year.

Created, designed, edited and/or wrote semi-annual CIS Update newsletter and the Annual Conference Program. Prepared them in-house on desktop publishing equipment. Became "communication guru" for organization.

Represented CIS at study abroad fairs at colleges - result, maintained high level of enquiries in spite of economic and political climate. Also initiated contacts with faculty and persuaded them to consider membership - result, increased net membership by 25% in the face of budget cuts at colleges.

Selected and purchased new IBM AT personal computer and suitable word processing and database software, as well as new Macintosh 2CX computer and desktop publishing software; also acquired laser printer.

> Result, reduced errors and thereby saved 90% of typesetting costs, cut production time from 2 weeks to 2 days for newsletter.

Replaced manual accounting system with computerized small business financial software - result, provided accurate, on-time financial, tax and management reports.

Designed and set up database of members and non-members - result accelerated distribution of newsletter, conference notices, mailings, dues notices, and other communication.

Louise M. Shields   page 2

FREELANCE ADMINISTRATOR   1986 to 1988
Various Professional Offices

Structured and installed accounting systems and controls, handled full
charge bookkeeping, filed payroll taxes, maintained cash flow procedures,
advised on investments. Provided expertise in choosing appropriate
computer systems.

VETERINARY HOSPITAL ADMINISTRATOR   1985 to 1986

Instituted cash flow control system - result, cash balances grew from zero to
$5,000 a month.

Invested balances in money funds that increased to $75,000 within 18
months.

Set up inventory control system - result, eliminated problem of "outages."

Hired and supervised veterinary assistants and receptionists; scheduled
staffing in all areas of hospital.

ASSISTANT TO THE PRESIDENT   1982 to 1984
Ventech, Inc.

Managed entire President's Office, acted on his behalf in relations with
stockholders, directors, clients, FDA representatives and suppliers.

Coordinated directors' meetings including travel, accommodation and
meeting arrangements.

Worked closely with new National Sales Manager to establish department:
set up sales programs, assisted in appointment of representatives and
dealers. Contacted sales leads and followed up on enquiries about products.

EDUCATION

Associate in Mechanical Engineering, Sommerville Technical College, U.K.

Courses in General Nursing, Ammerman Hospital, Hampshire, U.K.

Courses in business administration, accounting, bookkeeping.

TRACEY P. HAGGERTY

15 Chuck Road   bus 609-555-1234
Princeton, NJ 08540   res 609-555-1234

CAREER SUMMARY

Take-charge administration and facilities executive with a record of building a growing organization from start up to full operational level.

PROFESSIONAL ACCOMPLISHMENTS

SYRACUSE UNIVERSITY, Department of Electrical Engineering1985 to date
Department Manager

Developed and established entire administrative structure for newly-created department - facilitated its growth in eight years from an operating budget of $275,000 to $800,000; a research budget from $2.2 million to $6.0 million; and a program of 105 doctoral students (biggest in University).

The components of this start-up and growth included the following:

FACILITIES

Built and renovated hardware-intensive new computer engineering research facility, set up four new laboratories.

Acquired and set up two off-campus satellite buildings.

Expanded main facility by 22,000 square feet of offices, labs, and instructional facilities.

Handled start-up of $30 million interdisciplinary research and educational activity - Advanced Technology Center for Photonic and Opto-Electronic Materials - comprising seven university departments - that interacts with other New York educational institutions and with industry.

PUBLIC RELATIONS AND EXTERNAL AFFAIRS

Coordinated establishment of Corporate Affiliates Program:

> planned and implemented semi-annual all-day programs for affiliates, and

> prepared and distributed materials such as resumes and technical research library updates.

Tracey Haggerty   page 2

Syracuse University (cont'd.)

PERSONNEL

Hired, trained and evaluated all permanent and part-time support staff, grew
department from 14 faculty to 22, 8 technical to 10, and 4 support to 8.
Handled all administrative aspects of appointment and evaluation of
technical and visiting staff from abroad.

Evaluated and processed requests and recommendations for staff additions,
upgrades, changes in duties, and reorganizations.

ADMINISTRATION

Developed and implemented administrative policies; initiated, designed,
and evaluated effectiveness of procedures covering structure, personnel,
allocation of space, and schedules.

BUDGET AND CONTROL

Created and managed budgeting and control processes. Set up chart of
accounts used to forecast fiscal needs. Ensured maximization of return on
departmental funds. Managed proposals, plans and budgets for industry-
sponsored projects.

PERSONAL

Born May 14, 1939, married, two grown children

B.A. 1960, Ithaca College, major psychology

Hobbies and interests: travel, reading.

ANDREW ELLIS

461 Floyd Parkway   Telephone
Ewing, New Jersey 08638   609-555-1234

CAREER SUMMARY

Purchasing and accounting executive with a track record of using my
business ingenuity to make and save money for my employers.

BUSINESS ACCOMPLISHMENTS

ERICSON BUSINESS NETWORK   1989 to date
Controller   1990 to date
Assistant Controller   1989

Did the "impossible" by exporting dangerous aerosol cans to Mexico for
Ovelo Bros. in ten days compared to an already very tight two week
schedule - resulted in client increasing its account from $40,000 to $150,000
a year and promising further growth in future.

Negotiated with Nelson Espo, a new vendor of prestige products, to open
$200,000 line of credit by presenting excellent financial statements and
obtaining cooperation of bank and other vendors for reference checks -
became the vendor's first new credit customer in two years and did not have
to make any downpayment for deliveries.

Overcame Allen Sports's objections to invoice by presenting accurate facts
and enabling client to take physical inventory - obtained payment and
increased sales to $100,000 a year thereafter.

Computerized and consolidated parent and subsidiary accounts, provided
analyses that enabled owner to determine that one of five businesses was
highly profitable and another was not paying off - owner now targeting
profitable business opportunities at CVL.

Purchased incentive items directly from manufacturer instead of from
fulfillment house - increased profit margin from 9% to 35%; extended
program to all products and increased profits by 30%.

Negotiated with Mail-Ex to get on-site computer tracking system enabling
company to track shipments from suppliers and to customers - shipping
deadlines were met 100%.

Expanded local area network (LAN) from four stations to 16, upgraded
software, found right company to do installation - installation was up and
running in one week without any disruption to regular routine, performance
of new LAN is excellent.

Andrew Ellis   page 2

ELLIS CONTRACTORS   1986 to 1989
Principal and Owner

From date of founding, increased business to $100,000 in three years.

Expanded scope of business from only painting to full service home improvement - increased dollar volume per customer by 40%.

VALUETEX, INC.   1984 to 4/86
Branch Manager   1985 to 1986
Assistant Sales Manager   1984
Sales Representative   1984

Initiated telemarketing program that increased yield of sales calls by 10%.

PERSONAL

B.S. Business Administration, 1984, Ithaca College

Born Jersey City, December 29, 1961, married

Hobbies and interests: flight instructor

JANNA D. CAREY
200 Rumble Lane
Cranbury, NJ 08512

date

name
title
company
address
city, state ZIP

Dear name:

Assistant to the President of one of the hottest start-up production companies at **Castle Studios**; Assistant to **Frank Meyers**; Casting Assistant at **JL Network Television**; Assistant Production Office Coordinator at **Bohemia Films**; Staff Assistant at the **Maryland Governor's Film Office**; and Production Intern at **Dell Monica Associates**!

That is the track record I bring to you.

Plus, I get things done with and through other people: calmly, efficiently, competently, quickly. I am organized, focused, perceptive, direct, down-to-earth, businesslike, a voice of reason. I get to the heart of the matter and move things. And people like working with me and on my team.

I quickly know what you want and give it to you before you want it. I take in the big picture and filter it down to action. I thrive on diversity.

That's not my opinion. It is what my employers and colleagues say about me.

Best of all, I know L.A. - no matter where in the world it may be on location. I know the players, the people who matter to the success of a film or a start-up production company.

If you can use this kind of ability and energy, we need to get together. I will call you on [date] at [time] to set a time when we can meet to see how I can contribute to your success.

Yours sincerely,

P.S.   If you can't wait until I call you, phone me at 609-555-1234.

JANNA D. CAREY

200 Rumble Lane, Cranbury, NJ 08512   **Telephone 609-555-1234**

PROFESSIONAL ACCOMPLISHMENTS

ASSISTANT TO PRESIDENT   1994 to date
Norman Entertainment, Burbank, CA

During the first four months this start-up production company was in business, managed the combination and relocation of two separate offices into new studio offices; company was able to move into new space over holiday weekend and be up and running Monday morning.

Set up systems that provided for immediate growth to manage 15 active projects. Managed daily office activities.

Evaluated three to six prospective scripts each week of the 20 to 35 received by the office.

The end result was that one of the hottest companies at Castle Studios was fully functional right from the start.

ASSISTANT TO FRANK MEYERS   1993 to 1994
Philly Productions, Culver City, CA

Completely facilitated all communication between the Producer/Director, his Los Angeles office, and distant foreign locations. Acted as the key U.S. liaison with accountants, lawyers, agents, and studio representatives in Los Angeles and interacted with Toronto office.

CASTING ASSISTANT   1993
JL Network Television, Century City, CA

Coordinated international talent search for casting director, scheduled all casting calls with agents, actors and community representatives for Hollywood's only Native American talent specialist; produced the cast for *Geronimo*, the highest-rated original in JLNT history.

Janna Carey   page 2

ASSISTANT PRODUCTION OFFICE COORDINATOR   1992
Bohemia Films, Studio City, CA

Established the temporary headquarters for a production company in Dover, Maryland:

> created all necessary vendor relationships, managed logistics and supply for all departments,
>
> expedited contracts and deal memos,
>
> organized and distributed all shooting schedules, script pages, as well as cast, crew, and contact lists,
>
> ensured consistent overnight delivery of exposed film for processing in Los Angeles.

Coordinated location production office with Los Angeles production company, press and vendors.

STAFF ASSISTANT, INTERN   1991 to 1992
Governor's Film Office, Dover, MD

Assisted in developing marketing strategies for State of Maryland. Researched state-wide location possibilities and communicated Maryland location potential to production company representatives and local officials.

Created and structured Production Services Guide and Vendor lists.

Evaluated scripts, generated breakdowns in response to producer's individual needs.

PRODUCTION INTERN   1991
Dell Monica Associates, Studio City, CA

Coordinated set, location office, and Los Angeles production office during pre-production.

As a Set Production Assistant, ensured smooth functioning of film set during production period of 95-hour weeks.

Worked closely with producers, director, actors, crew on Emmy-Award-winning film.

EDUCATION

B.A. in Journalism, Georgetown University, GPA 3.2

PERSONAL

Born July 13, 1970, New Haven, Connecticut, single.

ANTHONY M. WHITMAN
8 Winona Street
Chestertown, MD 21620
410-555-1234

date

name
title
company
address
city, state ZIP

Dear name:

You may need an employee who has five years of practical experience in the whole range of television technology and production management:

> working behind the camera,
> designing the lighting,
> handling the audio,
> maintaining the equipment,
> directing and producing the programs,
> managing the crews,
> raising the funds,

and who has just completed his university degree and a postgraduate year in telecommunications.

If so, you may wish to read my attached resume for more information about the work I did at college and in part time employment.

In addition to having an unusually wide background in the film and television industry, I have strong leadership abilities and a strong desire to put my skills as a grip to work in an organization such as yours where I can make a maximum contribution right away.

In a week, I will call your office to make an appointment to discuss how my abilities will fit in with opportunities you might have in the technical end of your company.

Yours sincerely,

enclosure

ANTHONY M. WHITMAN

8 Winona Street, Chestertown, MD 21620   Telephone 410-555-1234

CAREER OBJECTIVE

To make a contribution to the success of a video production company based on my technical experience and education.

PROFESSIONAL ACCOMPLISHMENTS

TECHIE VIDEO INC.   1993
Production Assistant

Handled all aspects of post-production including chyron, dubbing, editing, library, equipment assessment, and day's preparation.

KROB PUBLIC ACCESS STATION   1993
Producer of *Camera 1*

Produced and directed biweekly TV program, *Camera 1*.

Assistant

Assisted with monthly university live production, *Grapevine*, and with two weekly sports programs, *Golden Bear Sports* and *Sportscene*.

NYU GRADUATE CLASS PROJECT   1993
Producer

Overcame problems of unexpected schedule change, unavailability of planned location, shortage of equipment, lack of budget, and tight timetable - all of which prevented production of original program - by brainstorming with five-member crew and negotiating with other producers for equipment to produce a short television commercial as an alternative project.

Learned how to use video camera as a film camera; developed a better understanding of how a camera sees an image.

NYU DRAMA CLUB   1991 to 1993
Lighting Designer

Designed lighting for Readers' Theatre Showcase, *An Evening of Performances*, student production, *Beyond Therapy*, and university theater production of *Lysistrata*.

Anthony M. Whitman   page 2

NYU OFFICE OF STUDENT ACTIVITIES   1989 to 1993
Manager of Production Crew   1991 to 1993

Directed five-member production crew in maintaining extensive audio and
lighting equipment.

Production Crew Member   1989 to 1991

NYU STUDENT ACTIVITIES COMMITTEE   1992 to 1993
Chairperson/Interim Director

Produced three concerts. Negotiated with parent group during two difficult
situations to obtain funding.

Ran SAC during interim period when there was no Director and helped to
install new incumbent.

ALPHA EPSILON RHO   1992 to 1993
President

Revitalized and rebuilt this National Broadcasting Honor Society society by
gathering group of students to act as Executive Committee; organized fund
raising projects.

Organized trips to local TV stations.

THE MORGAN SCHOOL   1990
Founding Editor of Yearbook

Conceived and created first ever yearbook for school; conducting fund
raising; secured computer and darkroom time; found company to print it at
minimal cost. The book continues to be used to attract students to this
private school.

EDUCATION

B.S. 1993, New York University, major telecommunications; extensive
classes in Gripping

Courses in Graduate Studies program, 1994

Leadership Scholarship from Student Government Association, 1992 to 1993

PERSONAL

Born New Haven, Connecticut 1968, married

Hobbies and interests: resided and traveled in Saudi Arabia 1983 to 1986

SANG MOY-SU, Ph.D.

59 Oak Terrace, Princeton Junction, NJ 08550-1509   609-555-1234

CAREER SUMMARY

Microbiologist with a record of accomplishment in research, teaching and business.

PROFESSIONAL ACCOMPLISHMENTS

SIGNA CORPORATION   1991 to 1993
Postdoctor

Conducted independent research studies of apolipoprotein B expression. Determined the effect of progesterone and 25-hydroxycholesterol on apolipoprotein B expression.

Improved methodology in molecular biology techniques and wrote them into standard protocol.

Instructed associate scientist in molecular biology techniques.

UNIVERSITY OF TENNESSEE   1990 to 1991
Postdoctor

Devised and executed new approaches in studying receptor-binding domain of hemopexin. Localized the receptor-binding site within a 30 amino acids region.

Maintained mammalian cell lines.

Supervised research projects of two graduate students.

COLUMBIA UNIVERSITY   1985 to 1990
Ph.D. Candidate

Conducted research projects into the unraveling of plasmid transfer mechanism in *Enterococcus faecalis*. Study was published in Journal of Bacteriology.

Wrote thesis on localization and sequence analysis of genes involved in ferryman-inducible conjugation of pCF10. Study was published in Journal of Bacteriology.

Arranged set up of and purchased supplies for advanced molecular laboratory course. Wrote laboratory manual.

Taught graduate level molecular biology and undergraduate level microbiology laboratory.

Sang Moy-Su, Ph.D.   page 2

TRENTON STATE UNIVERSITY   1984 to 1985
Research Technician III

Performed different experimental tests in studying the microbiological impact of using chemicals that generate oxygen-free radicals in foods.

M.S. Candidate

Determined biological mechanisms for Paraquat-resistance in *Escherichia coli*. Thesis published in Journal of Biological Chemistry and FEMS Microbiology Letters.

ECKO PHARMACEUTICAL COMPANY, TAIWAN   1976 to 1980
Administrative Secretary

Managed office operation for a sales force of 25 representatives. Coordinated customer service. Served as liaison between company and exclusive sales agent. Prepared sales reports.

Maintained company's reputation in market by giving personalized attention to customer complaints.

Translated promotional literature into Chinese - saved company 16% of my monthly salary for each piece translated.

LABORATORY EXPERIENCE

[Insert]

PUBLICATIONS

[Insert]

EDUCATION

B.S. 1975, Taiwan University, major, entomology.

M.S. 1984, Trenton State University; major, microbiology, minor, biochemistry.

Ph.D. 1990, Columbia University; major, microbiology, minor, genetics and biochemistry.

Awarded Columbia Biotechnology Program two year pre-doctoral fellowship

Affiliations:

American Society for Microbiology
Sigma Xi

J. STEVEN CAPLAN
56 Bardin Street
Bloomfield, NJ 07003
bus 201-555-1234, ext. 47
res 732-555-1234

date

name
title
school
address
city, state zip

Dear name:

Getting and keeping the attention of elementary school children is a constant challenge for any teacher in any school.

I have done that in *multi-cultural, multi-age classrooms* in inner city and suburban public and private schools—and then have engaged the students' imaginations and creativity. I even got the students to teach themselves and each other.

For examples of the methods I use, please see my attached resume. My secret added ingredients are exploration, enthusiasm and excitement. The youngsters really love learning in my classes.

Having obtained my Master of Elementary Education degree from Syracuse University, I am now ready for a permanent position as a teacher in an elementary school in Manhattan.

I look forward to meeting with you to discuss how my teaching skills and techniques can benefit the students in your school. If I may, I will call to set up an appointment.

Yours sincerely,

enclosure

J. STEVEN CAPLAN

46 Bardin Street, Bloomfield, NJ 07003   W 201-555-1234, ext. 47; H 973-555-1234

CAREER SUMMARY

Elementary school teacher (Grades 1-8) in multi-cultural schools and multi-age classrooms.

EDUCATION

Bachelor of Arts 1995, Cornell University. Double major in elementary education and English literature. Dean's List two years.

Master of Elementary Education 1997, Syracuse University

Certification New Jersey

PROFESSIONAL ACCOMPLISHMENTS

NEWARK FRIENDS SCHOOL, Newark, NJ   1995 to date
Teacher (advisory grades 6-7)

Pulley Project: Brainstormed and predicted the effects of the use of one, then two, then three or more pulleys on an object. Students then collaborated and designed a pulley system that enabled each of them to lift their 175 pound teacher (me) into a tree (grades 6-8).

Butterfly Project: Students researched the development of a caterpillar throughout its various life cycle stages and prepared reports on their findings. They learned scientific techniques as well as cooperation in a laboratory setting (grades 1-2).

Keeping the Peace: Developed a collection of cooperative games designed to build community and reduce conflict among students of different socio-geographic backgrounds (grades 3-8).

Village: Gave students a chance to form their own communities, solve problems and develop social skills and teamwork through building structures with natural materials (grades 1-3).

Sukkoth: Enabled students of multicultural backgrounds to appreciate various religions and philosophies by coming together to build an outdoor structure (grades 5-8).

Drama: Students performed plays designed to evoke their ability as actors to think on their feet in various dramatic situations. The class also enabled the students to deal with relevant issues common to adolescence (grades 3-8).

J. Steven Caplan   page 2

Newark School (cont'd.)

Basketball Team: Assembled a group of interested students during unstructured lunch times into a co-ed basketball team. They developed a sense of teamwork and fair play. Empowered girls on the team who developed confidence through their interaction with older, bigger, boys.

Soccer Club: Developed and implemented a soccer program during lunch hours. Gained coaching experience.

Villanova Elementary School, West Windsor, NJ   1994
Student Teacher (grade 3)

Davis Street Elementary School, Trenton, NJ   1993
Student Teacher (grades 1-2)

Bilingual first and second grade combined classroom. Initiated *Math Fraction Fruit Salad*, a math game used to show the "real life" uses for fractions.

Northside Elementary, Trenton, NJ   1992
Intern (grade 2)

Implemented math stations. Students were broken down into small groups in order to better facilitate peer learning and exploration. The groups switched stations and activities in 15 minute increments, then came together to share discoveries and questions.

HOBBIES AND INTERESTS

Running, skiing, soccer, basketball

Rider University:
    International Student Organization, represented Guyana, South America
    Student Advisory Board
    Resident Advisor, junior and senior years

CAITLYN BARRINGTON
37 Anders Way
Monmouth Junction, NJ 08852
908-555-1234

name   date
title
company
address
city, state zip

Dear name:

Question: Why do employers have company cafeterias on their premises?
Answer: To make sure employees stay on site instead of going out for
               lunch.

Question: What makes sure that employees eat in the company dining
               room?
Answer: Great and varied food, day after day, week after week.

Question: What makes an employer contract with and keep a food service
               company?
Answer: Great food at low cost.

Question: Why would you hire me as an Assistant Food Service Director?
Answer: My record of pleasing employees with great food at low cost and
               of keeping them coming back for more day after day, week after
               week. And my record as a supervisor who employees really put
               out for because of my ability to motivate their pride in what
               they do.

As you see in my resume, I have the combination of hands-on experience as a
chef and as a manager that gets great results. I know all facets of running a
kitchen from creating menus, cooking meals from scratch, and presenting food
appetizingly, to controlling inventory and costs, and ensuring sanitation. I have
cooked in volume, created *special days* and gourmet menus, and catered small
VIP parties. As a former Diet Technician at a hospital and a convalescent center,
I emphasize health consciousness and nutrition as well as taste.

In addition to my skills as a chef and manager, I am energetic, fast, and hard
working; train and delegate well; and have my certificate as an emergency
medical technician.

I look forward to meeting with you to discuss how my abilities can contribute to
the success of your food service company. In a week, I will call your office to set
up an appointment at a convenient time.

enclosure

CAITLYN   BARRINGTON

37 Anders Way
Monmouth Junction, NJ 08852

Telephone
908-555-1234

CAREER SUMMARY

Chef manager/dietetic technician with a record of creating and preparing
nutritious and tasteful foods in executive dining rooms, hospitals,
convalescent centers and colleges.

PROFESSIONAL ACCOMPLISHMENTS

OLGIVE CORPORATION   1988 to date
Chef Manager

Managed executive dining and VIP functions from start to finish for from 10
to 120 people. Planned creative menus, prepared, cooked, and served
meals.

Catered VIP lunches in executive dining room.

MONAHAN'S GOURMET DELI   1986 to 1988
Assistant Chef

Constantly created novel gourmet items for display cases for parties and
other functions.
Standardized recipes for catered parties, prepared cold and hot salads.
Taught cooking classes.

OAKDALE MEMORIAL HOSPITAL   1985 to 1986
Supervisor, Diet Technician

Managed patient service, cafeteria, and special functions. Coordinated
communication among nursing, medical, and food service staffs. Developed
and maintained department's Quality Assurance program.

SAYVILLE CONVALESCENT CENTER   1980 to 1984
Relief Supervisor, Diet Technician

Managed all aspects of food services.

AMHERST COLLEGE   1979 to 1980
Food Production Aide

MARTHA'S RESTAURANT   1978 to 1979
Waitress

Caitlyn Barrington   page 2

EDUCATION

A.A. 1984, Dietetic Technology, Food Service Management, Middlesex
County College, Deans List.

Courses in:

>Merchandising, Amherst College, 1979
>Food Service Supervision, Ithaca College, 1982
>Certified Food Service Sanitation Management, Suffolk University,
>1982
>Leadership Workshop, Nassau County College, 1984

PERSONAL

Associations: Member, American Dietetics Association and Culinary
Institute of America.

Hobbies and interests: sports, athletics, health-conscious cooking,
emergency medical technician.

LAWRENCE DOLLINGER

462 Canterbury Court
Robbinsville, NJ 08691
609-555-1234

date

name
title
company
address
city, state zip

Dear name:

Chase Cuisine Gourmet Food + Victory's Pizza = L.A. Pizza Kitchen. It all adds up!

As a Manager for Victory's, I have learned that total commitment to customer satisfaction produces business success. Quality, promptness, price: those are the watchwords that made Domino's the leader in the order-out business.

As Assistant Manager, Gourmet Food for Chase Cuisine, I have learned how to please the discriminating upscale, full service restaurant customer. To obtain and satisfy the corporate clientele we served, I developed the market strategy to identify them and the methods to turn prospects into customers. I also created the innovative menus that this kind of restaurant calls for.

But, success in the restaurant ultimately requires outstanding leadership of the people who work for you. When I arrived at Victory's, the store had been in a slump for two years. By developing rapport with and good morale among my employees, I improved sales by 10%. In my personal life, I hold leadership positions in all my activities.

If you wish to learn more about how my accomplishments can contribute to the success of L.A. Pizza Kitchen, please read my enclosed resume. It also includes my salary history.

I look forward to interviewing with you about the excellent opportunities you offer in the Washington, D.C., area or in New Jersey.

Yours sincerely,

enclosure

LAWRENCE DOLLINGER

462 Canterbury Court, Robbinsville, NJ 08691   **609-555-1234**

CAREER SUMMARY

Restaurant Manager with a record of building sales and improving profits through leadership and strategic planning.

PROFESSIONAL ACCOMPLISHMENTS

VICTORY'S PIZZA   1993 to date
Store Manager ($16,900)

Improved customer satisfaction - increased weekly sales by 15% from previous year.

Accurately completed daily and weekly reports, analyzed profit statements - cut food and labor costs from 52% to 48% of revenues.

PENNSYLVANIA LIFE INSURANCE COMPANY   1991 to 1992
Sales Representative, Life Insurance ($22,000)

Evaluated customers' financial needs; devised promotional marketing program; developed, and conducted seminars - sold $10 million of life insurance.

CHASE CUISINE, GOURMET FOOD   1989 to 1991
Assistant Manager, Gourmet Food ($15,000)

Developed marketing strategy to solicit corporate clientele - built this business from scratch.

EDUCATION

A.A.S 1985, Syracuse Institute of Technology/National Technical Institute for the Deaf, major, computer science.

B.S. 1989, Gallaudet University, major, business administration.

Courses in computer programming.

PERSONAL

Born Montreal, Canada, January 5, 1962; single.

Hobbies and interests:

Syracuse Institute of Technology/National Technical Institute for the Deaf nominated for Alumni Board Member

New Jersey Golf Association for the Deaf, Board Member, Chairperson of annual tournament

Quiet Money Investment Club, portfolio manager

Skiing, swimming, volleyball, travel.

MERIDITH LOCKE
73 Sutton Landing
Princeton, New Jersey 08540
609-555-1234; mlocke@tmail.com

date

name
title
company
address
city, state ZIP

Dear name:

As Controller of a start up venture capital firm, I ran the business while the owner found investors and ventures. Together, we built the business from $1 million to over $40 million in capital in five years.

As interim Assistant Corporate Secretary of a start up high tech firm, I consolidated and corrected all ownership records in anticipation of initial public offering or sale of firm.

As Executive Assistant to the President of the New York Museum of Art, I interacted with trustees, donors, high level members, and legislators to ensure their continuing loyalty and support.

If you would like to know more about my accomplishments, please read my attached resume.

In addition to my record of professional dealings with high level finance and financiers, I get things done - on time, on budget, and at or above expectations. I have the analytical ability to get to the heart of a matter and fix problems so that they stay fixed. My output is so reliable that investors, attorneys and accountants accept it without question.

I also have the ability to communicate clearly and persuasively orally and in writing. I gain the confidence of people so that they respond to my requests even though they have other priorities. I have excellent planning and organizing skills.

I would appreciate the opportunity to meet with you to discuss how my achievements and abilities can contribute to the success of your firm. If I may, I will call you next week to set a mutually convenient time to get together.

Yours sincerely,

enclosure

MERIDITH LOCKE

73 Sutton Landing, Princeton, New Jersey 08540   609-555-1234; mlocke@tmail.com

SUMMARY

Versatile, energetic, and problem-solving administration manager with record of achieving results - on time, on budget, and above expectations - in a wide variety of industries including high technology, finance, professional service, and not-for-profit.

PROFESSIONAL ACCOMPLISHMENTS

Promise Tech, Inc., Princeton, New Jersey   2000
Director of Administration (Interim)

Developed and installed a benefits plan in six weeks for high tech start up manufacturer. Result: plan had elements of a big company program without the complexity and expense.

Edited and published user-friendly employee benefits handbook. Result: employees understood and appreciated value of plans.

Purchased equipment, established credit, and instituted procedures as company grew from zero employees to over 15. Result: company was able to get into operation effectively.

Grassman, Inc., Princeton, New Jersey   1998 to 1999
Assistant Corporate Secretary (Interim)

Researched and compiled complete and accurate investment data for medical products company seeking additional financing. Result: buyer conducted its due diligence process expeditiously and completed the deal.

Organized and researched private equity financing documents to verify stock ownership for compliance with securities and accounting regulations. Result: company avoided misrepresentation and forestalled lawsuits and fines.

Health Care Strategies, Inc., Princeton, New Jersey   1995 to 1997
Administrative Assistant to President

James Bannon, Princeton, New Jersey   1993 to 1994
Staff Accountant

Freeman Partners, Belvedere, California   1984 to 1992
Business Manager

Set up and managed operations of start up venture capital business. Result: business grew from $1 million to over $40 million in capital in five years.

Coordinated with underwriters and attorneys on initial public offerings, calculated complicated allocations of stock, and prepared lists of investors and their shares. Result: stock was distributed efficiently and accurately.

Meredith Locke   page 2

Freeman Partners (cont'd.)

Interpreted private equity financing documents and created systems to record and
monitor investment information. Result: portfolio valuations and payouts were
correct.

Informed venture capital investors about product launches, sales performance, and
other business updates on companies they funded. Result: investors were confident
in ability of firm and invested additional funds.

Initiated and prepared quarterly and annual financial reports and tax returns
accurately and on time for 17 partnerships. Result: investors were able to file their
tax returns on time.

Organized audit preparation. Result: fees were reduced by one-third.

Managed overall operation of office, administered payroll, and recruited and
supervised support staff.

New York Museum of Art, New York, New York   1981 to 1982
Executive Assistant to President

Received and welcomed visiting trustees, major donors, members, and legislators.
Arranged lunches and tours. Recruited and supervised support staff.

Barlin, Naslow and Larson Inc., New York, New York   1971 to 1978
Manager Compensation and Benefits

Developed and administered support staff compensation programs; administered
expatriate compensation; and planned and managed professional staff salary and
bonus plans. Administered various employee benefit plans, including ERISA
compliance.

EDUCATION

B.A. in economics *cum laude*, University of Chicago   1981

Strong math skills: courses in algebra, calculus, statistics and accounting.

DEBORAH HOWELL
35 Goldbach Avenue
North Brunswick, NJ 08902
732-555-1234

date

name
title
company
address
city, state zip

Dear name:

Within six months of setting up a multi-level marketing business, I had organized and trained 50 members of my sales team and produced a total revenue of $25,000 in one month.

If you need an aggressive, persuasive, and innovative sales producer to start, turn around or build your revenues, you may wish to read more of my accomplishments in my attached resume.

In addition to my entrepreneurial capabilities, my strengths include:

a professional, problem-solving approach to producing sales results,

a flair for motivating and training people,

a sense of urgency to get things done fast and well,

a dedication to serving customers,

an ability to be both a team player and a leader.

I am sure that my track record in starting businesses, marketing, sales, and service can increase the success and profitability of your organization. I would be pleased to meet with you to discuss further how my skills and achievements can contribute to your specific needs.

Yours sincerely,

enclosure

DEBORAH HOWELL

35 Goldback Avenue   Telephone
North Brunswick, NJ 08902   732-555-1234

CAREER SUMMARY

Top revenue and profit-producing Entrepreneur, Sales Representative, Trainer and Manager.

BUSINESS ACCOMPLISHMENTS

FEEHAN MARKETING INTERNATIONAL - Principal   1990 to date

JANELL MARKETING - Partner/Trainer   1990 to date

NATIONWIDE SAFETY ASSOCIATES - Sales Representative 1990 to date

Simultaneously established multi-level marketing business, provided sales training services, and functioned as independent sales representative. Have built sales volumes and other revenues to a current personal income rate of $60,000 per year.

> Organized and trained 50 members of my sales team - produced a total revenue of $25,000 within one month.

> Demonstrated effectiveness as a sales and marketing orientation trainer; initiated the opening of a new office.

MEDIA PUBLICATIONS   1990
Account Executive

Cold called 15 to 20 prospects per day, secured numerous new, diversified accounts; created special "Highlights" section.

Revitalized existing accounts by performing cost analyses and preparing proposals that increased advertising revenues.

Wrote advertising copy, designed layouts and artwork, which resulted in an innovative flair in the appearance of the publication.

MAYFIELD HOTEL CORPORATION   1985 - 1989
Princeton Mayfield Hotel   1986 - 1989
Supervisor of Concierge (Customer) Services

Lead start up team for three new hotel facilities with respect to specialized sales presentations and customer services.

Deborah Howell   page 2

Princeton Mayfield (cont'd.)

Developed training manual for all new hires to expedite and improve training
- reduced customer complaints and raised satisfaction rating to 95%, the
highest rating in the hotel.

Wrote Standard Operating Procedures manual still used by staff to ensure
complete and thorough standards of service.

Somerset Mayfield Hotel   1985 - 1986
Front Desk (Sales) Clerk

Received recognition and monetary award for outstanding performance.

CAPITAL AIRLINES Newark International Airport   1986
Gate/Ticket Sales Agent, Station Agent, Ramp Agent (part time)

Maintained and improved on high standards of "on-time" performance thereby
avoiding heavy penalties imposed by airport for lateness.

WILSON HOTEL New York City   1981 - 1982
Concierge (Customer Service Representative)
Front Desk (Sales) Clerk

Provided personalized hotel services to VIPs and dignitaries.

McKINNEY PUBLISHERS   1981 - 1985
International Sales Assistant (summer jobs)

Coordinated Latin American sales.

Prepared promotional materials in Spanish.

EDUCATION

B.A. 1981, Pace University, White Plains, N.Y., majors Spanish and pre-law;
Dean's List.

PERSONAL

Born June 28, 1959, married, three children

Hobbies and interests: numerous community, fund raising and sports
activities.

MATHEW LORIA
920 Carleton Avenue
Plainsboro, New Jersey 08536
Telephone 609-555-1234; Fax 609-555-1234

name   date
title
organization
address
city, state zip

Dear name:

"Boy, I'm going to sue your ass.

That was what I heard on the phone within days of starting my new job as Vice President of a deeply troubled insurance company from the President of one of our best clients. He was calling to complain about an unpaid refund of several million dollars for the past three years. It turned out that my predecessor had frozen the payment for negotiating leverage. Now he was gone, and so were our files on the account. After doing strenuous detective work, I found out that the balance was legitimate and paid it. This salvaged the relationship and we went on to grow the business volume.

Not long after, my boss, the new President, said that we should drop catastrophe coverage (which was an important line of business) because it did not produce much revenue - and because he had a fundamental prejudice against it. But, this was the very time that a large hurricane had hit Florida and prices for such insurance were beginning to skyrocket. I demonstrated that this was the time of great opportunity so instead we stayed and eventually doubled our premium income.

When I arrived, our annual forecasting process was a simplistic projection of premium dollars. I turned it into a complete five year forecast by line of business and type of coverage and then into a strategic planning process that documented sources, profitability and quality of business partners. As a result, we identified profitable new lines and the internal and external resources needed to support them.

It was this unusual combination of paying attention to customers, seizing opportunities, and seeing the big picture that enabled me to manage revenue growth from less than $20 million to over $150 million in 14 years. If you would like to see more examples of my accomplishments, please read my resume.

I would be very pleased if you and I could get together to discuss how my record of achievement can contribute to the success of your company. If I may, I will call your office to set up an appointment to meet at a convenient time. Many thanks.

Yours sincerely,

MATTHEW LORIA
920 Carleton Avenue, Plainsboro NJ 08536   Telephone 609-555-1234, Fax 609-555-1234

CAREER SUMMARY

Turnaround marketing and underwriting executive with record of creating long term revenue and profit growth and extensive market contacts in property and casualty insurance industry.

PROFESSIONAL ACCOMPLISHMENTS

Charles Lipman Corporation
Senior Vice President
Vice President

1984 to date
1990 to date
1984 to 1990

Reversed owners' decision to close down the business by demonstrating statistically the positive profitable growth of the market and the success of competitors during the time that company was losing money - result: gained consensus support from owners for commitment of resources necessary to achieve strategic goal of top-ten market standing in ten years.

Converted annual forecasting process from simplistic projection of premium dollars into complete five year forecasts by line of business and coverage type and strategic plans that documented sources, profitability and quality of business partners - result: identified profitable new lines and internal and external resources needed to support new ventures.

Identified potential new line of business by analyzing lucrative new geographic market not serviced by competitors, developed contacts with and selected best brokers and prospective clients, and determined optimum ways of doing business - result: grew premium revenue from zero to $70 million in seven years and became a market leader.

Overcame industry-wide inability in to estimate losses from catastrophes by designing a pioneering computer model - result: was able to calculate losses from events of various magnitudes in different parts of country and create an early warning claim tracking and processing system.

Following Hurricane Andrew in 1992, used a computer model to calculate a credible worst case scenario, bought re-insurance against it, and insured otherwise threatened market - result: became largest broker-market reinsurer for this program and realized 50% profit margin.

Revealed that lack of actuarial support limited company's credibility in eyes of brokers and competitors and impeded profitable underwriting due to inconsistency in hazard analysis and pricing - result: hired in-house actuaries and thus reassured owners that efforts to enter "perilous" new lines were prudent.

Matthew Loria   page 2

Charles Lipman (cont'd.)

Rationalized supplier network by eliminating 10 direct reinsurers and reducing number of brokers from four to two - result: redirected time and effort from administration to business development.

Thurston Reinsurance Company	1979 to 1984
Assistant Vice President	1983 to 1984
Assistant Secretary	1981 to 1983
Underwriter	1979 to 1981
IAMCO Insurance Companies	1972 to 1979
Senior Home Office Underwriter	1977 to 1979
Senior Property Underwriter	1975 to 1977
Branch Office Underwriter	1972 to 1975

EDUCATION

B.A. 1972, Tulane University; Newberger Scholarship

PERSONAL

Born June 3, 1950, Washington, D.C., married, one son

Hobbies and Interests:
Director and Treasurer, College Bound of Trenton, Inc.
Financial Advisor, start-up Trenton Music School
photography, music, skiing, scuba diving, golf

VICTOR K. HUGHES
5 Marberry Circle
Kendall Park, NJ 08824
908-555-1234

date

name
title
company
address
city, state ZIP

Dear name:

What do you do if your $7 million highly-specialized military equipment manufacturing market disappears with the end of the Cold War? Either you can go out of business - or you can develop a whole new set of products serving a whole new mix of customers.

We decided to stay in business and it was my job to make sure that we made it.

Before the words were even in general use, I initiated Re-engineering, Total Quality Management, and Just-in-Time manufacturing as well as adopting Computer Aided Design/ Computer Aided Manufacturing (CAD/CAM)software to achieve the successful Rightsizing of the company.

As the head of operations and chief design engineer, I worked directly with prospective customers to develop the products that now provide $3.5 million profitable revenues. As a result, I also raised the annual productivity of the remaining workforce by 3.7 times.

If you would like to know more about my accomplishments, please read my attached resume.

In addition to my manufacturing and engineering inventiveness, I can offer leadership ability to your firm. In spite of the tremendous upheaval caused by the down-sizing of the company, I kept morale high, maintained loyalty, and ensured improved productivity. I get the job done.

I would be pleased to meet with you to discuss how my abilities can contribute to the profitability and future success of your firm. I will call your office next week to set a time when we can get together.

Yours sincerely,

enclosure

VICTOR K. HUGHES
5 Marberry Circle, Kendall Park, NJ 08824   Telephone 908-555-1234

CAREER SUMMARY

Versatile manufacturing operations executive with a record of making money.

PROFESSIONAL ACCOMPLISHMENTS

L.A. MACON, INC.   1978 to date
Manager Manufacturing Operations

Rightsizing

Due to reduction of business from $7 million a year to $3.5 million, had to cut staff from 90 employees to 12. However, increased productivity per employee from $78,000 to $290,000

Product Diversification

Worked directly with prospective customers to determine precise needs and designed and built products to fit them. Replaced $7 million military revenues with $3.5 million in very diversified commercial products and kept company in business.

Instituted system of requiring payment for custom-design engineering work that previously had been given away at no cost.

Re-engineering

Tracked production flows on computer to see what was happening with materials and labor at each step of the process; identified specific materials that could be eliminated; determined minimum economical levels of production at each stage - improved yield from 34% to 90%.

Set up system to salvage gold used in process - saved 25% of costs.

Total Quality Management

Initiated quality tests at each step of the labor intensive production line from incoming inspections to final output - eliminated processing of faulty components and reduced labor requirements by 50%.

Vendor Relations

Analyzed what aspects of military specifications were essential and which allowed for flexibility in terms of the effects on quality of end products - in a typical case, cut costs per piece from $25 to $13 by relaxing unnecessary requirements.

Worked with vendors to ensure more timely deliveries - reduced in-house inventories by 60%.

Victor K. Hughes   page 2

L.A. Macon (cont'd.)

Computerization

Used computer aided design (CAD) software and FAX to send a sketch of a test set layout to a customer as soon as specifications were received - customer doubled normal year's order.

Installed computer aided manufacturing (CAM) software to run cutting equipment - reduced irregularities from 15% to 0.5%.

Researched, acquired and installed cutting-edge computer software to capture manufacturing data on the fly - resulting analytical reports enabled company to spot early trends in demand and respond ahead of time.

Just-in-time Management

Implemented Just-in-Time manufacturing system to fit our company's needs. However, instead of adopting consultants' advice to build a new $250,000 facility, I re-arranged the existing plant at a cost of $20,000.

Purchasing

Persuaded Japanese manufacturer of SOT to provide a large sample of CD-ROMs at no charge as a way of breaking into a new European missile program with OEM equipment.

PRO CAM AIRCRAFT   1977 to 1978
Supervisor Printed Circuit Manufacturing

TANKA ELECTRONICS CORPORATION   1969 to 1977
Plant Manager

EDUCATION

University of Minnesota, B.S. Business Administration candidate (two years)

DBL Institute, 1970, Associate in Electronic Technology

Associations: IEEE member

PERSONAL

Born July 27, 1947, married, two children

Hobbies and interests: scuba diving, snow skiing, boating, racquetball, tennis, golf, trap and skeet shooting; Special Olympics.

Christopher Carter
91 Lincoln Avenue
Vineland, New Jersey 08360
res 856-555-1234; bus 856-555-1234

date

name
title
company
address
city, state zip

Dear name:

Think of a church as a Training & Development Center and it is easy to think of me, a clergyman, as a Training & Development Manager and a hands on trainer. Because that is what I want to become.

After eight years as a successful Presbyterian minister, I am ready to move into a related occupation where there is the potential for upward mobility that the church simply does not provide.

I teach, motivate, communicate, organize, plan, schedule, and manage programs and courses, develop and use audio/visual aids, build teams, train trainers, develop leaders, teach problem solving, goal-setting, and decision-making skills, modify behavior, change culture, improve morale, impart ethics, assess needs, test learning, teach conflict resolution and management, demonstrate group dynamics, and do all the other myriad tasks that T&D performs.

A sample of my accomplishments is shown on the attached resume.

I am articulate, perceptive, and organized. I am a team player who can also work autonomously. I have strong leadership and interpersonal skills. I have a finely-honed ability to juggle a multitude of tasks simultaneously; I prioritize them and follow through to get them finished.

If training and development are about behavior change, no one spends more effort and energy on this than the clergy. I use ingenuity and creativity to get attention paid to a subject that has not really changed in 2000 years, yet I make it fresh and new for each person.

Now I am ready to move into an operation where I can apply my abilities at higher and broader levels. I would be pleased if we could get together to discuss how my achievements can benefit your organization. Therefore, I will call your office to set a date when we can meet.

Yours sincerely,

CHRISTOPHER CARTER

91 Lincoln Avenue   res 856-555-1234
Vineland NJ 08360   bus 856-555-1234

PROFESSIONAL ACCOMPLISHMENTS

PASTOR   1991 to date
Memorial Presbyterian Church, Gibbstown, NJ

Determined that deficiencies in congregation's lay leadership stemmed from the dominance of two members and passivity of the rest of Board - empowered all members and thereby created greater balance and effectiveness.

Identified lack of vision and ability to plan as reasons for failure to move the organization forward - established mechanisms that enabled each member to express feelings about the organization; gathered the feedback; reported results; and ran retreat on how to set goals and objectives based on information received.

Discerned that the reason donations were inadequate to sustain church financially was lack of knowledge of theological reasons and practical methods: gave sermons, led study sessions and ran workshops on stewardship; organized committee to handle giving program.

Prepared congregation for forthcoming change in the order of worship by explaining reasons for the change at each of four services - achieved smooth transition.

Discovered that Vacation Bible School was strong in content but lacking in fun; introduced and led recreation part of program - created opportunities for fellowship as well as community building.

ASSOCIATE PASTOR   1987 to 1991
First Presbyterian Church, Budd Lake, NJ

Addressed discomfort of leaders with having to conduct Every Member Visit program: developed instruction booklet covering all aspects of campaign and on active/reflective listening skills.

Found that new members did not feel accepted in congregation - set up orientation that built on their past experiences; trained them in worship style; outlined "the way things are done;" and described volunteer opportunities.

Was chosen to lead implementation in New Jersey of new nation-wide confirmation curriculum: attended national training session; led discussion period during state-wide meeting on program; led leadership training sessions.

PROGRAM CONSULTANT 1983 to 1991
Old Greenwich Presbyterian Church, Toms River, NJ

Set up orientation and training program for new and continuing members of
church council regarding their roles and responsibilities; used team building, role
playing, skill inventories, organization planning, explanation of procedures, and
instruction in church's mission.

Designed workshop to introduce new curriculum: personally taught a lesson to
the teachers using new lesson plan; taught a kindergarten class with teachers
present as observers.

Discovered that teachers lacked creative ways to use new curriculum materials -
brought one of authors to conduct a workshop that gave teachers examples to
adopt and adapt.

STUDENT PASTOR 1986 to 1987
United Presbyterian Church, Kinnelon, NJ

STUDENT PASTOR 1985 to 1986
Second Presbyterian, Philadelphia, PA

Was required to lead class on inclusive (non-sexist) language to co-students at
seminary who had already been given too many such courses - to gain
seminarians' attention, brought drawings of "God" done at my request by
children in my Sunday School class and sparked lively discussion and
understanding based on the diversity of images used by the children.

CENTER MANAGER 1980 to 1983
Pro Value, Inc., Rochester NY

Devised program for On-The-Job training for new employees in operations and
organization of store.

PERSONAL

Born July 3, 1960, Rochester, NY, single

Bachelor of Arts 1984, Syracuse University; major, sociology

Master of Divinity, 1987, Virginia Theological Seminary

Associations: Association of Presbyterian Church Educators, New Jersey Cluster
of Church Educators

Hobbies and interests: piano and voice performance, opera buff, creative writing

INDIRA KUMAR
22 Carlough Road
Lawrenceville, NJ 08648
609-555-1234

date

name
title
company
address
city, state zip

Dear name:

Why should I as a dietician and school teacher want to start as an entry level trainee stock broker?

Because I have been investing in the stock market ever since my daughter was born as the way to pay for her university education. I have become increasingly interested in the securities market as I have become increasingly involved in it, and I now want to work in the industry on a professional level.

Why should you as a broker want to hire me in this position?

Because I bring the communication skills and intelligence to the job that will make me succeed for you and your clients. These abilities have come as a result of the kind of work I have done over the years as both a teacher and a dietician. I have had to communicate well with all ages to make certain that they received the services they needed. And I have had to know my subject matter to be effective.

I believe that these qualifications will also make me effective as a broker-trainee. I look forward to meeting you to discuss working with you in your new office in Princeton.

Yours sincerely,

INDIRA KUMAR

22 Carlough Road   Telephone
Lawrenceville, NJ 08648   609-555-1234

PROFESSIONAL ACCOMPLISHMENTS

Teacher, Substitute Teacher, or Teaching Assistant   1982 to date

Pearl Street School, Pennington, NJ   1990 to date

Middlesex County Vocational-Technical School   1984 to 1986

Care for Tots, Mt. Holly, NJ   1982 to 1984

Consulting Dietician   1978 to 1979

Crestwood Nursing Home, Maple Shade, NJ
Abel Valley Nursing Home, Maple Shade, NJ

Dietician   1978
Carro Heart and Lung Center, Browns Mills, NJ

Food Service Technician   1976 to 1978
Morgan Charity Hospital, Cleveland, OH

EDUCATION

B.Sc. 1972, Sayajirao University, India, Home Economics, major, food and nutrition.

Courses: Dietetics, Western University, 1972 to 1973

Dietetics, Orville College, Chicago, IL, 1974 to 1975; accumulated 120 credits for dietetic internship

PERSONAL

Born May 3, 1950, Mombassa, Kenya; married, one child

Hobbies and interests: investment, personal financial management, interior decorating, travel, outdoor activities, aerobics.

ROBERT COLLINS
125 Split Oak Drive
Princeton, NJ 08540
609-555-1234

name   date
title
organization
address
city, state zip

Dear name:

As a neophyte fund-raiser in the southeast for the Thomas Young Evangelistic
Association, I raised over $500,000 in deferred gifts and cash in my first year. As
a real estate sales person, I became a member of the Million Dollar Club. As
Senior Pastor of a small suburban church, I overcame opposition both inside the
church and in the community to raise $1 million to build a new church facility.

What do these accomplishments have in common?

My ability to use a low key, carefully organized approach to help people arrive at
decisions that are good for themselves and for others.

Why such an unusual career?

In common with so many other clerics, I suffered mid-life burnout and, five years
ago, sought a career change.

In doing so, I discovered that my ability to establish rapport, my skill in
listening, my powers of explanation and persuasion, my persistence, my
knowledge of strategic planning, and my leadership talents were
transferrable from the ministry to sales. I was successful, but I still felt a
need to be involved in work that had broader social significance.

I then realized that I could use these same capabilities to help worthy
causes in their development activities, so I joined one of the best fund-
raising organizations in the country. I am successful here too, but I am in
a remote area that requires me to be away from home five nights a week -
every week.

Now I wish to apply my unusual combination of abilities to help your organization
raise funds in the northeast where my effectiveness can be even greater because
I know the people.

I would be pleased, therefore, to meet with you to discuss how my fund raising
capabilities can contribute to the success of your organization. If I may, I will
call you next week to set up a time when we might get together.

Sincerely,

ROBERT COLLINS

125 Split Oak Drive
Princeton, NJ 08540

Telephone
609-555-1234

CAREER SUMMARY

Fund raiser with a background in building church ministries.

ACCOMPLISHMENTS

THOMAS YOUNG EVANGELISTIC ASSOCIATION, St. Louis, MO   1991 to date
Field Representative

Raised over $500,000 in deferred gifts and cash in one year:

> used computer databases and to identify and track prospects and donors;

> pre-qualified donors based on amounts and frequency of previous giving, age and marital status;

> persisted in fund-raising efforts in spite of the reality that only 3% of contacts are responsive and only one third of those actually close;

> lead prospects to establish goals, educated them in appropriate instruments to achieve goals, and lead them to make their decisions:

>> one lady set up a Charitable Remainder Trust to schedule limited payout of the estate to her children and then give the residual to charity,

>> an 82 year old farmer was suffering loss from his bank accounts because of the drop in interest rates, set up an annuity to triple his income.

HALVERT REALTIES, Princeton, NJ   1987 to 1991
Salesperson

Achieved $1 Million Dollar Club membership:

> used low pressure approach to determine peoples' needs, desires, and financial capabilities;

> determined from computer which houses fit their criteria;

> helped them reach decision to buy from me.

Robert Collins   page 2

MULLADY EVANGELICAL FREE CHURCH, Somerset, NJ   1981 to 1987
Senior Pastor

Raised $1 million to build new church facility:

> established cohesive direction in a divided congregation through use of such techniques as needs analysis, common goal setting, and preparation of a coordinated plan of action;
>
> overcame resistance of pioneer church founders who did not want to grow, obtained their cooperation;
>
> organized lay committee, prepared literature, supervised calling program, collected and evaluated statistics;
>
> trained groups in fund-raising techniques and followed up to ensure that they performed their assigned tasks;
>
> gained trust and agreement of hostile townspeople at new location;
>
> organized the building committee and completed construction.

Increased church membership by over 100% and annual giving by 300% in seven years.

FIRST EVANGELICAL FREE CHURCH, Sanford, IL   1977 to 1981
Associate Pastor

EVANGELICAL FREE CHURCH , Blue Lake, WI   1967 to 1977
Senior Pastor

LAKEFIELD EVANGELICAL FREE CHURCH, Sanford, IL   1965 to 1967
Pastor

EVANGELICAL FREE CHURCH, Salisbury, CT   1961 to 1965
Pastor

PERSONAL

Doctor of Ministry candidate, Deerfield Evangelical Divinity School, Deerfield, IL
Master of Divinity, 1960, General Seminary, New York, NY
Bachelor of Arts, 1957, Brown University, majors history and bible

Born Foxboro, MA, January 7, 1935; married, three grown children

Hobbies and interests: antiques, clocks, gardening, carpentry, classical music, live theater, sailing, cycling, golf, football, basketball, baseball.

LUCILLE T. FREY
62 Hawkins Avenue
Lawrenceville, NJ 08648
609-555-1234

name   date
title
organization
address
city

Dear name:

Do you know what the hardest sales job in the world is?

Teaching school to kids who don't really want to buy what you are trying to get them to learn.

The reality is that to be a successful teacher, you have to be a top-flight salesperson. All the same attributes, attitudes, skills, steps, persistence, and personality that make a successful salesperson make a successful teacher.

I have been a successful teacher of environmental and biological sciences for 22 years. During that time, I have followed a tried and true method:

I find out students' needs, I get their attention, I arouse their curiosity, I convince them by showing them the benefits to them of the subject, I stimulate their desire to learn, I overcome their objections, and I use questions, tests and examinations to "close" what was learned.

But potential is not all I have to offer:

I also am licensed to sell real estate - I have sold!

I have been a Guest Service Representative and Manager on Duty at a Ramdell Inn - I can deal with all kinds of people.

I have been a recruiter and counselor - I can help people make decisions.

And I have even acquired a degree in industrial engineering - I know how to make people, processes, and equipment work together.

If you would like to learn the specifics of my career, please see the attached resume.

Now, after 22 years in the classroom, **I am ready to convert those skills to selling** your goods and services to your customers.

I would be happy to meet with you to discuss how my capabilities and energy can be applied to meet your needs and build your business. In about a week, I will telephone your office to set a time for us to get together.

Sincerely,

LUCILLE T. FREY

62 Hawkins Avenue
Lawrenceville, NJ 08648

Telephone
609-555-1212

CAREER SUMMARY

Extensive experience in environmental and biological sciences, statistics, education and training, recruiting, sales, and computer applications.

PROFESSIONAL ACCOMPLISHMENTS

HALLOW HILLS HIGH SCHOOL, Morgantown, NC   1974 to 1991
Teacher

Sparked team-planning, role-playing, educational experimentation, curriculum-planning, and large and small group discussions among teaching staff.

Educated department about new areas of research and study.

CRESTHAVEN SCHOOL, Morgantown, NC   1971 to 1974
Teacher

Wrote course offerings. Purchased science equipment.

FRANKLIN WEST SCHOOLS, Franklinton, NC   1969 to 1971
Teacher

PART TIME SUMMER EMPLOYMENT

FERES, HALPERN & ASSOCIATES, Morgantown, NC   1987 to 1989
Real Estate Broker

Listed, showed and sold properties.

Performed public relations for the firm.

WESTERN TENNVILLE COLLEGE, Morgantown, NC   1985 to 1986
Recruiter and Counselor

Recruited new students into the college.

Counseled students regarding their major courses of study.

Lucille T. Frey   page 2

RAMDELL INN, Morgantown, NC   1981 to 1984
Guest Service Representative

Acted as Manager on Duty when management was off property.

Provided customer service.

EDUCATION

B.A. 1969, Georgetown University, major, biology; minor, English and
education

A.A. 1988, Western Tennville Community College, major, industrial
engineering

Graduate programs in education, Ohio State University, West Virginia
University

Real Estate Licence 1978 Mackey Technical Institute

Effective Speaking and Human Relations, 1989 Dale Carnegie

PERSONAL

Born Rutherford, NC, 1948, married

Hobbies and interests: reading, canoeing

Index

About the Author

Niels H. Nielsen, president, Princeton Management Consultants, Inc., Princeton, New Jersey, founded the company in 1979 to provide a full range of human resources and general management consulting services including human resources strategy, human resources needs analysis, human resources policies, organization planning, compensation planning, employee benefits planning, human resources information systems, employee communication, employee relations, outplacement counseling, business strategy, marketing strategy, start-up consulting, executive coaching, and turnaround consulting. Company clients include Fortune 500, Inc. 500, and start-up companies, plus nonprofit institutions.

Nielsen rose in management with DuPont, Massey Ferguson, Domtar, Allis-Chalmers, Johnson & Johnson, and JC Penney, before becoming corporate vice president, Personnel Services, at Aramark. He is the author of *Managing Human Resources: Forms and Reports* (Prentice Hall, 1989) and many articles. He won WorldatWork's first annual award "In Recognition of Outstanding Written Contribution to the Field of Compensation" for his article, *The Strategic Use of Compensation and Benefits in a Changing Environment.* He is a frequent lecturer and seminar leader. He received a BA with honors in economics and political science and an MA in economics (magna cum laude) from McGill University in Canada.